I0764054

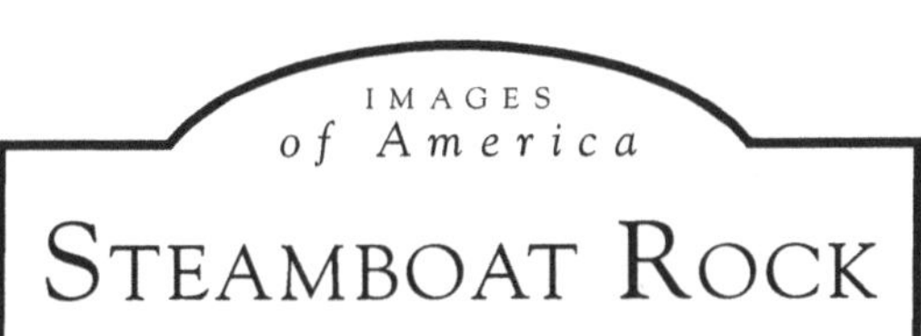
IMAGES
of America
STEAMBOAT ROCK

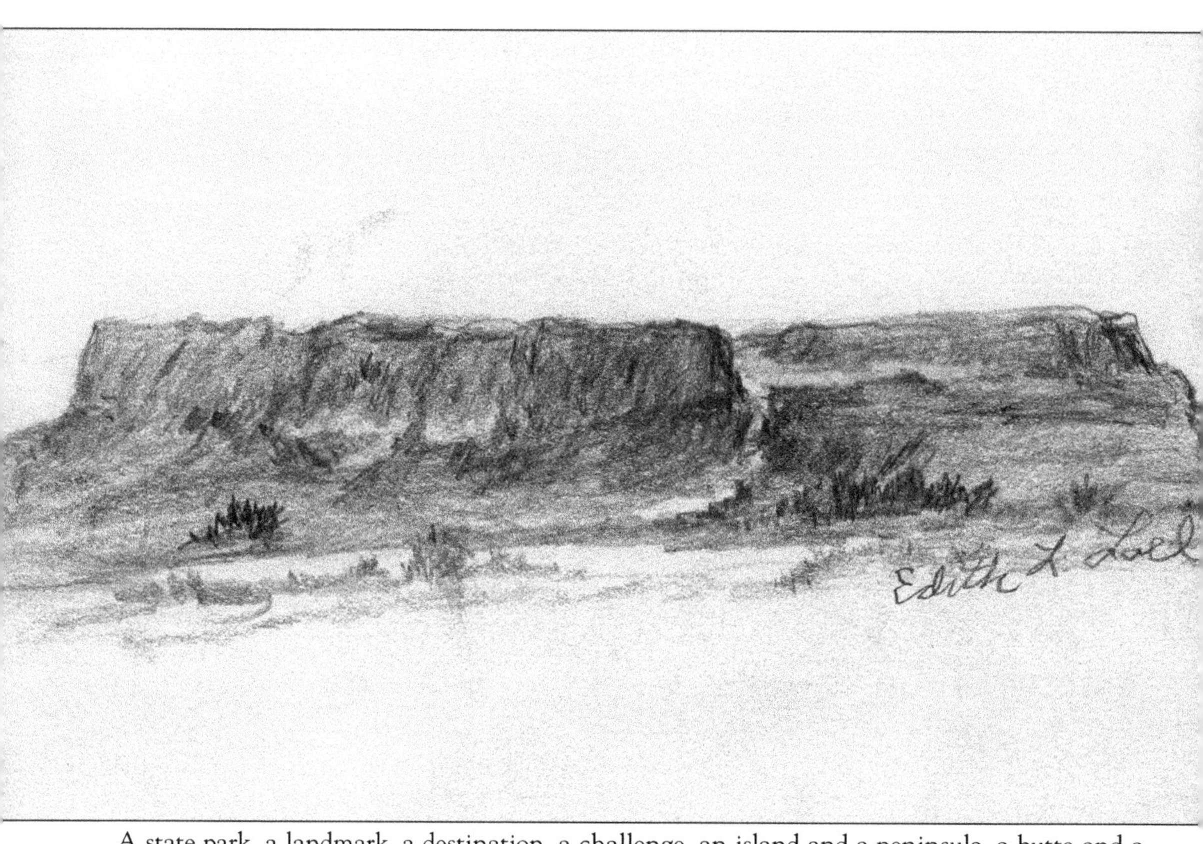

A state park, a landmark, a destination, a challenge, an island and a peninsula, a butte and a mesa—over the centuries, Steamboat Rock has been many things to many people. Steamboat Rock now once more sits surrounded by water and people, a mixture of its own past, present, and future. (Courtesy of Edith Lael.)

On the Cover: The Speedball Highway makes its way past the south end of Salishan Mesa headed north toward Steamboat Rock. Taken sometime before 1951, this picture shows the coulee before it was flooded with Banks Lake and predates the cutting of the Million Dollar Mile. (Courtesy of Washington State Archives.)

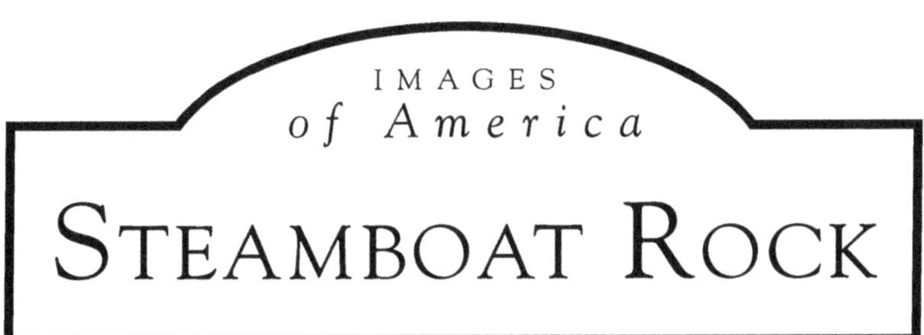

John M. Kemble

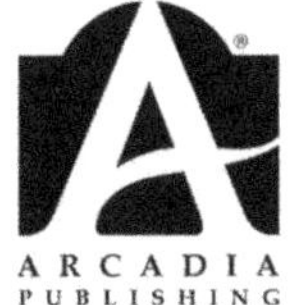

ISBN 978-1-4671-0471-5

Published by Arcadia Publishing
Charleston, South Carolina

Library of Congress Control Number: 2019952772

For all general information, please contact Arcadia Publishing:
Telephone 843-853-2070
Fax 843-853-0044
E-mail sales@arcadiapublishing.com
For customer service and orders:
Toll-Free 1-888-313-2665

Visit us on the Internet at www.arcadiapublishing.com

This book is for everyone.

Contents

Acknowledgments

A great, big thanks to all the following people: Birdie Hensley and the Coulee Pioneer Museum, Steamboat Rock State Park, Dan Bolyard, Dennis King, Gaylene (Pryor) Green, George Kuzminski, Liz Palachuk, Edith Lael, Don Nutt, Nora Egger, Keith Powell, Dani Bolyard, Mike VanderWerff, Pheenix Wonder, Alicia Marie McGuckin, Darlene Morava, Bill Kemble, Pat Witham, Ryan Holterhoff, Jared Liening, Art "Cowboy" Brown, Melissa Walker, Edward J. Powell, Sean Eaton, Windy Bolger, Michele Ricks, Machelle Martin-Rzepka, Kyle Bryant, Scott Hunter, and Jacob Wagner at the *Star*. Thanks also go to the US Bureau of Reclamation, the City of Grand Coulee, the Grant County Museum, the Grant County Historical Society, Grant County Public Utilities District, the Spokane Public Library, the Grand Coulee Public Library, the Coulee City Public Library, Washington State Digital Archives, Cousin Sam, Big Bend Rail Road History, Cariboo Trail Studio, Little Virtual Museum in the Coulee, and of course, Them Dam Writers. Extra special thanks go to my family—they made me. Thanks to my nephew Randahl Kemble for being himself.

Images courtesy of Coulee Pioneer Museum in Electric City, unless otherwise noted.

INTRODUCTION

At one time, before recorded history, Steamboat Rock was an island that was created by repeated floods down the Columbia River. At the mouth of the Grand Coulee, where the coulee meets the river, was a large ice dam that deflected the water south toward Ephrata. As time passed, and this channel was repeatedly used by floodwaters, the land became scoured, and the chasm we know as the Grand Coulee slowly appeared. In the center of the upper coulee was an island that could not be swayed by the erosive currents of the Columbia River and tons of debris rafting down the floodwaters. As the centuries passed, the coulee dried out, leaving Steamboat Rock washed up in the middle of a huge, dried-up riverbed filled with rich volcanic soil and spotted with seasonal lakes. The story of Steamboat Rock transcends geology, becoming a story of people and places.

Rising 800 feet from the lake below, Steamboat Rock is now a destination for recreation and outdoor enthusiasts. It sits in the middle of a well-maintained Washington State Park that fills to capacity every summer. People travel from all over the world to camp, hike, or launch a boat on Banks Lake, the huge equalizing reservoir that surrounds Steamboat Rock on three sides. The rock itself is 600 acres, but the state park is 3,522 acres, containing approximately three miles of trails. The state park is named after the butte—Steamboat Rock State Park—and surrounds the landmark, spreading out into other, more primitive natural preserves like Castle Rock, Jones Bay, and Osborne Bay.

The only real way to get to any of these destinations is by driving State Route 155, which runs from Coulee City to the south of Steamboat Rock and north into Electric City and Grand Coulee. At one time, there were plans for trains, airplanes, and more than one way into Steamboat Rock, but that was before Banks Lake was filled, and the landscape around Steamboat Rock was vastly changed. Where waves now push against artificial riprapped shores, fields of grain and luxuriant bunch grass once grew. Cows, sheep, and horses once wandered around the coulee floor in great herds. Hay and alfalfa crops could be seen bordering farms, and orchards with various types of fruit grew in the coulee where people now water ski and fish. A new way of farming was put on show at the base of Steamboat Rock called dry-land farming, which was about irrigation and moving water to land once thought unmanageable, using oil pull engines and gravity-fed pipes wooden pipes—a land tamed by pioneers and settled by homesteaders.

From the early 1900s to the late 1940s, a loosely knit community had been building slowly in the farmlands around the base of Steamboat Rock. At first, it was a community of lonely pioneers clinging to each other for comfort and success, and later, they were ranchers and farmers separated by great heads of cattle or fields of wheat. By 1910, a schoolhouse had been built and was in use for lessons as well as a community center. Dances and other events were held in the shadow of Steamboat Rock, as people married and children were born. The early ranchers of the coulee around Steamboat Rock soon gave way to fences and farmers and new ideas in irrigation, turning the dry land coulee around Steamboat Rock into a wealth of produce, feed, and livestock. Goods were sold in nearby Coulee City and went to marketplaces all over the country by rail. By 1915, the farmlands around Steamboat Rock and nearby Northrup Canyon were legendary in the area, but around 1917, a great drought began, and families were forced out of the Coulee and left abandoned farms dotting the countryside in an exodus to greener pastures. A few families remained on the drylands around Steamboat Rock, relying on each other to help make it through the lean times.

By the 1930s, the Steamboat Rock community was at a low, as many of the homesteaders had moved on, and the unmaintained land was becoming barren. But then work began on the Grand Coulee Dam, bringing a new wave of settler to the coulee that some called "modern pioneers."

Once more, the Steamboat Rock area came alive, and a couple new townships sprung up "in the Shadow of Steamboat Rock" to catch the overflow of new arrivals at the construction site. A new highway was built down the coulee, and as was a new railroad, the first-ever in the Grand Coulee. As the community grew, new landmarks were established, like the poplar trees, and old landmarks were moved or forgotten. Once more, the community around Steamboat Rock started to grow as money slowly trickled in. Several gas stations were located on the floor of the coulee around Steamboat Rock, and a small diner or two where locals would gather at to drink coffee and gossip about the changes or the good old days were established. But they were all living on borrowed time, for soon, a 27-mile-long reservoir would flood the land in which they sat drinking coffee and chatting about the weather. Big changes were coming to the Steamboat Rock community, where farmers redefined irrigation and fought to bring water to a parched land would soon be flooded with a massive lake of irrigation water; where cows once roamed the field, now fish would swim. Once more, Steamboat Rock would be surrounded by water, and that water would come from a diverted Columbia River and flood the coulee floor.

With a history that spans from the Missoula Flood to this very day, bits and pieces of the history of Steamboat Rock have been preserved in various books, newspaper and magazine clippings, oral traditions, personal memories, artwork, and rare photographs. I have assembled this collection from multiple sources spanning the decades in an attempt to piece together a compelling, relevant book that answers questions and preserves history. My hope is to both entertain and enlighten.

Now, let's catch up to a legend, as Steamboat Rock rolls along!

One

Origin Stories

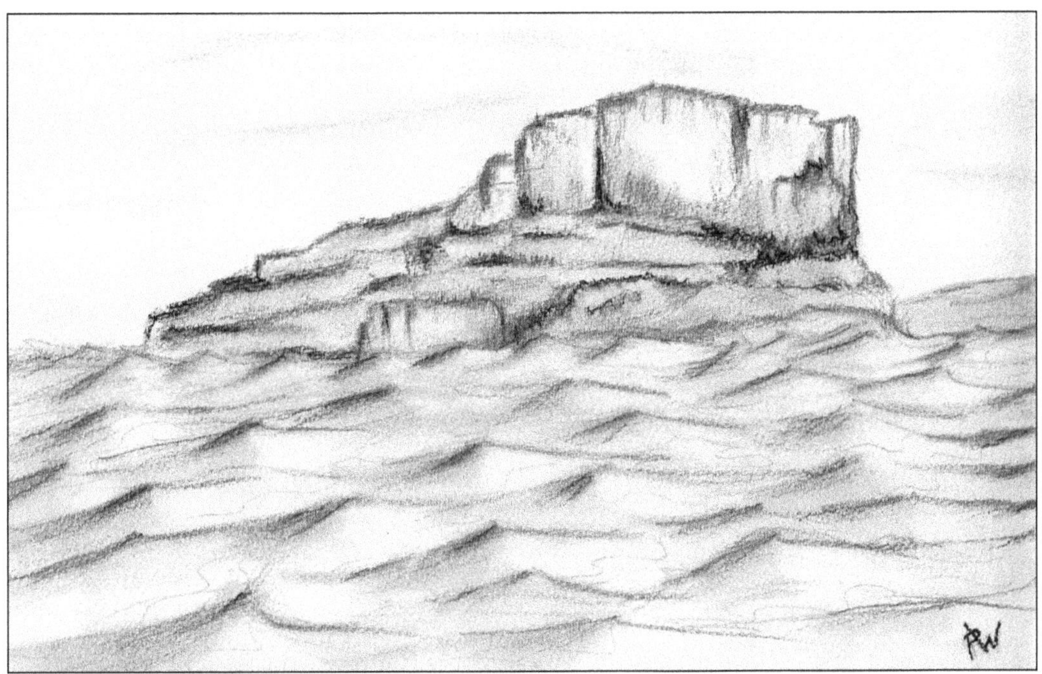

In the center of the upper coulee was an island that could not be swayed by the erosive currents of the detoured Columbia River and tons of debris cascading through the floodwaters. Named after the fabled riverboats due to its appearance, Steamboat Rock was once an island that was created by repeated floods from the Columbia River. (Courtesy of Pheenix Wonder.)

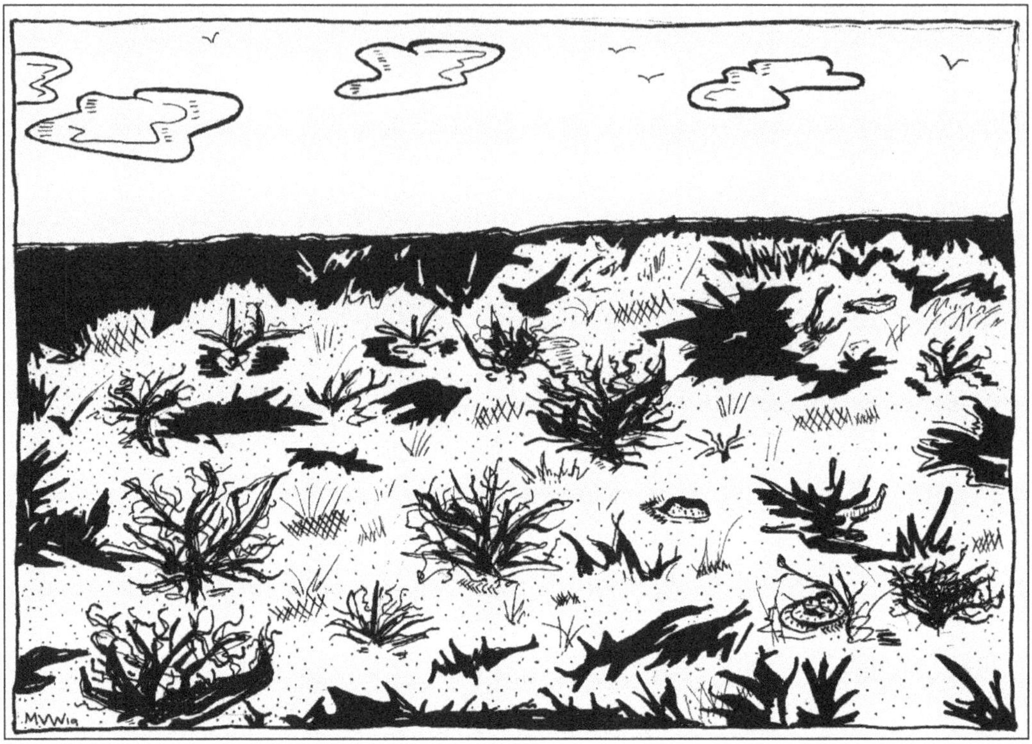

About 17,00 years ago, during the end of the last Ice Age, the late Pleistocene Epoch, the land around the Grand Coulee was all the same height and indistinguishable. It was the end of the Paleolithic Age, and it is unknown if any humans were around to witness the creation of the Grand Coulee or Steamboat Rock. (Courtesy of Mike VanderWerff.)

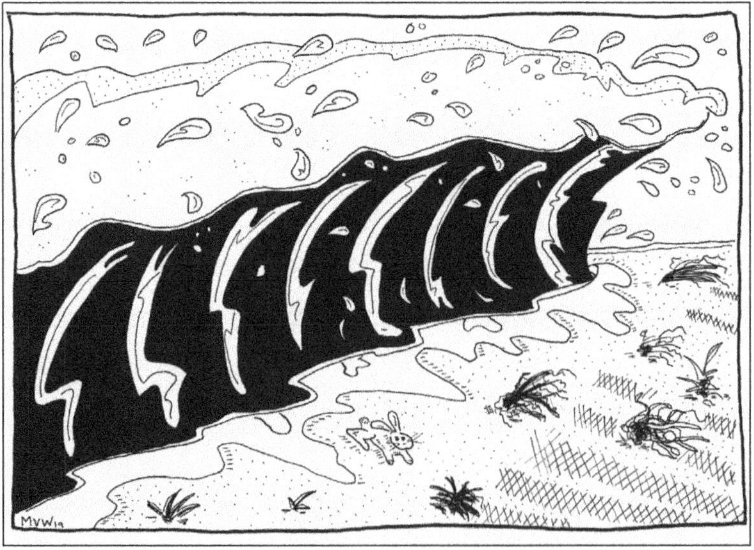

Up north, the great Missoula Ice Dam repeatedly burst over time, sending water and debris cascading down the Columbia River. The flood of water, glacier chunks, and boulders were diverted by an ice dam about where the Grand Coulee Dam sits now, sending the deluge south toward Soap Lake and Ephrata. (Courtesy of Mike VanderWerff.)

The Grand Coulee was created, and erratics were strewn, rafted, and rolled across the land. As the flood dug deeper and wider, a lone basalt mesa rose out of the water, largely unaffected by the cascading onslaught; the land strip became an island in the diverted waters of the Columbia River. (Courtesy of Mike VanderWerff.)

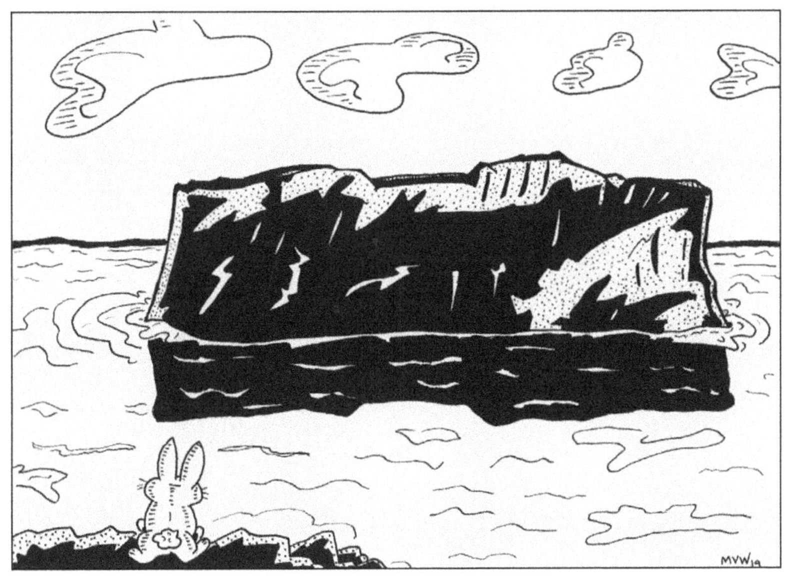

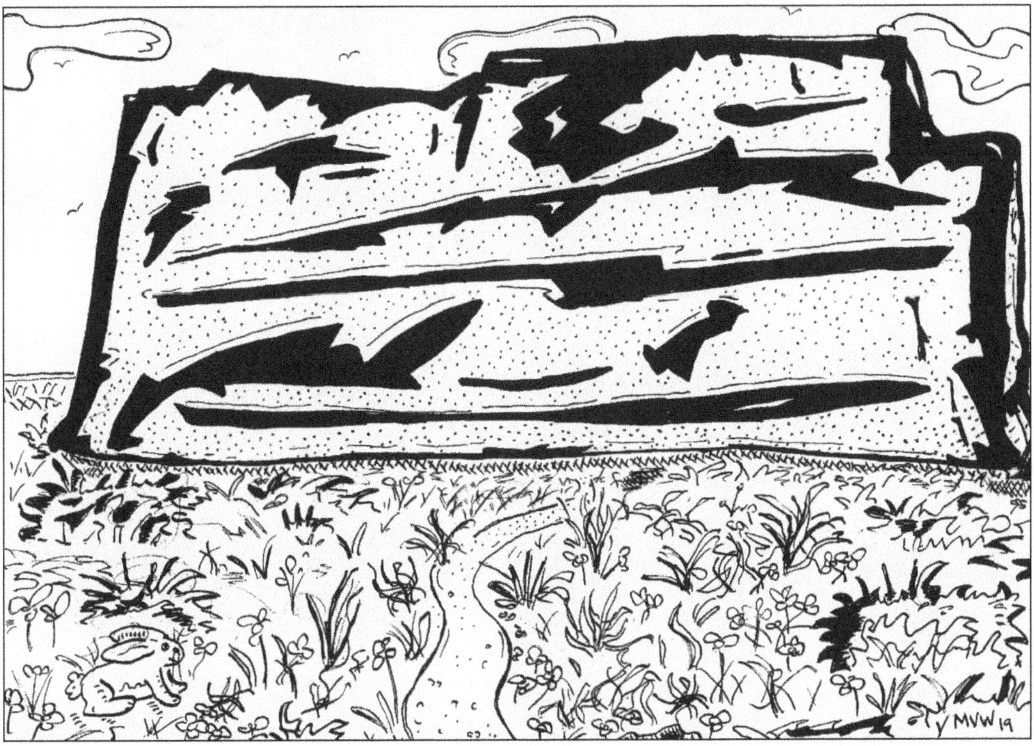

As time progressed, the land dried up, leaving the butte standing tall over the horizon. It was noticed by the original inhabitants who held it in reverence; later, when the fur traders and miners started to travel through the coulee, it was used as a landmark and received a new name, Steamboat Rock, due to its appearance. (Courtesy of Mike VanderWerff.)

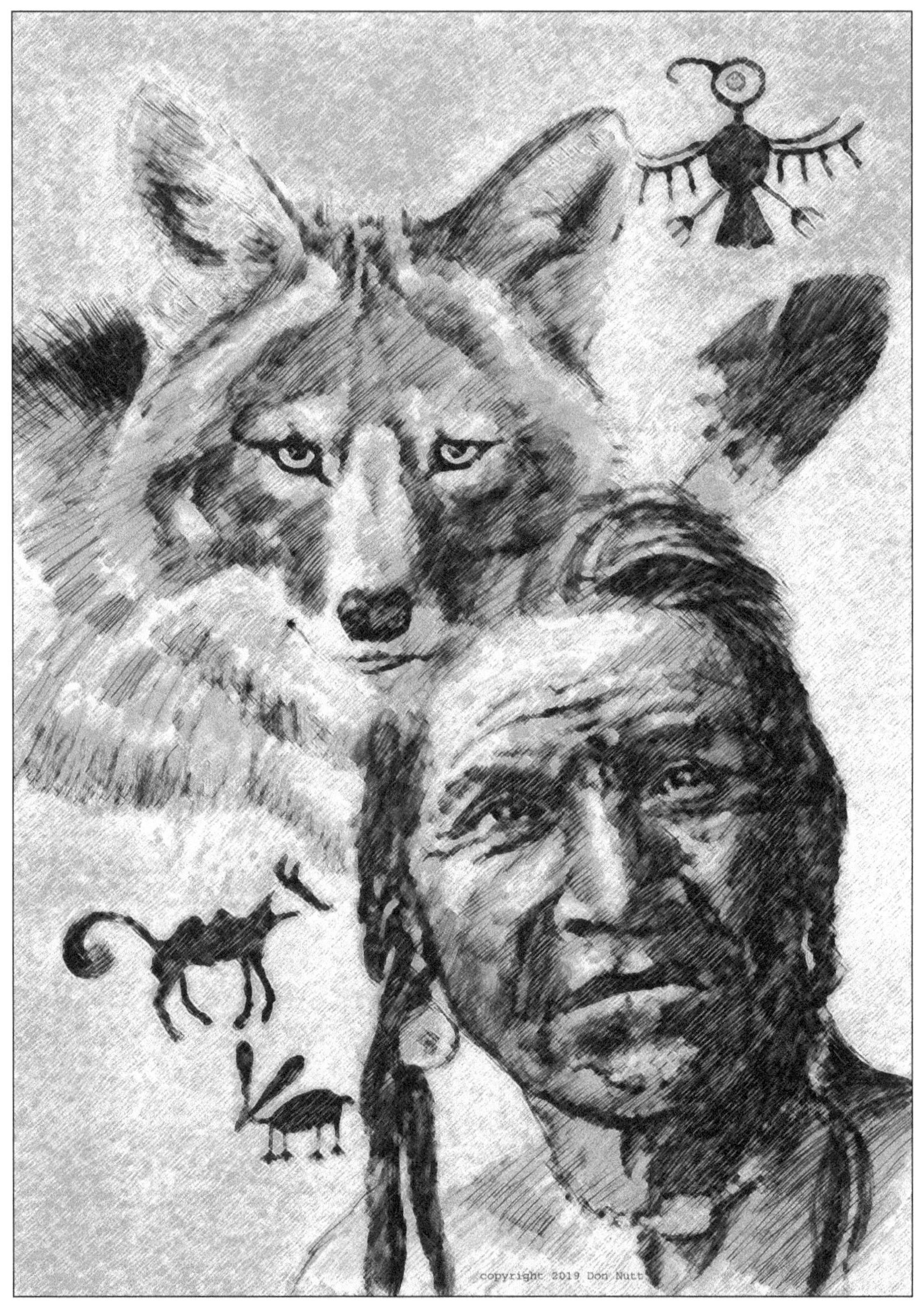

Another creation story about Steamboat Rock includes Coyote, Eagle, and Rabbit. There was a great drought leading to a lack of food. Eagle's father, facing starvation, turned to Coyote for help. In return, Coyote asked for the hand of Eagle's daughter. The wedding and a great feast were prepared, and the guests started to arrive. (Courtesy of Don Nutt.)

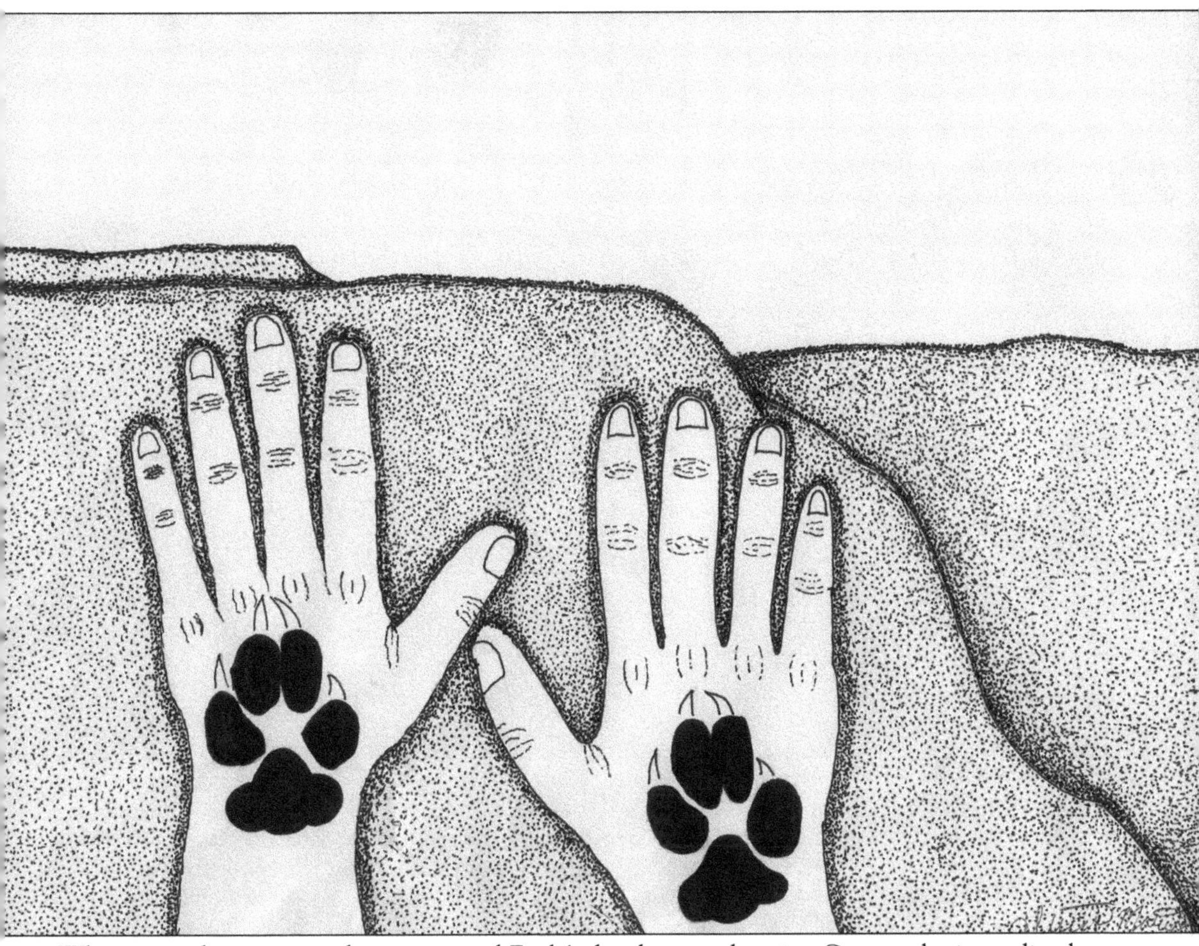

When everything was ready, out stepped Eagle's daughter, and spying Coyote, she immediately burst into tears, refusing to marry him, and disappeared back where she had come from. Rabbit laughed loudest, and Coyote flung him across the coulee, where he stuck on the wall near Salishan Mesa, forever changed to stone. Coyote then tossed the great wedding feast against the coulee wall, and it became the lichen and serviceberry found in the coulee today. Using his great power, Coyote then pushed Eagle's home far out into the coulee, cutting it off from the rest of the land and creating the mesa now called Steamboat Rock. (Courtesy of Alicia Marie McGuckin.)

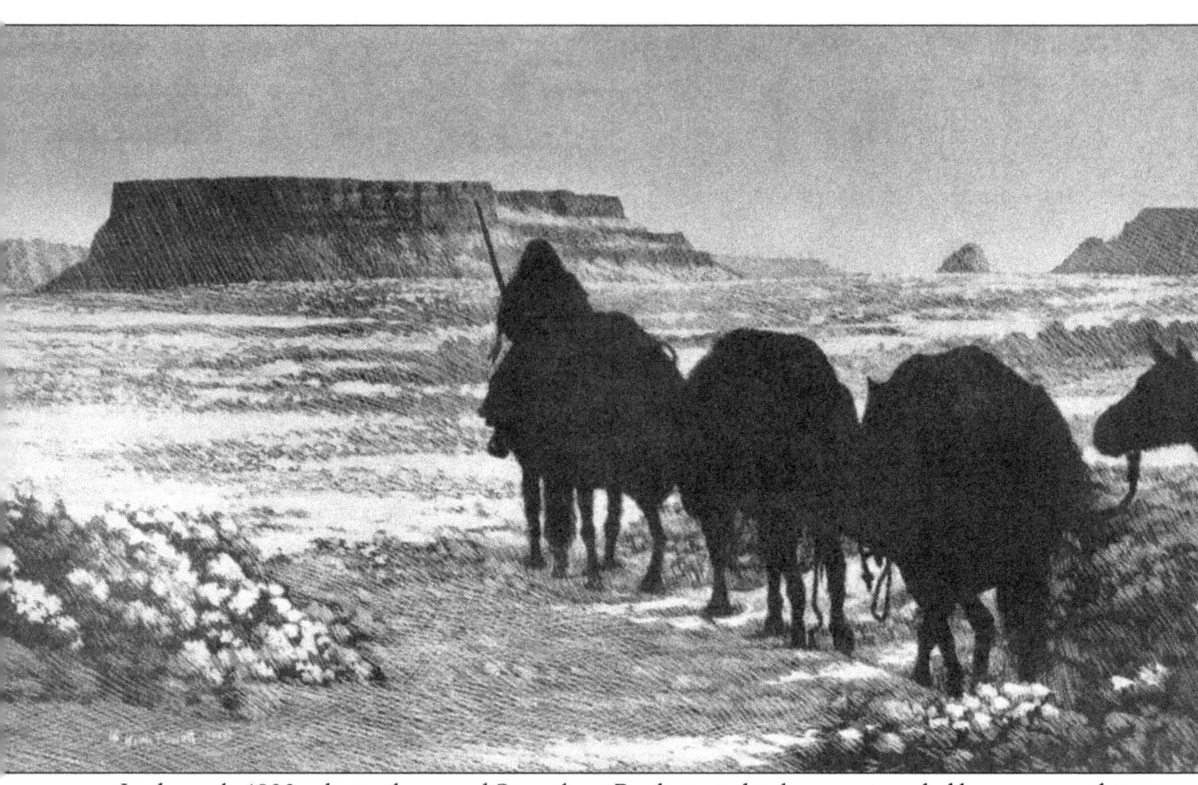

In the early 1800s, the trails around Steamboat Rock started to become traveled by scouts working for the Hudson Bay Company as well as miners headed to the Frasier Canyon Gold Rush up the Okanogan Trail. The Okanogan Trail was on the west side of Steamboat Rock and, on the east side of the trail, ran through Northrup Canyon up to Fort Colville or the Spokane House and was called the Point Trail. The two trails connected on the northeast side of Steamboat Rock near Pinnacle Rock and Devils Lake. (Courtesy of Keith Powell.)

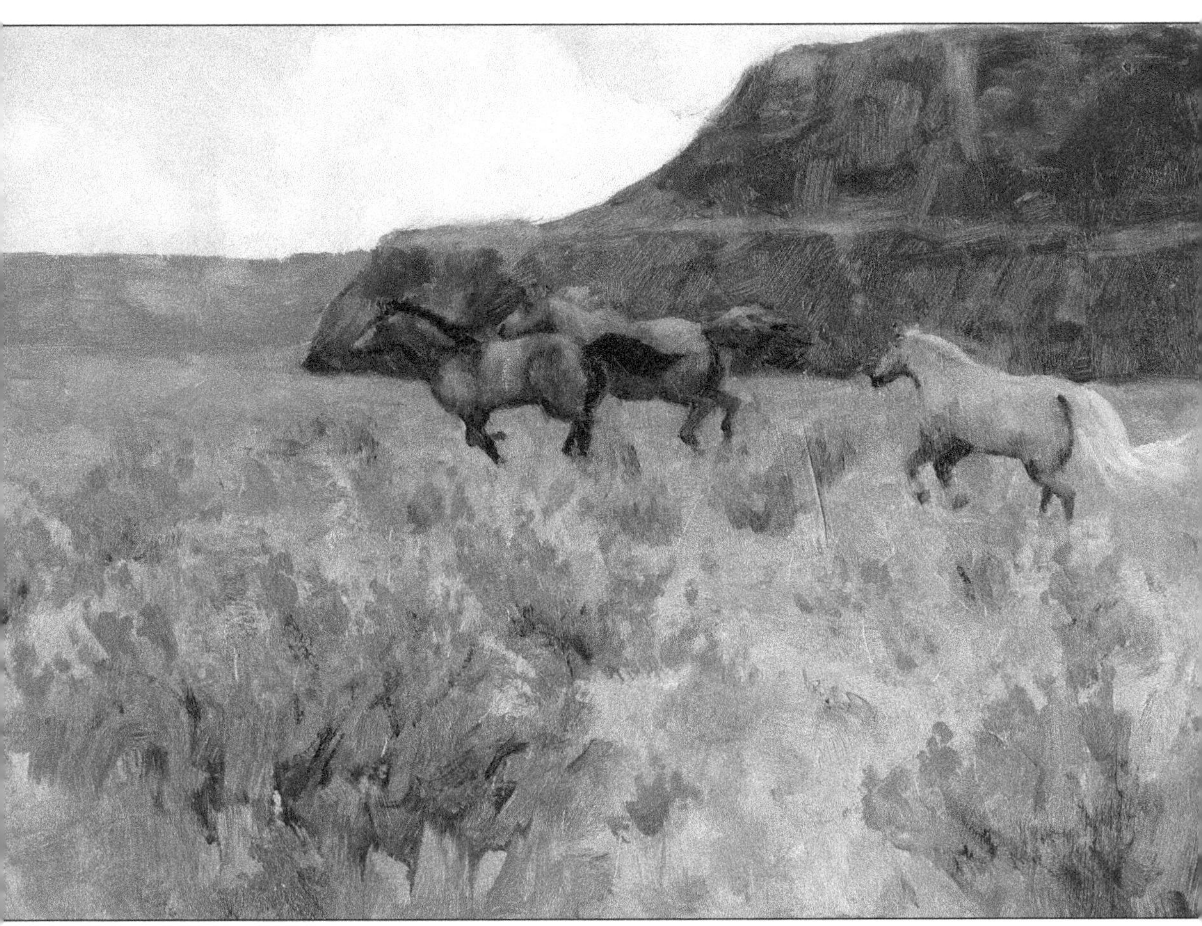

One of the earliest stories of Steamboat Rock is about horse thieves. The legend is the thieves would use the top of Steamboat Rock as a place to hide their stolen horses until they could move them into a different location to be sold. At the time, no one lived around Steamboat Rock, and even though it was a crossroads for travelers, days or weeks would pass without a single person being seen. As time passed, the horse thieves watched as more and more pioneers moved in, until their hideout was compromised and they were forced to move on. (Courtesy of Nora Egger.)

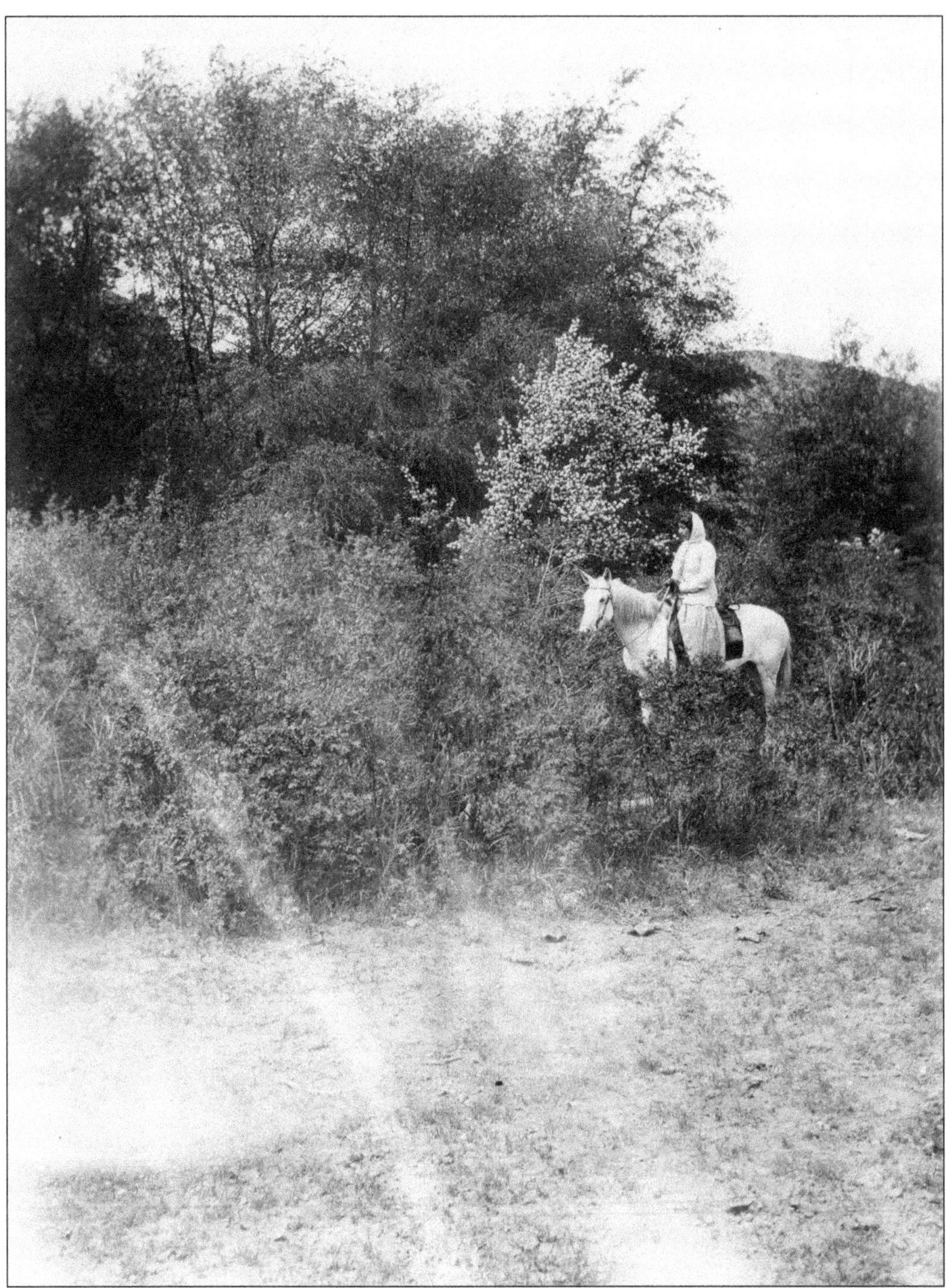

The land's original inhabitants also watched as pioneers moved into the coulee around Steamboat Rock. About 12 miles away, the Colville Reservation had been established in 1872. Under the guidance of Chief Moses, the various tribes coexisted peacefully with the newly arrived Steamboat Rock settlers. It is written that Chief Moses used to spend time at Steamboat Rock when he was younger and before the creation of the Colville Reservation. (Courtesy of Spokane Public Library.)

Two

Pioneers Arrive

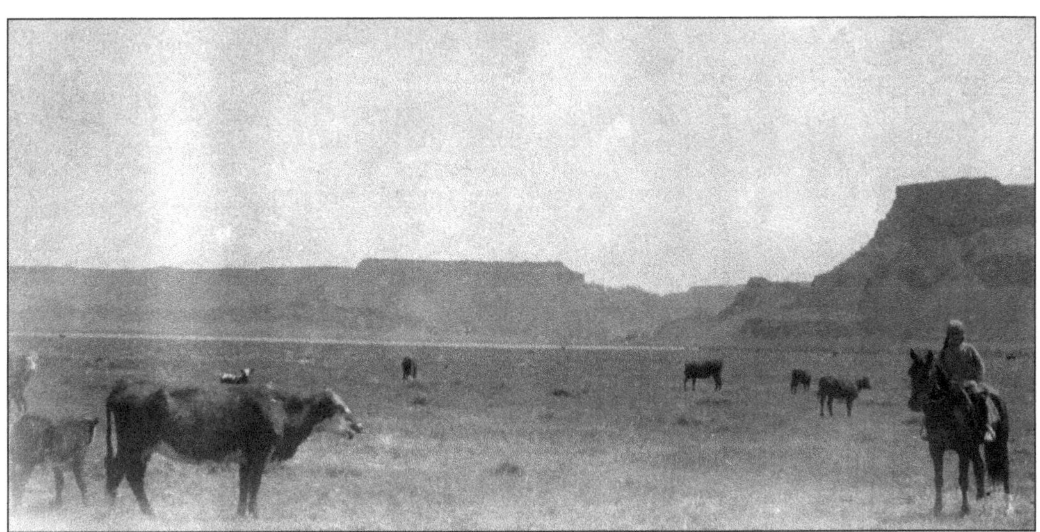

The Manifest Destiny attitude of the mid-1880s and Abraham Lincoln's Homestead Act of 1862 are the reason for most of the early Steamboat Rock pioneers. However, there were other claims that were also used by settlers to acquire land, such as the Timber Culture Act of 1873 and the Desert Land Act of 1877, which allowed settlers to purchase land for $1.25 an acre.

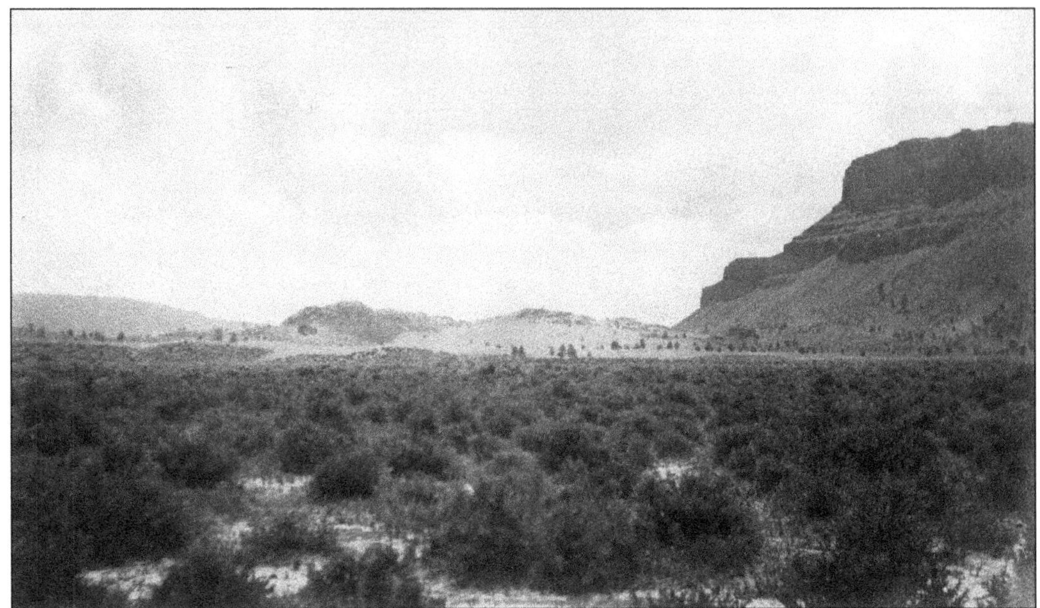

The land on the plateaus above the Grand Coulee had mostly been settled by the late 1880s. The Grand Coulee was viewed as an obstacle to get around more than a place to set up a homestead, and there were several well-used wagon trails that traveled down into the coulee and up out the other side.

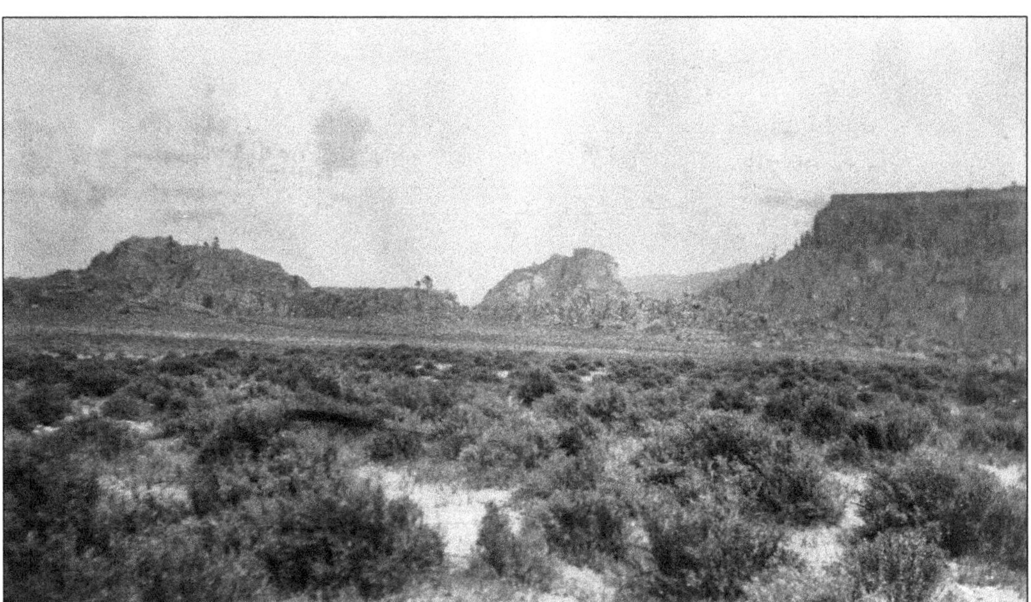

The land around Steamboat Rock, at first, seemed harsh, filled with sagebrush and sand dunes. Dry alkali lakes doted the coulee floor, their white soil shimmering in the sun, creating the illusions of water. It was an untamed land that seemed useless. However, the soil turned out to be rich volcanic ash, and crops of luxuriant bunch grass grew wild, providing perfect range conditions for cattle. Here, Pinnacle Rock can be seen in the center, with Castle Rock to the right.

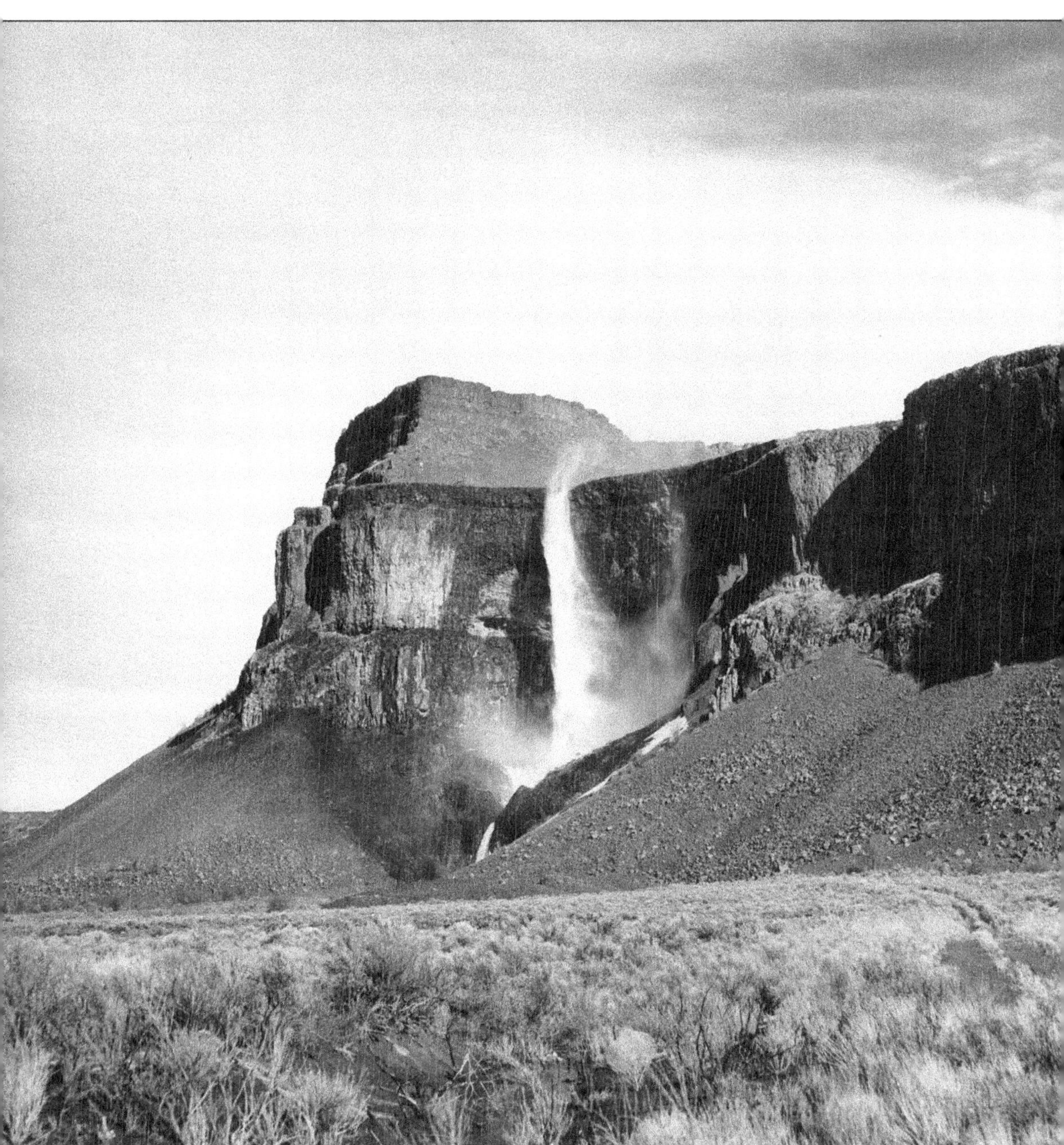

The first pioneers in the coulee around Steamboat Rock and Northrup Canyon discovered that despite being surrounded by sand dunes and seasonal alkali lakes, the land around Steamboat Rock had numerous springs and creeks that produced water all year round, and the spring run-off would flood over the coulee wall in multiple places, creating spectacular waterfalls, like the one seen here at Martin Falls/Devil's Punchbowl. There was plenty of water, but it tended to pool up in low elevation lakes, and what was left would dry up quickly under the hot summer sun. Despite the large run-off shown in the picture, Martin Falls only flows a few months every spring, when the snow from the highlands melts off or after an exceptional rain.

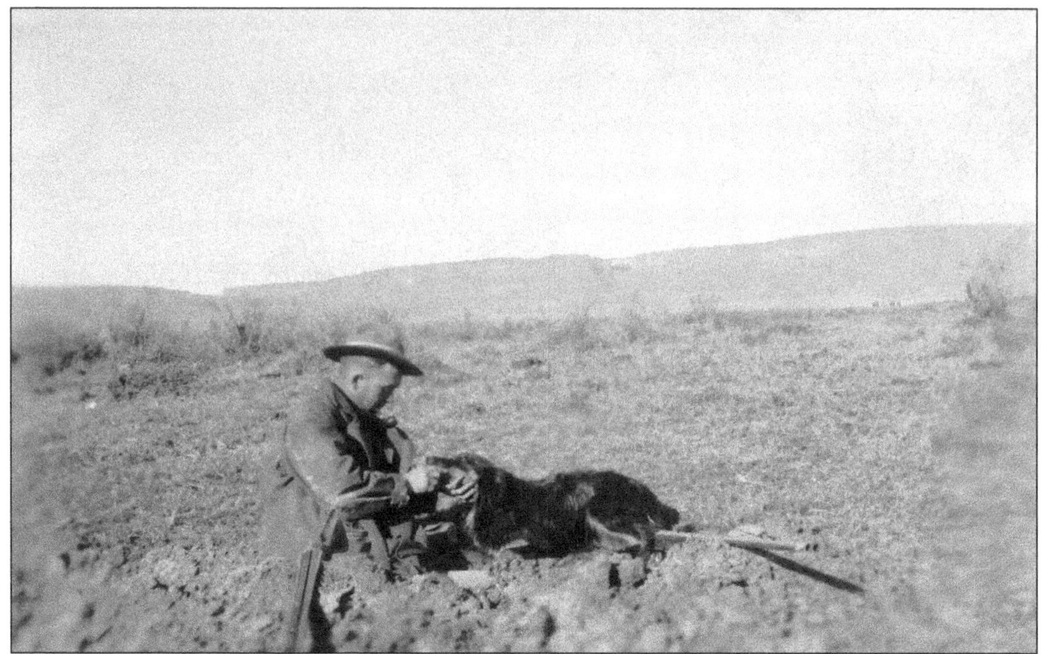

One of the earliest settlers around Steamboat Rock was Albert "Old Man" Barker. No one is sure when Barker took up residence on the west side of Steamboat Rock by the Okanogan Trail, but he was there when the earliest pioneers to the area started to arrive. Albert Barker had a small farm at the base of the cliff, and his water came from a natural spring.

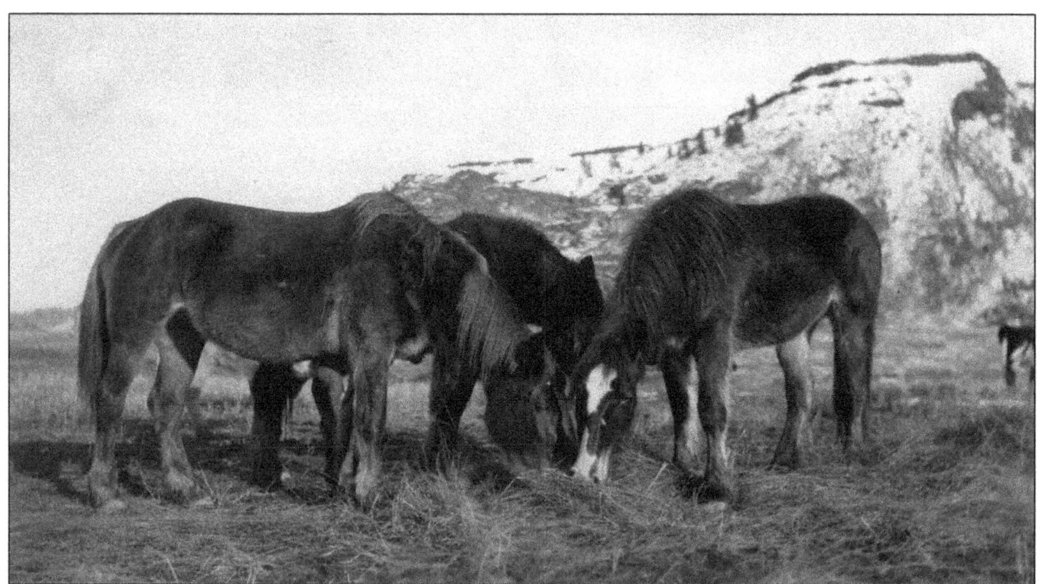

Albert Barker raised and sold horses in the canyon, utilizing the Okanogan Trail to move his livestock. The area was named after Barker, and even when he moved on and other families came to live on the old homestead, the name remained the same: Barker Canyon.

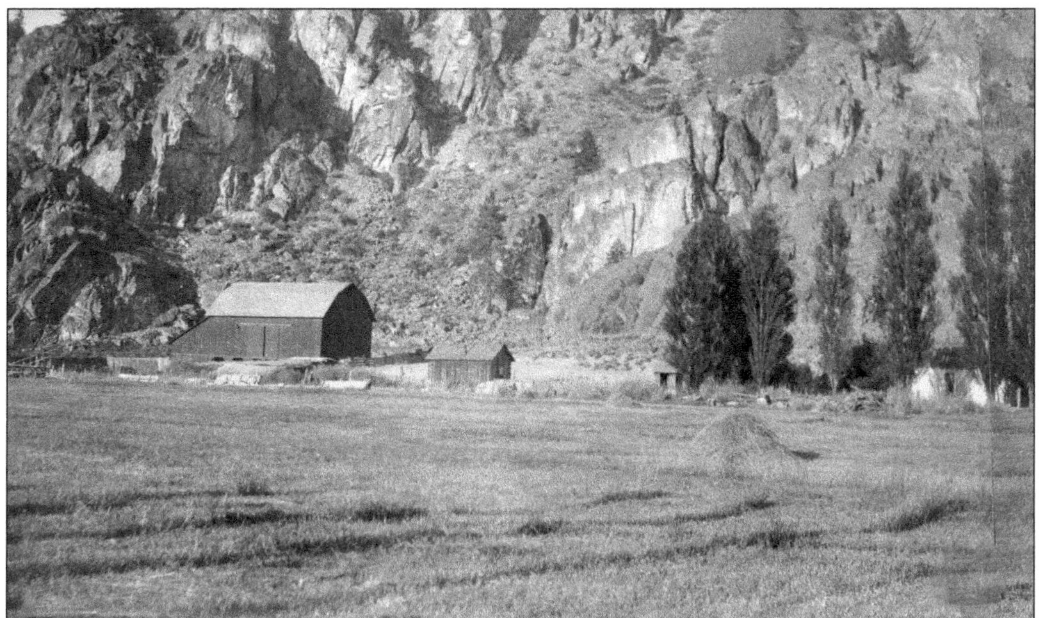

At the age of 19, William Fleet traveled into the Coulee region with historical Coulee City figure Dan Paul in the mid-1880s. Fleet continued up the Grand Coulee to Steamboat Rock and, just across from it, made his claim on the choicest land near Northrup Creek at the base of Castle Rock.

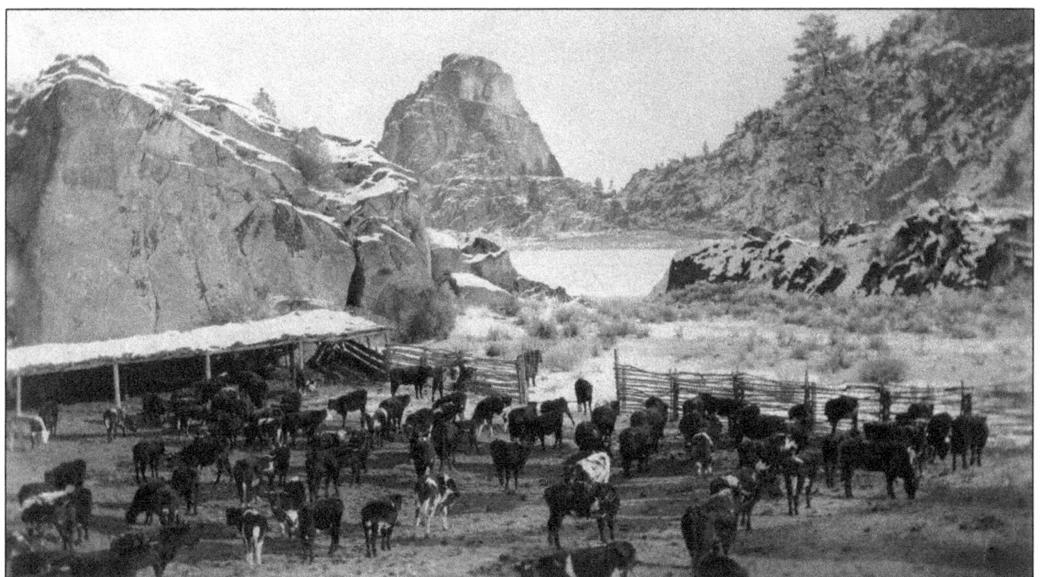

William Fleet imported and raised cattle; at one time, he ranged thousands of cattle for beef. During his time in the coulee, Fleet acquired and improved property up to the base of Steamboat Rock. In 1889, William Fleet decided to move back to his native homeland of New York and sold his ranch to Edward Schrock. In this picture, cattle are penned up on the old Fleet Ranch under Pinnacle Rock.

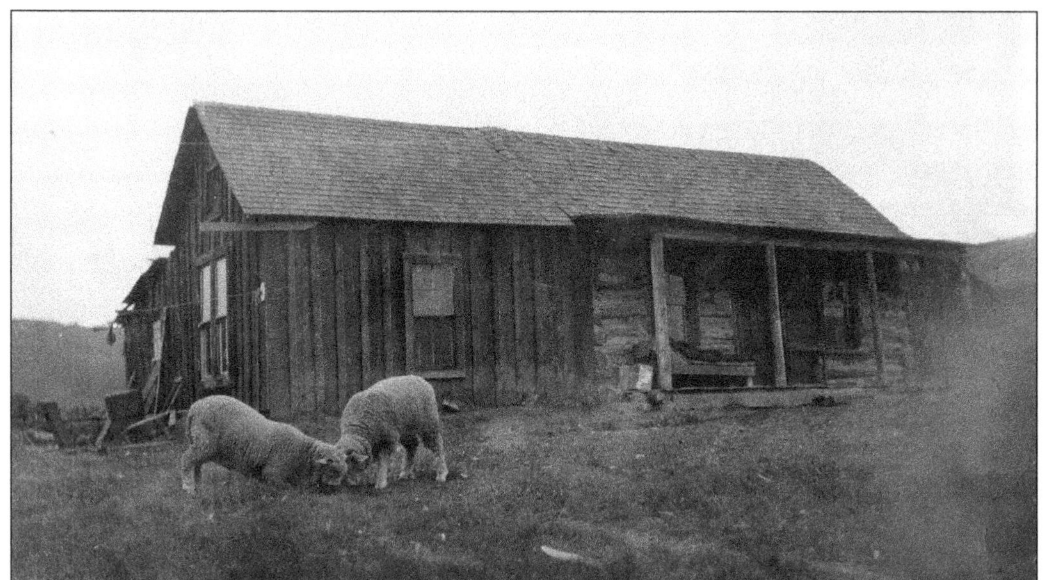

In 1886, newlyweds Hans and Matilda Lange arrived in the coulee and set up a small cabin a few miles to the northwest of Steamboat Rock. Hans was a cattleman who brought a small starter herd with him. At first, he let his cattle range and would ride the coulee with neighbor Charley Osborne. (Courtesy of the *Star*, Grand Coulee.)

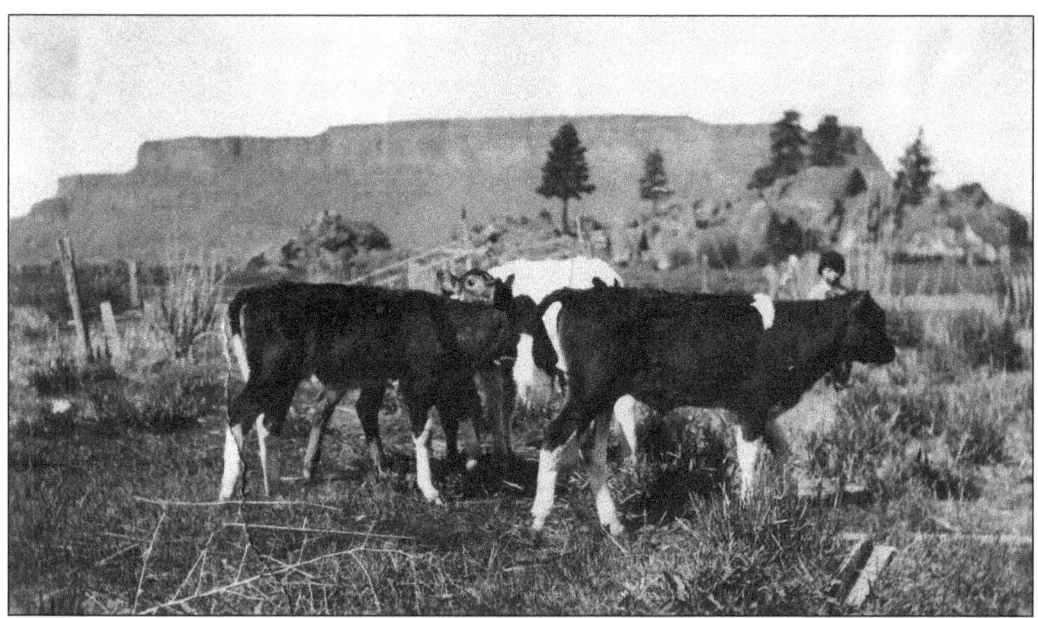

Successful cattle ranching earned the Langes a fair sum of cash, and Hans was able to build a deluxe two-story ranch house out of natural white granite quarried from his own land. Before his land was condemned and he was forced to move out, he was quoted as calling his white granite home the culmination of his work and time spent in the coulee.

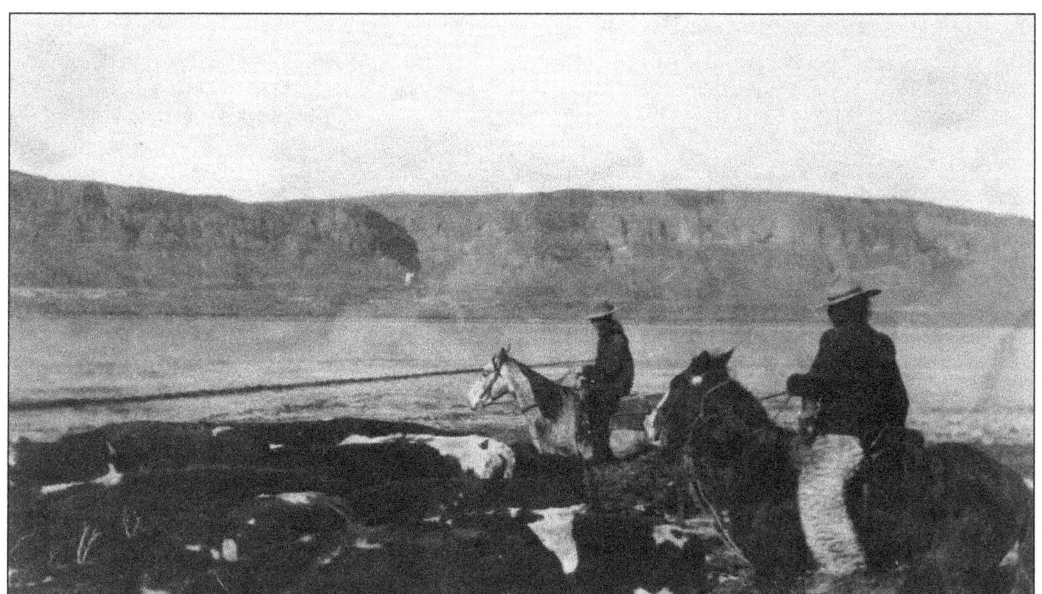

The traditional way to move cattle was by herding them on horseback, and this was done for many years in the coulee around Steamboat Rock. Sometimes, the cattle were herded hundreds of miles for a specific client, but most were bound for a railhead and far-off meat-packing plant.

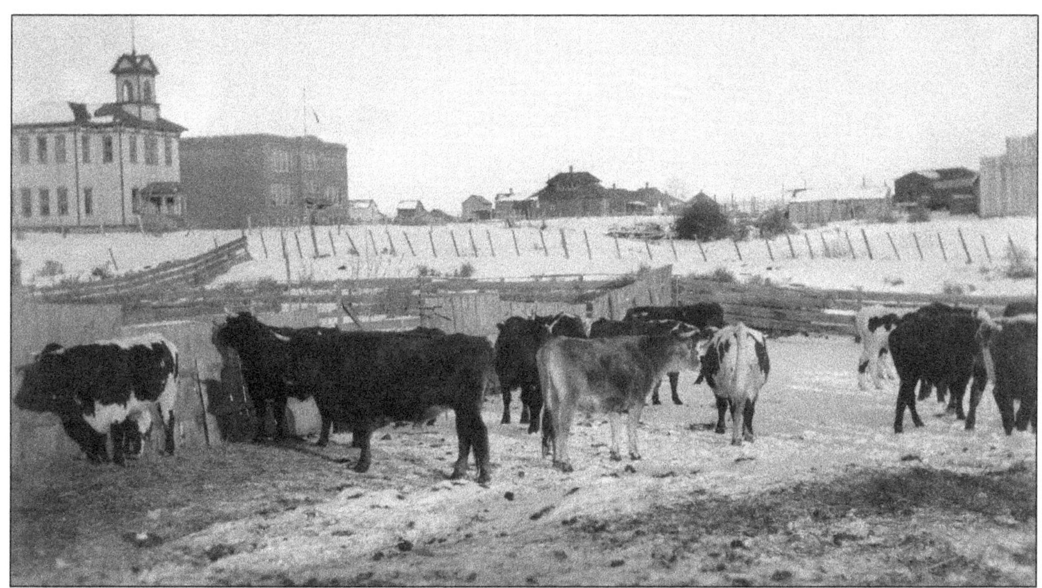

Most of the cattle raised around Steamboat Rock were moved down the coulee south to the railhead in Coulee City. From there, they could be either sold in town or shipped out by rail to packing plants on the East Coast. This c. 1910 picture shows cattle in Coulee City waiting for market. In the background, the old Coulee City school can be seen.

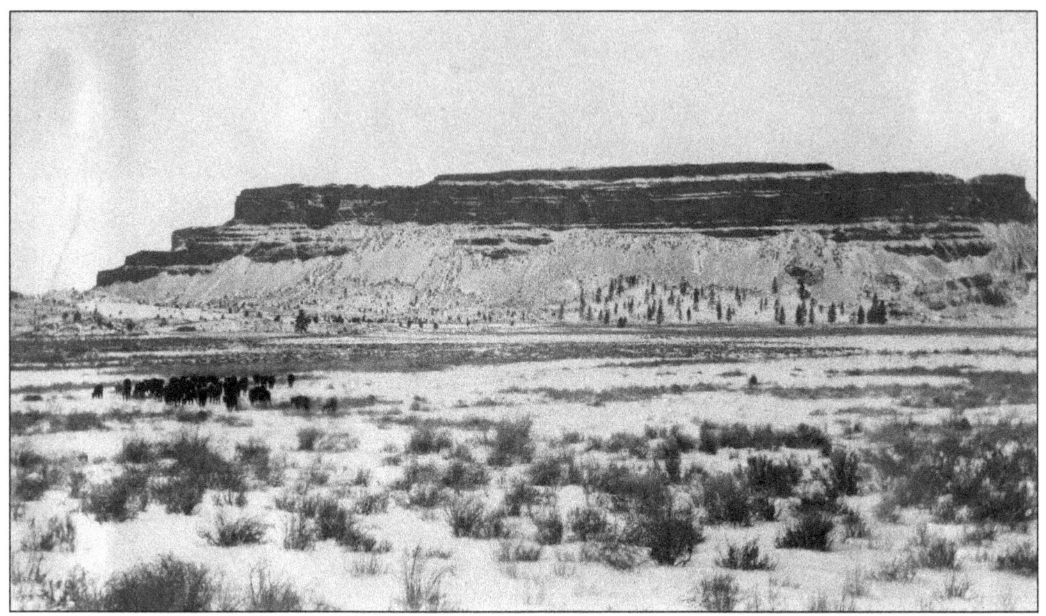

Winter around Steamboat Rock could be a terrible thing, often leaving pioneers snowbound. The winter of 1899 was especially bad. It came early and stayed late into 1900, with temperatures dropping into the minus degrees. Many cattle died that winter, and most froze to death. Other cattle could not get food, and starvation set in, thinning the herds.

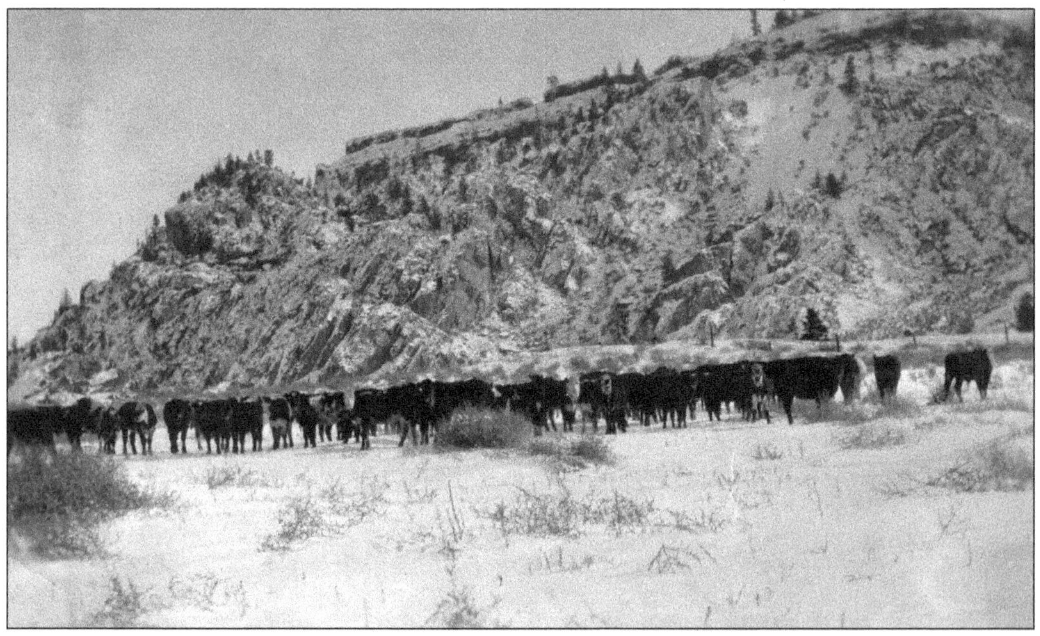

Neighbors Hans Lange and Charlie Osborne knew they had no choice but to go to Coulee City for feed. On their way back, they were met by a herd of starving cows that followed the men and their sleigh full of hay. To avoid being trampled by starving cattle, the two ranchers stashed the hay on a tabletop rock and returned later after the cows wandered off again.

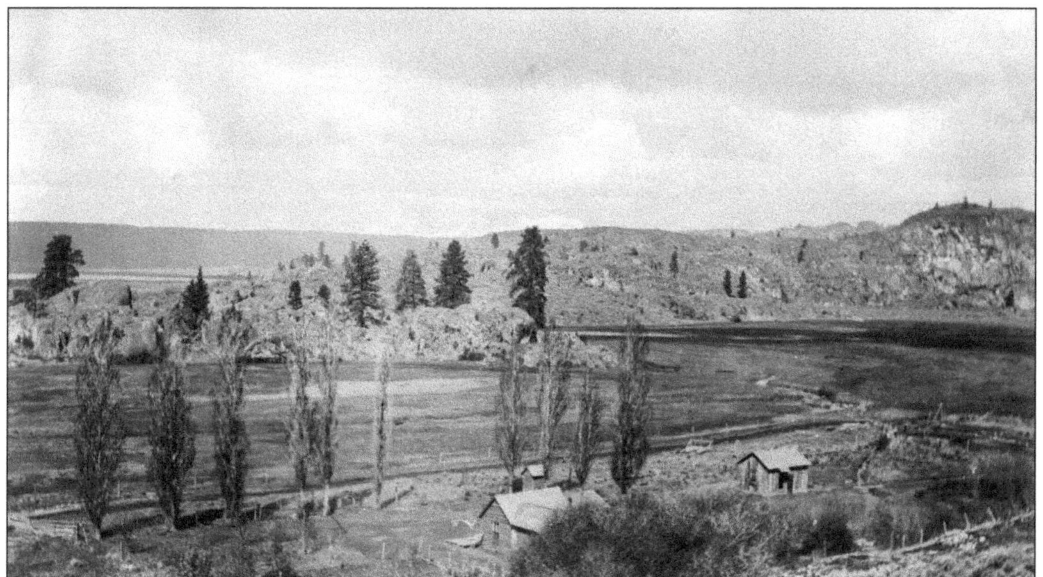

Ed and Willie Schrock had a cattle ranch up around Almira, and when they purchased the Fleet Ranch in 1889, they moved their livestock down into the coulee. Ed Schrock and his wife, Anor Bernard, moved into the old Fleet homestead. Anor gave birth to three children in the little farmhouse across from Steamboat Rock.

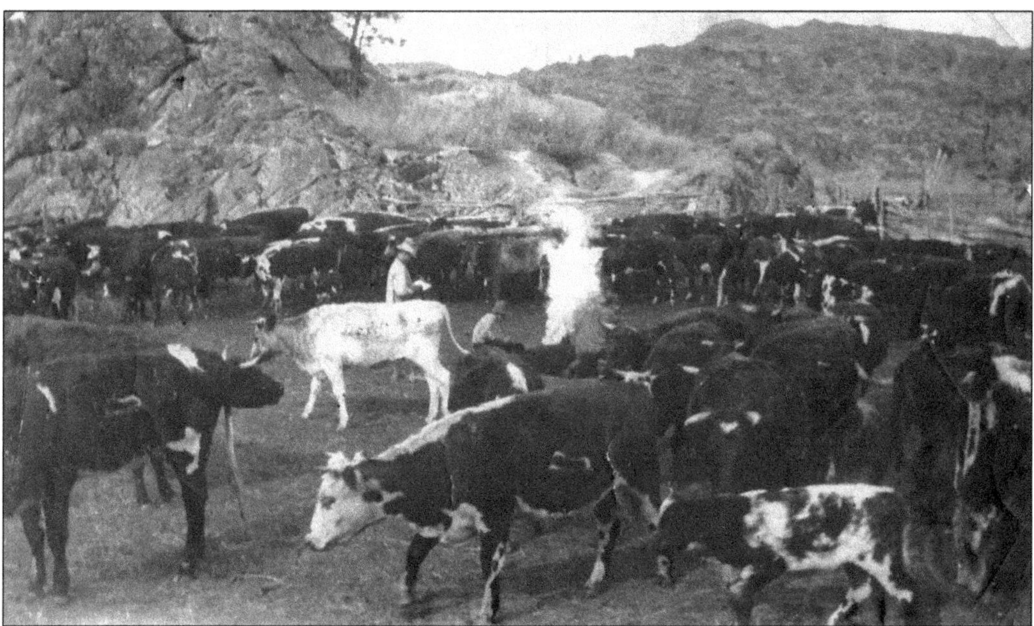

Ed Schrock ran thousands of cattle across the Columbia River at the Condon ferry into Okanogan Country. He usually ran a herd of 400 or 500 draft horses with his cattle, which he also sold. The Schrock herds ranged from the San Poil to the Okanogan River, and calves were often being brought back across the river to winter at the Steamboat Rock ranch.

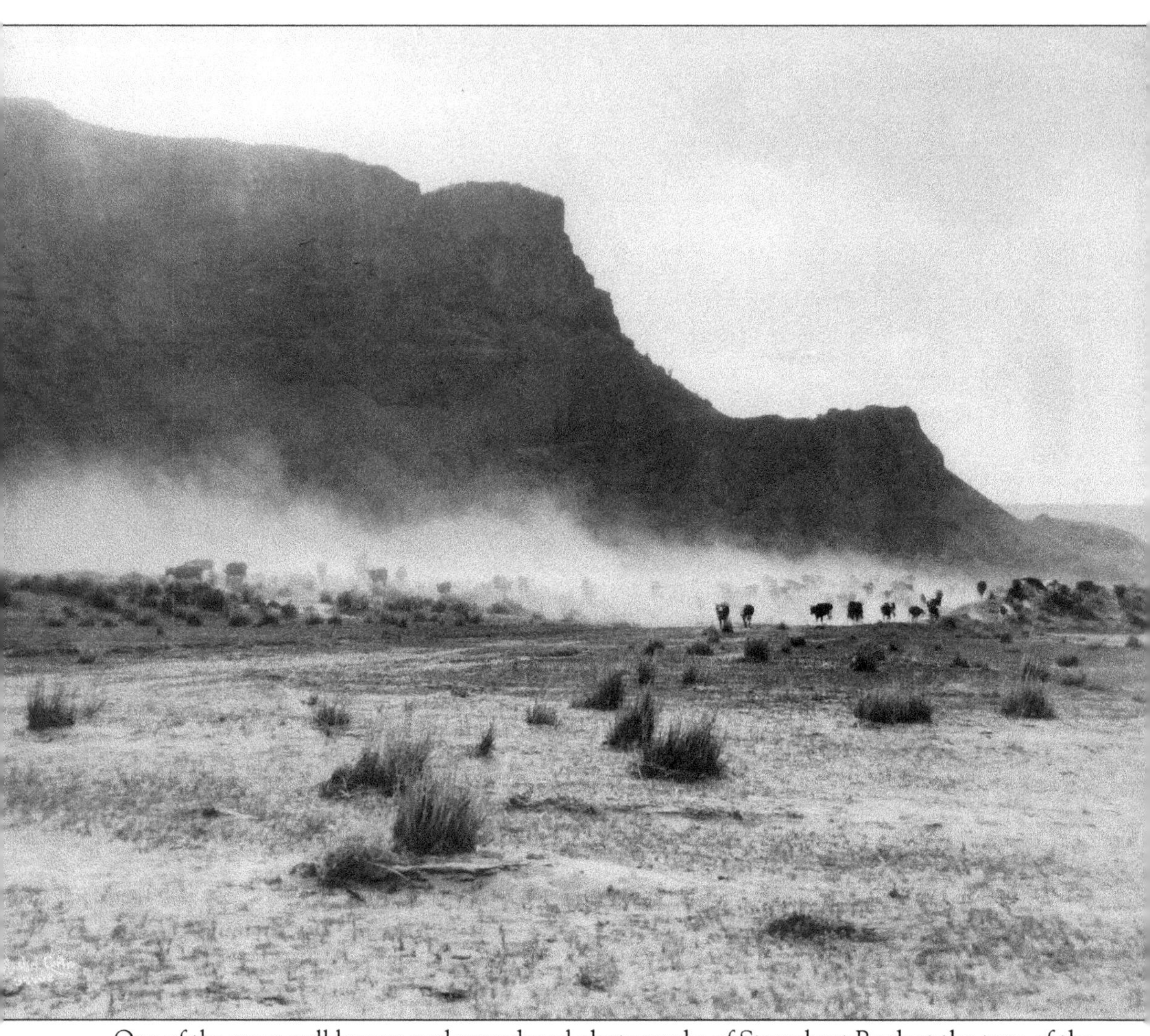

One of the more well-known and reproduced photographs of Steamboat Rock at the turn of the 20th century was Asahel Curtis's "The Phantom Herd." Taken around 1900, this picture shows Ed Schrock, the cowboy in the dust cloud, running his cattle around the northeast end of Steamboat Rock. Schrock was known for hiring some of the best range men of the area to herd his cattle back from Okanogan to his ranch at Steamboat Rock, where they would then be driven by horse to the nearest railhead in Coulee City.

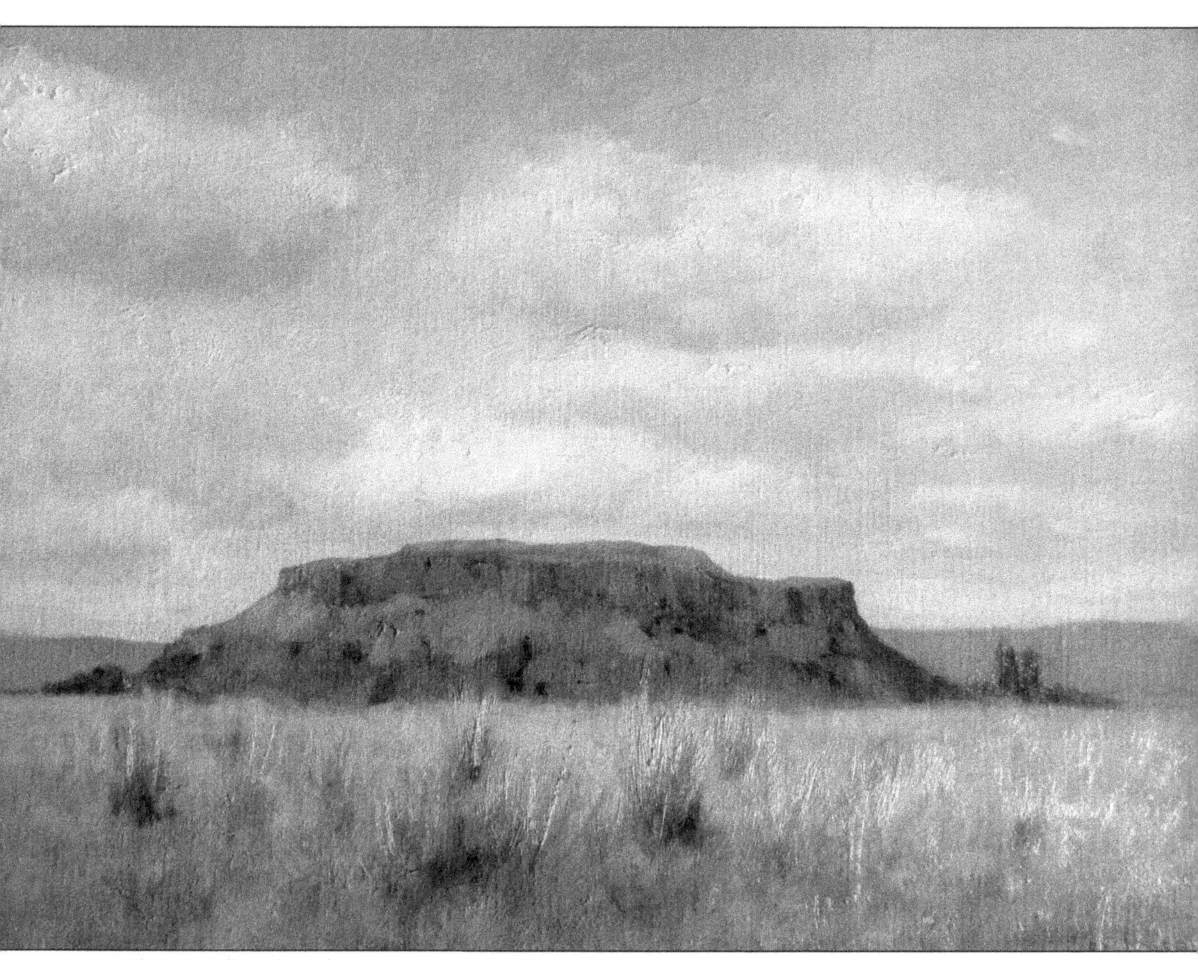

Arnor (Bernard) Schrock was an artist and used to oil paint the coulee walls and Steamboat Rock. The Schrock children all attended the Steamboat Rock School, and in 1909, Ed Schrock sold the farm to Baldwin and Barnhizle and moved to Okanogan County. Baldwin and Barnhizle had plans for the land, joining it with other properties to create one huge sprawling ranch they called the Steamboat Rock Stock Company. (Courtesy of Nora Egger.)

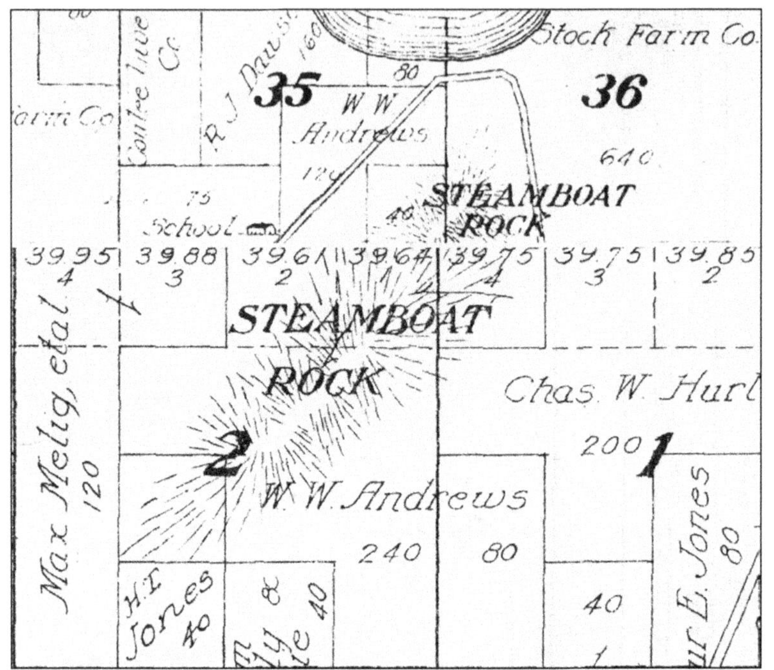

Around 1904, brothers William and Richard Andrews from Tennessee took up a homestead around Steamboat Rock, filing separate land claims. William's claim was directly on Steamboat Rock as well as a patch of land on the east side, while his older brother Richard's claim was on the more-populated west side in Barker Canyon. This land plat shows William's land claim of Steamboat Rock. (Courtesy of Dan Bolyard.)

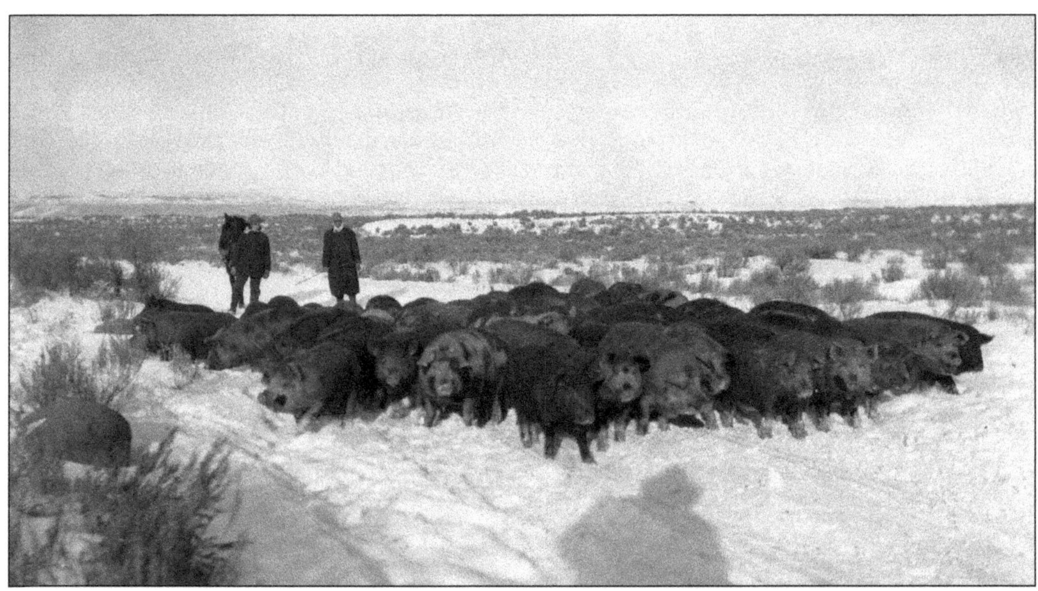

The brothers came from a refined Southern plantation life, and Richard was prone to the highlife, attending dances and courting the neighbor ladies. He raised hogs on his land and did fairly well. Together, the brothers would herd the hogs to market down the coulee, often on foot, with the help of a dog.

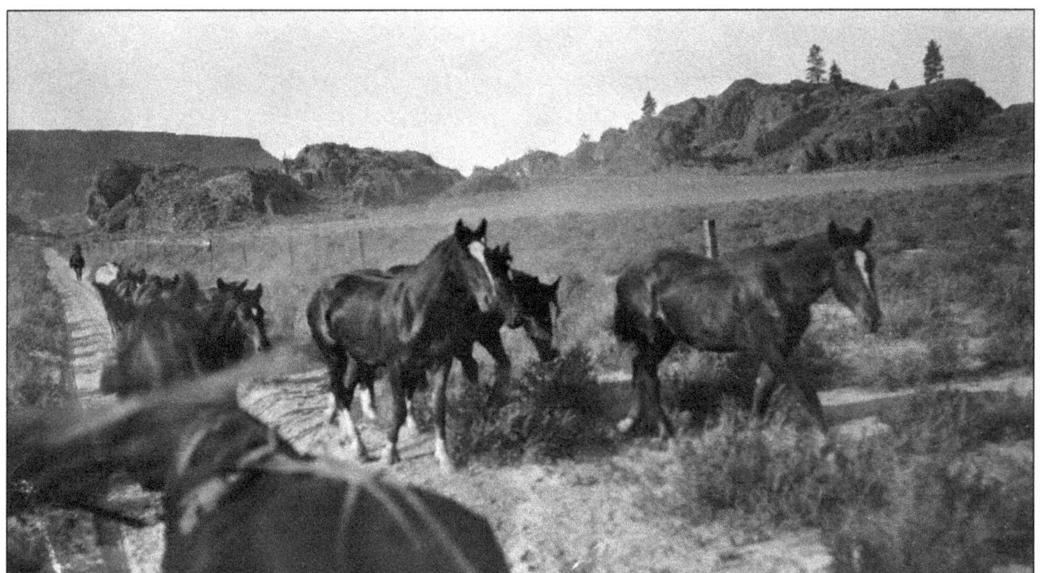

William Andrews, better known as "Steamboat Bill," laid claim to the whole of Steamboat Rock with the idea of creating a horse farm at the top. For a while, Steamboat Bill had some success with ranging the horses on top of Steamboat Rock. He would drive them up the same steep path traveled by hikers today and rumored horse thieves in the mid-1800s.

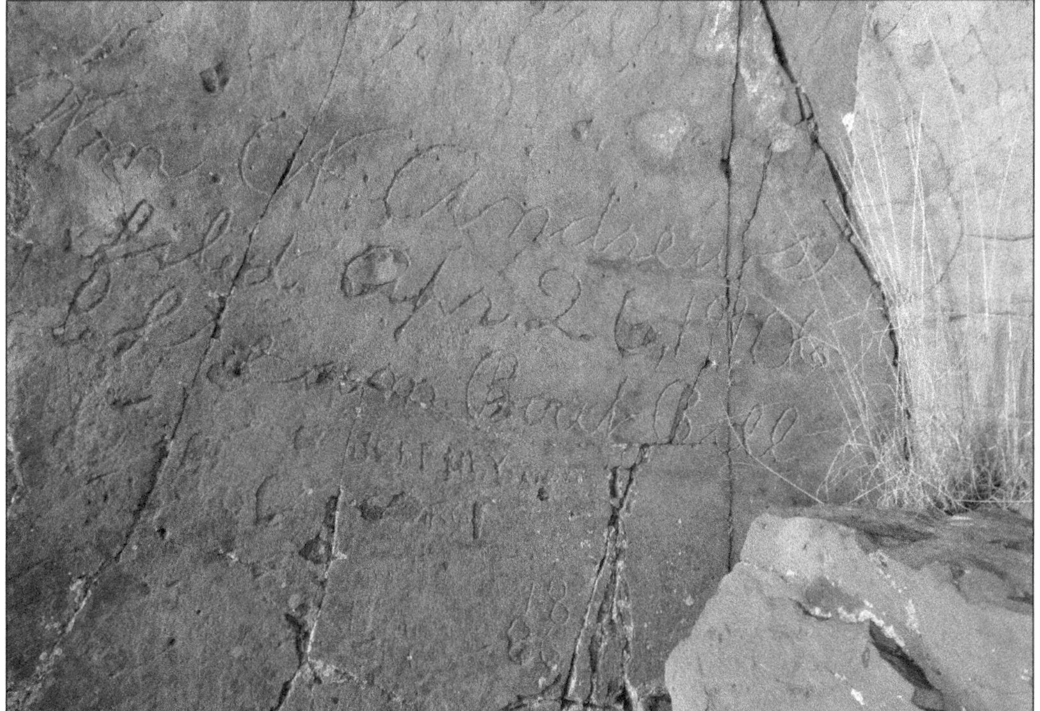

Steamboat Bill Andrews was the opposite of his brother—quiet and reserved. While waiting for his claim on the land to go through, he carved his name into solid rock along with the date of his claim; April 2, 1906. In 1911, their sister arrived from Tennessee, and the brothers escorted her back to the South. (Courtesy of J. Kemble.)

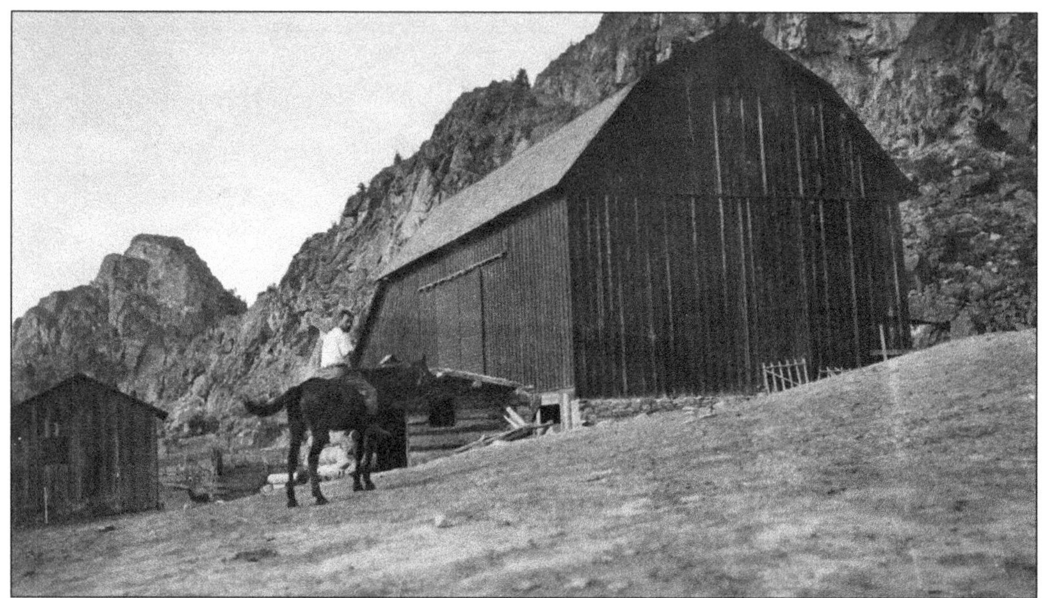

Often, the homesteaders would move out as fast as they moved in, but not always. By the early 1900s, there was an influx of pioneers settling around Steamboat Rock. A small, loose community started forming as homesteaders moved into the coulee with their entire families to take advantage of various homesteader acts and land claims.

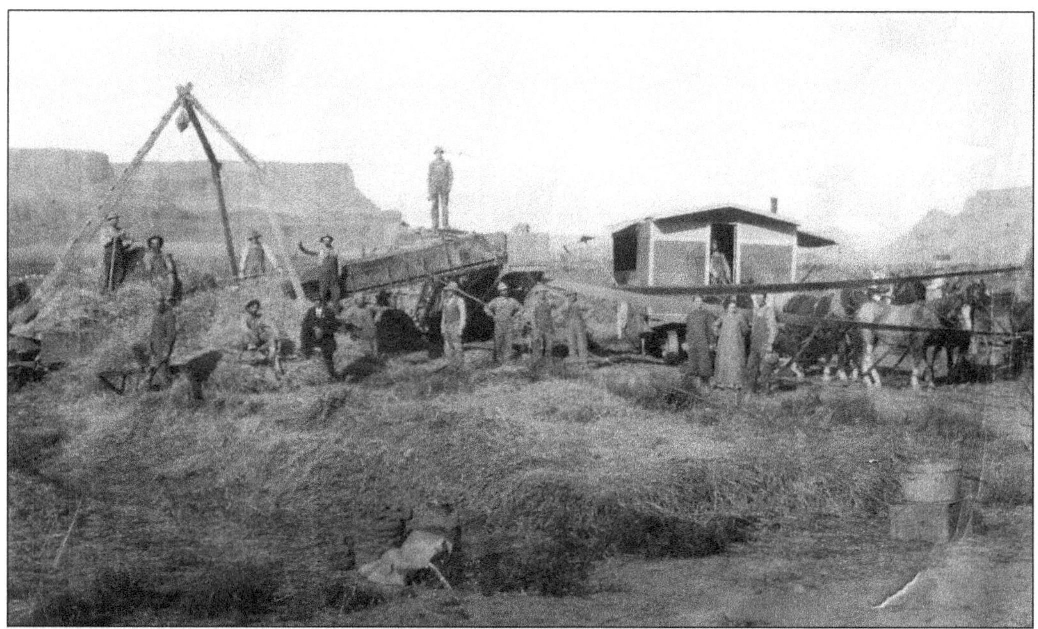

In the beginning, the land around Steamboat Rock was used almost exclusively for cattle, but as the 1900s approached, more land had been plowed up, and fields of wheat, hay, and alfalfa became more and more common. Cattle, sheep, and occasionally, horses were the primary livestock raised in the area. There were several other crops that were produced, orchards, smaller livestock, and dairy of all sorts.

Three

DRY-LAND FARMING

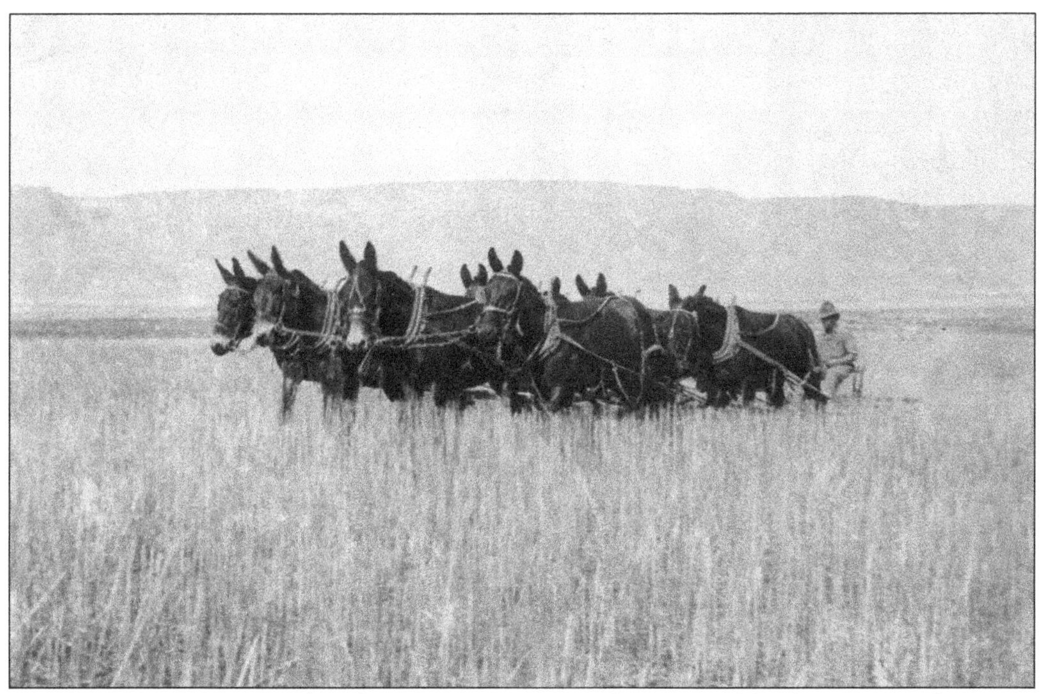

With so many pioneers and settlers moving west into dry untamed lands, irrigation became a key factor in success or failure. Some people believed that irrigation was the key to taming the west, and there was much talk, study, and speculation on farming and the distribution of water to crops. In 1902, Congress passed the Reclamation Act, later renamed the Bureau of Reclamation; its first task was to bring water to the arid lands of the West.

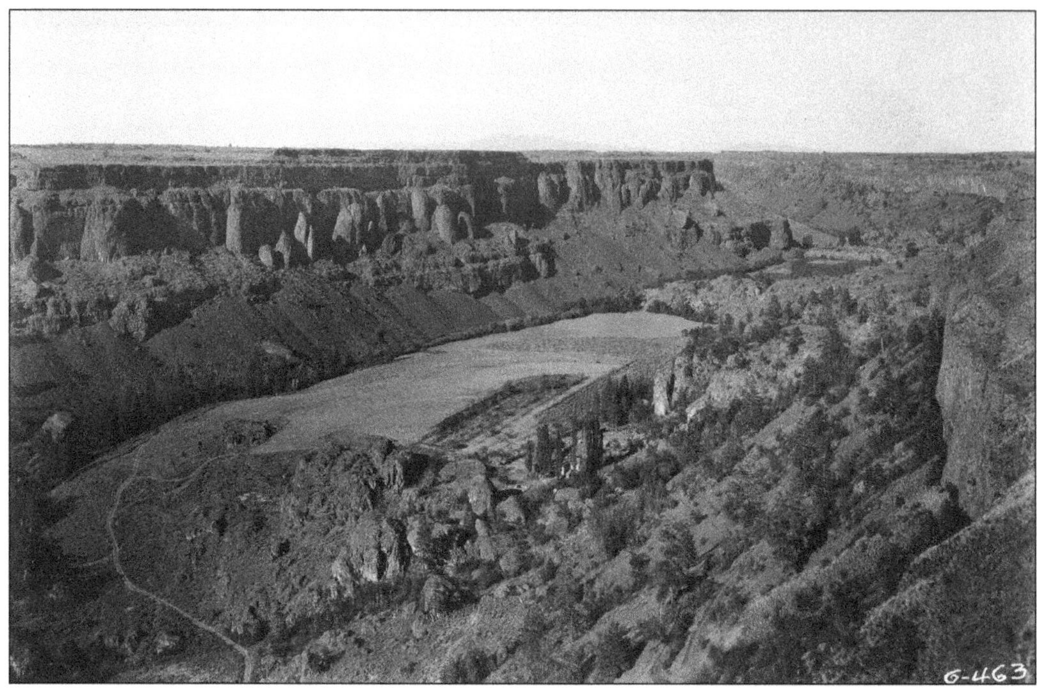

Near Steamboat Rock, Northrup Creek flowed year-round, along with natural springs it fed Devils Lake. The creek flowed from a canyon that pioneers had settled since the late 1880s, utilizing the running water and natural springs to irrigate orchards. People would travel from all over to purchase fruit in Northrup Canyon. (Courtesy of Spokane Public Library.)

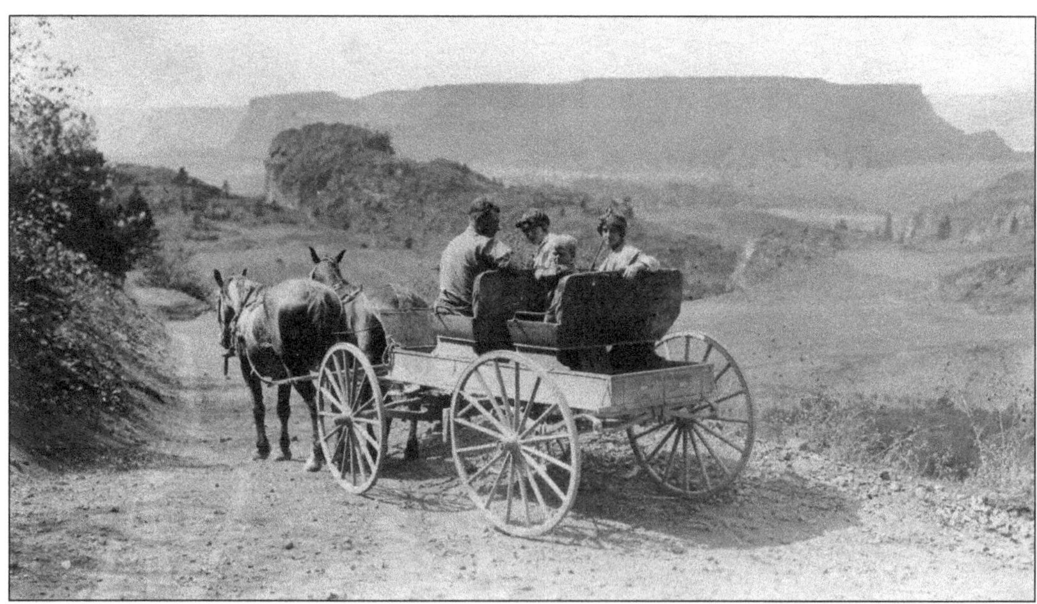

The Scheibner Grade ran down the south basalt wall of Northrup Canyon; it was built and maintained by the Scheibner Brothers. It became a quick route from the trains in Wilbur down through the coulee past Steamboat Rock and onto Leahy Junction. Here, the Baldwin family makes their way down in the transport of the day.

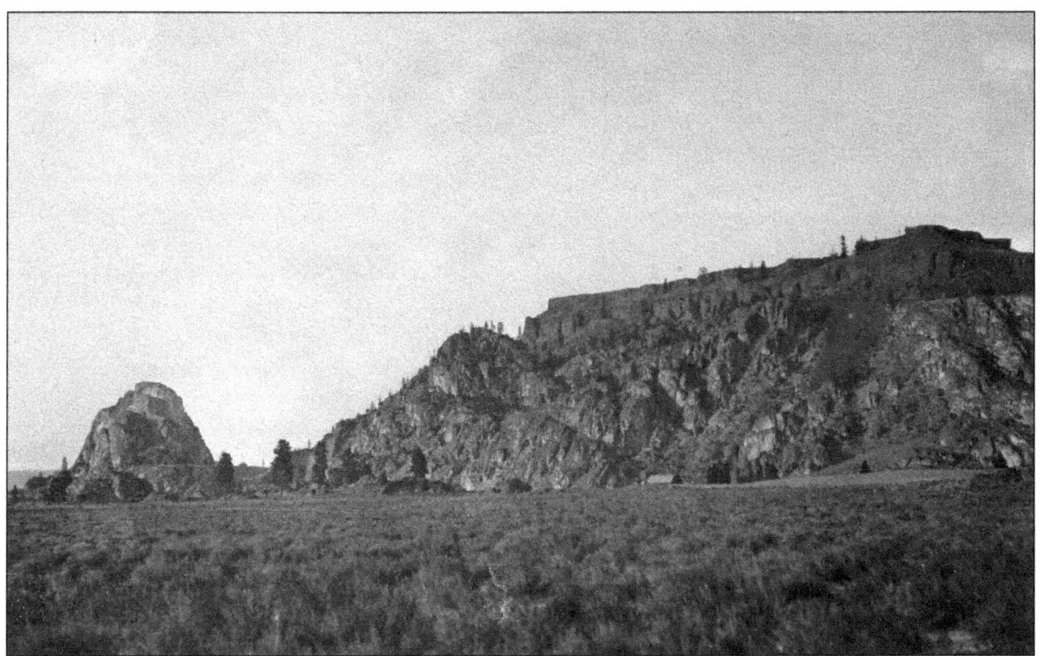

In 1909, Ed Schrock sold his ranch into the interest of Baldwin and Barnhizle. The two young men were college-educated and had a lot of cash and big dreams. Their idea was to combine several of the large ranches around the base of Steamboat Rock and up to the shore on both sides of Devils Lake into one big diversified ranch.

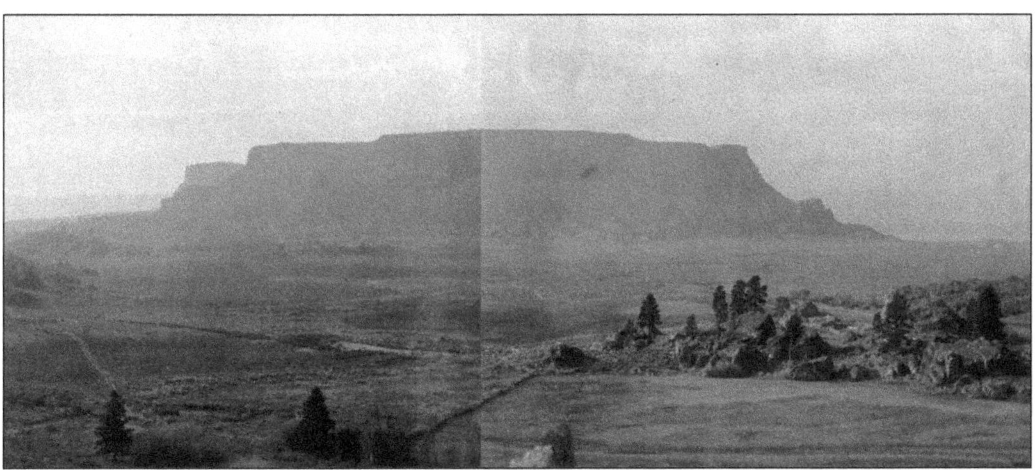

The partnership of Baldwin and Barnhizle acquired 5,000 acres and three sprawling ranches, including the Fleet/Schrock Ranch. They named their newly acquired ranches by number, and the Fleet/Schrock Ranch was called Ranch One.

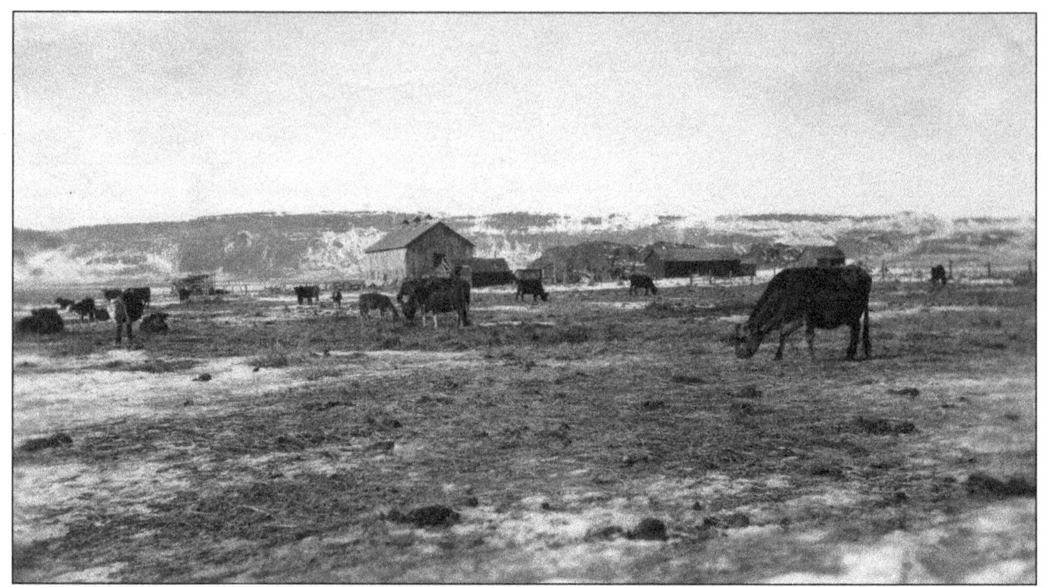

Ranch Two was located on the west side of Steamboat Rock, and Ranch Three was further up into Barker Canyon. Ranch Two had a huge dairy barn and rich, fertile volcanic ash topsoil. George Baldwin and his family moved into Ranch Two. From here, among other things, the Baldwins raised a herd of dairy cattle and sold the fresh cream directly to Seattle and Spokane.

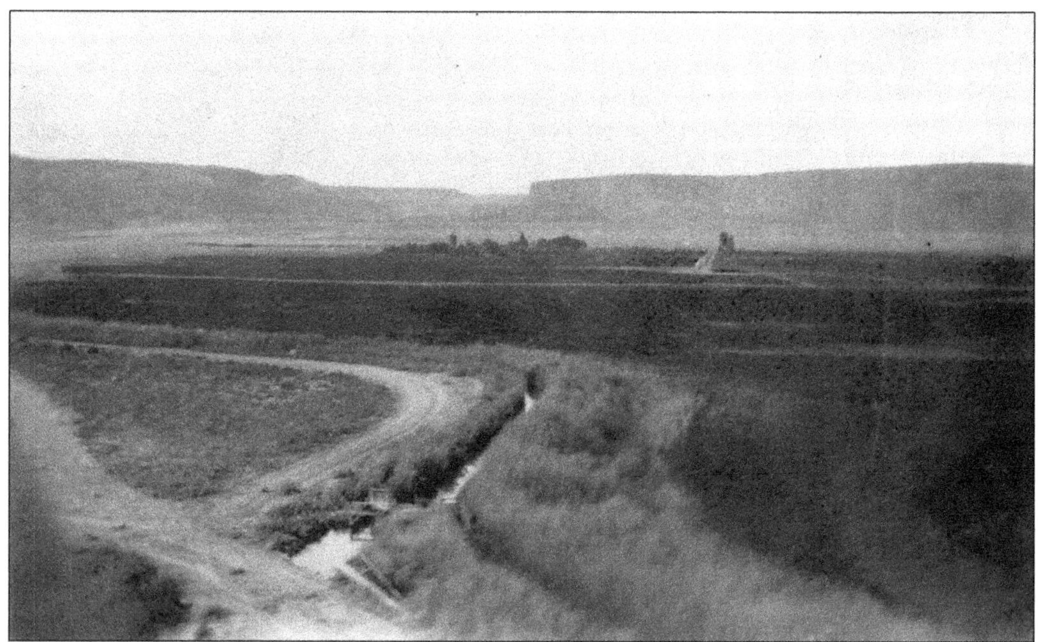

A big part of the Baldwin and Barnhizle plan was to irrigate their lands from nearby lake Devils Lake. At the turn of the 20th century, as more and more people migrated into the desert areas, irrigation became a fine science. The traditional way was irrigation ditches, as seen here, delivering water to an orchard southwest of Steamboat Rock.

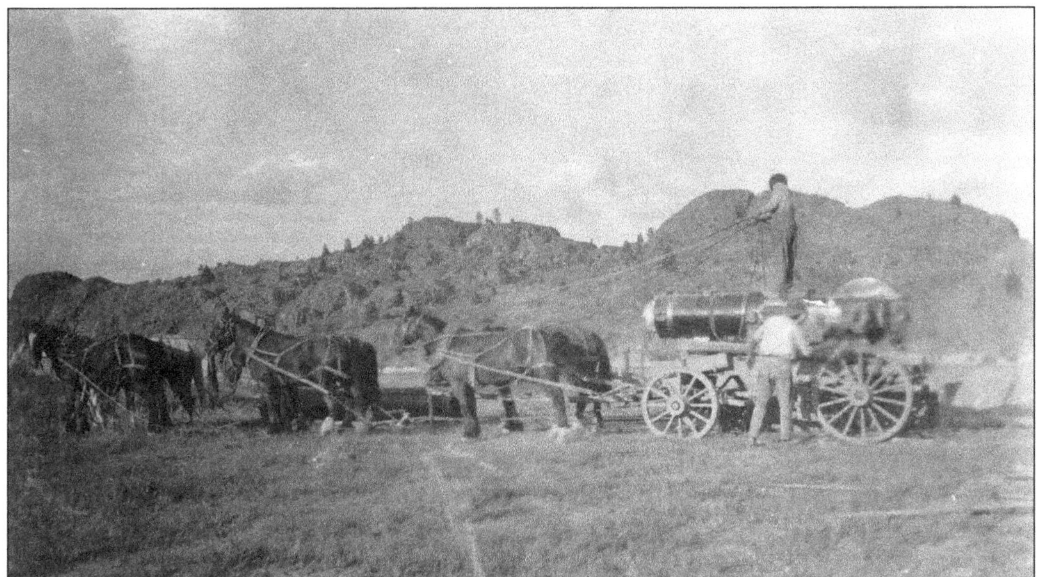

Here, the Steamboat Rock Stock company is moving the huge Rumley oil pull engine that will power the pump on Devils Lake and irrigate the dry farmlands. Farming in what appeared to be desert areas with irrigation was referred to as dry-land farming, and new techniques appeared in periodicals and were studied with great seriousness at universities around the country.

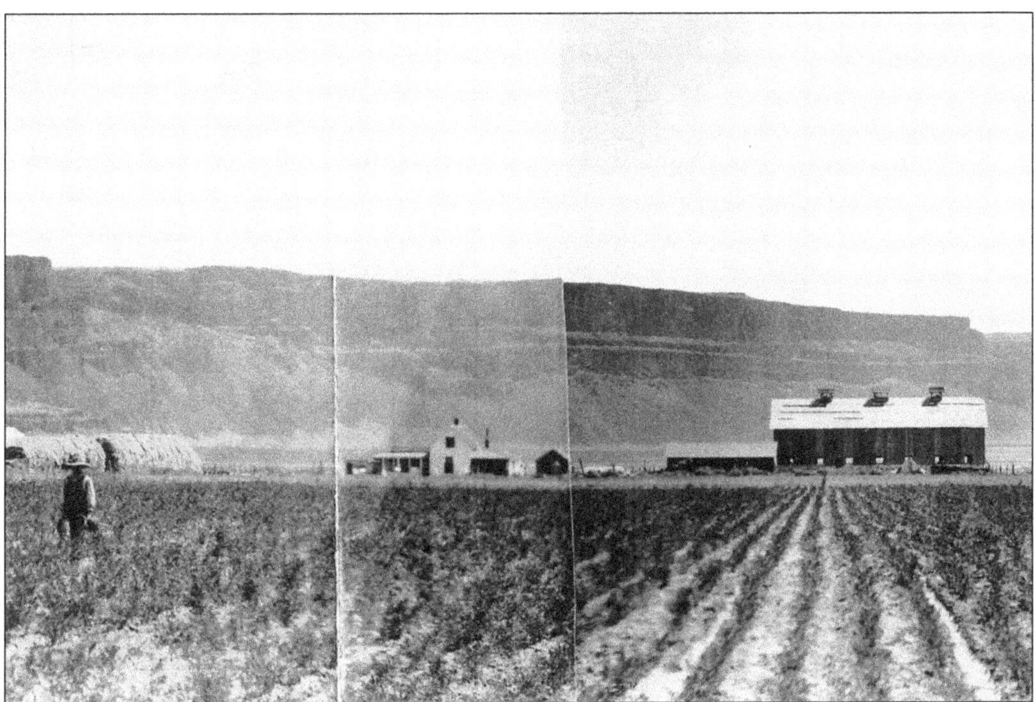

The topsoil was rich volcanic ash, and the water was also high in nutrients; the combination of the two produced large unseasonal crops. The weather in the coulee was also affected by the sheer cliff walls, creating a shorter growing season than seen on nearby plateaus.

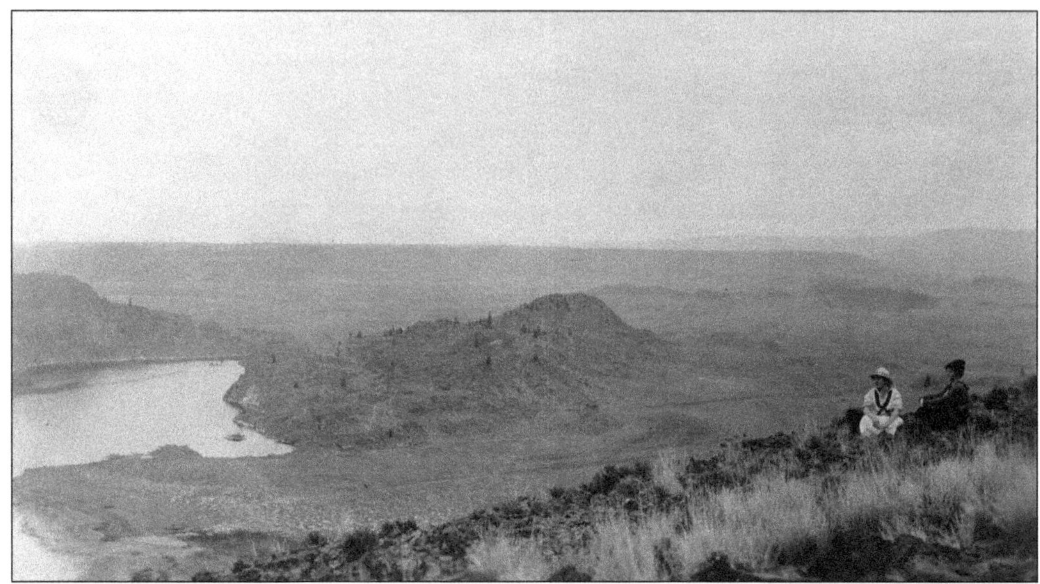

A couple of ladies overlook Devils Lake from the top of Steamboat Rock around 1910. Devils Lake was, on average, a mile long and a hot spot for wildlife—deer, ducks, geese, and rabbit, to name a few—plus, the lake had various types of fish, making Devils Lake a valuable resource for generations.

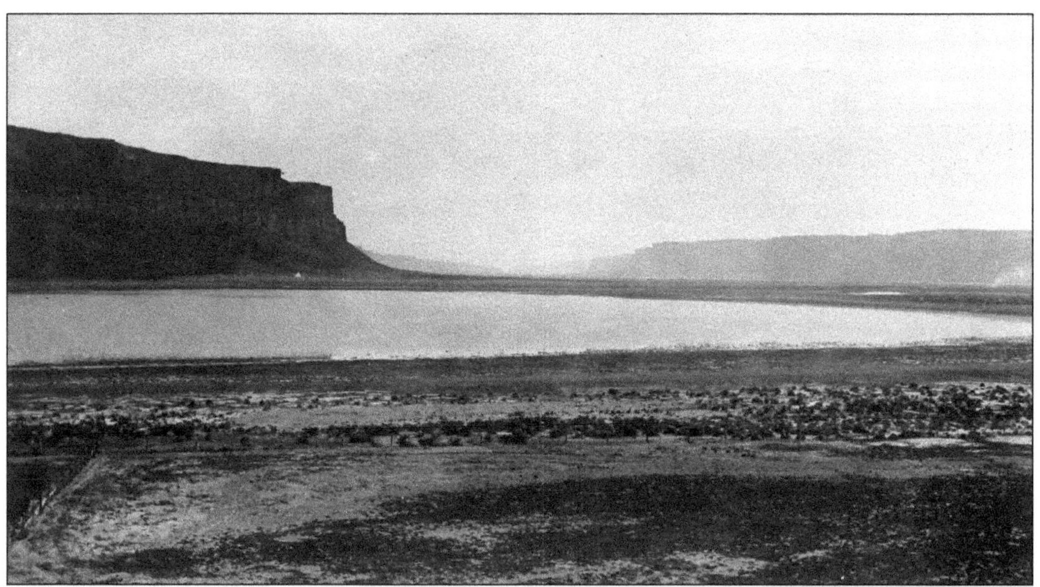

Devils Lake was located at the northwest point of Steamboat Rock, and when the water was high in the spring, it gave the mesa the appearance of floating in water. In the winter, when the lake froze, pioneers would gather ice to fill their icehouses; the harvested ice would last long into the summer months. In this picture, the old Steamboat Rock school can be seen in the distance.

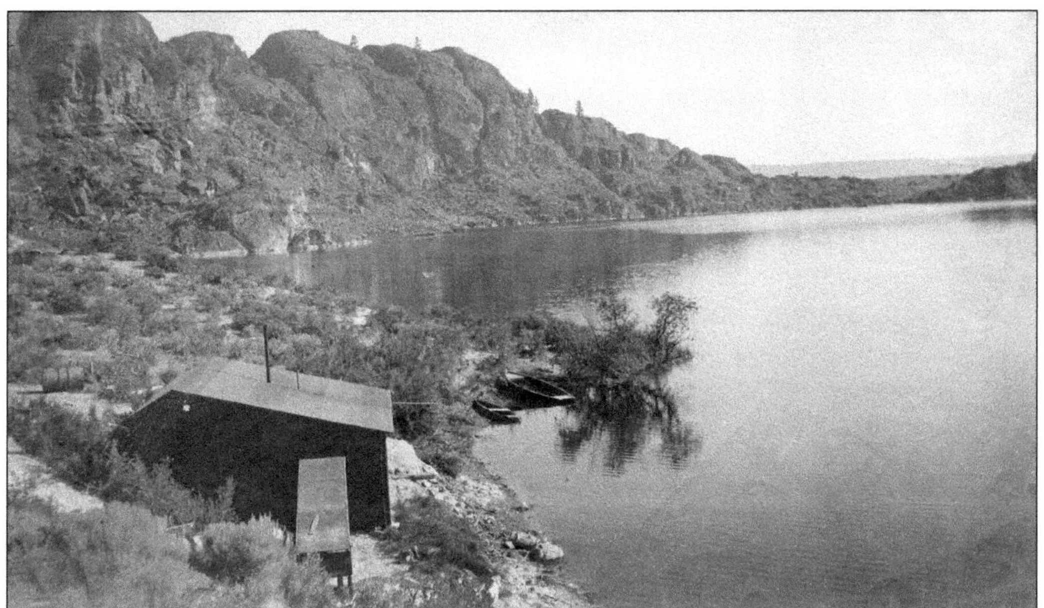

This is a c. 1910 picture of the pumphouse on Devils Lake. Because of the irrigation, crops of alfalfa started to grow and flourish in Barker Canyon and around Ranch Two, where George Baldwin and his family lived. In time, over 300 acres of alfalfa were produced, and the business became lucrative enough to support year-round help, who also lived on the land at the base of Steamboat Rock.

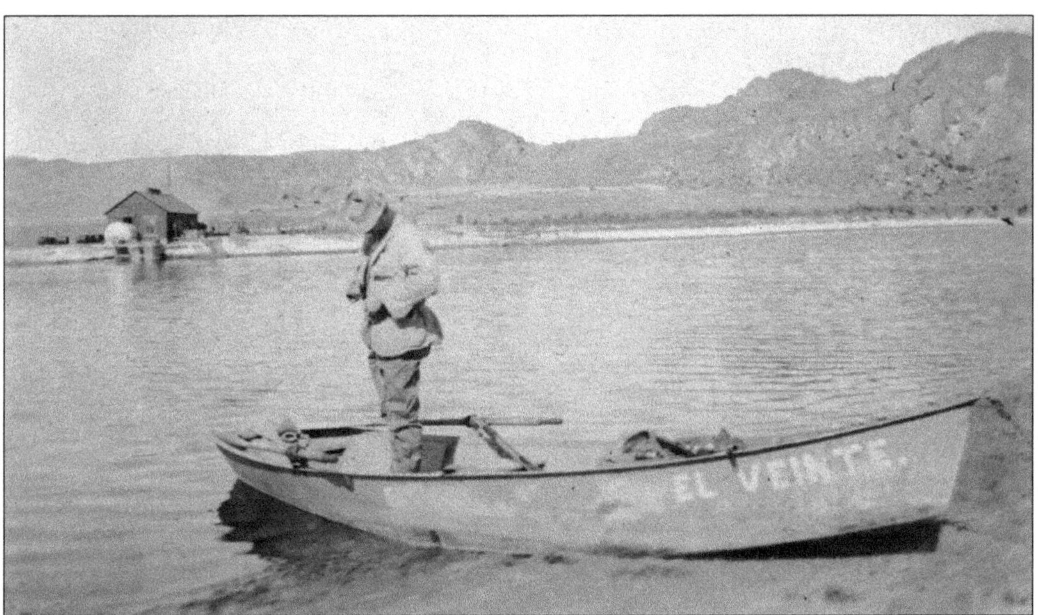

The Baldwins' dry-land farming was a complete success at first. Orchards were watered, and crops like carrots, wheat, and alfalfa were grown and sold to foreign markets. Here, a worker mans a rowboat on Devils Lake, and behind him is the pumphouse.

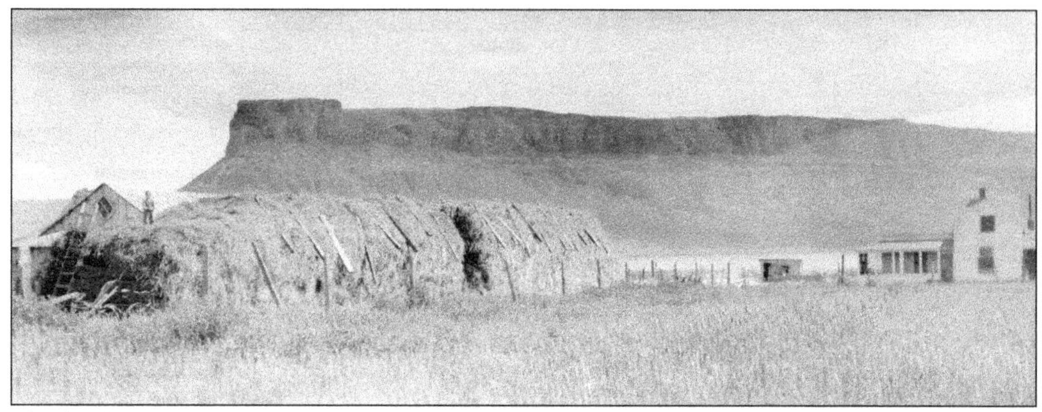

The land was transformed from dry, arid desert to rich, fertile farmlands capable of supporting a variety of products. The coulee had a slightly quicker growing season than the neighboring plateaus, and the soil meant that crops would often grow to award-winning country-fair size. Seen here are two 50-ton stacks of alfalfa at Ranch Two.

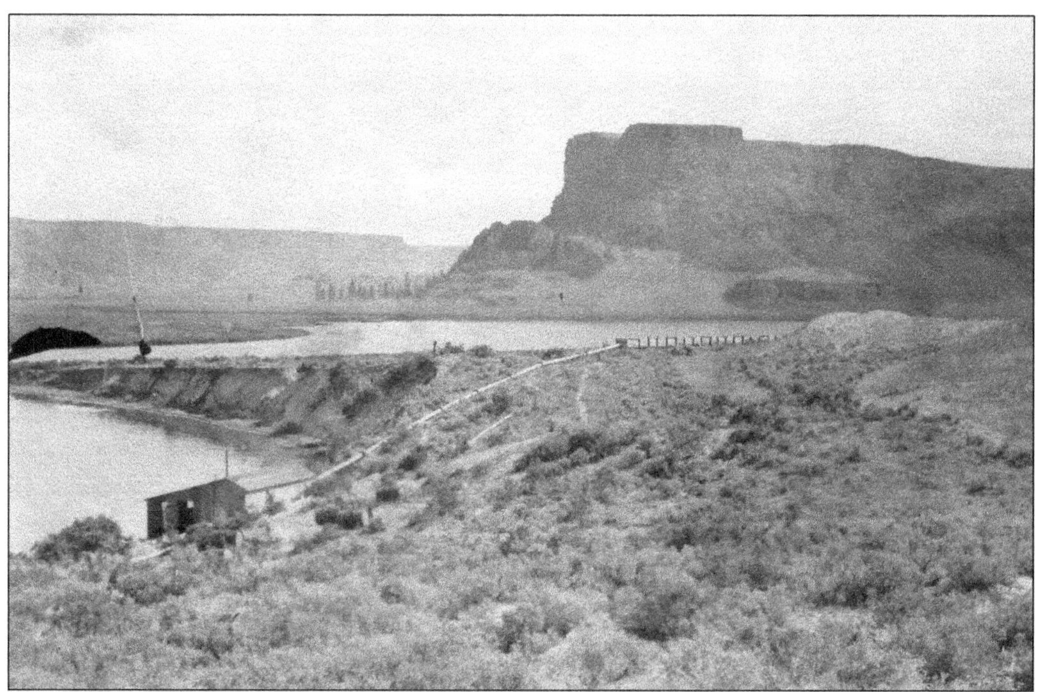

Water from Devils Lake was pumped out by the Rumley diesel engine and up a 27-foot incline into irrigation canals and gravity fed to the crops. Devils Lake was fed by both nutrient-rich springs that came up from the ground, as well as Northrup Creek, which flowed from the nearby canyon.

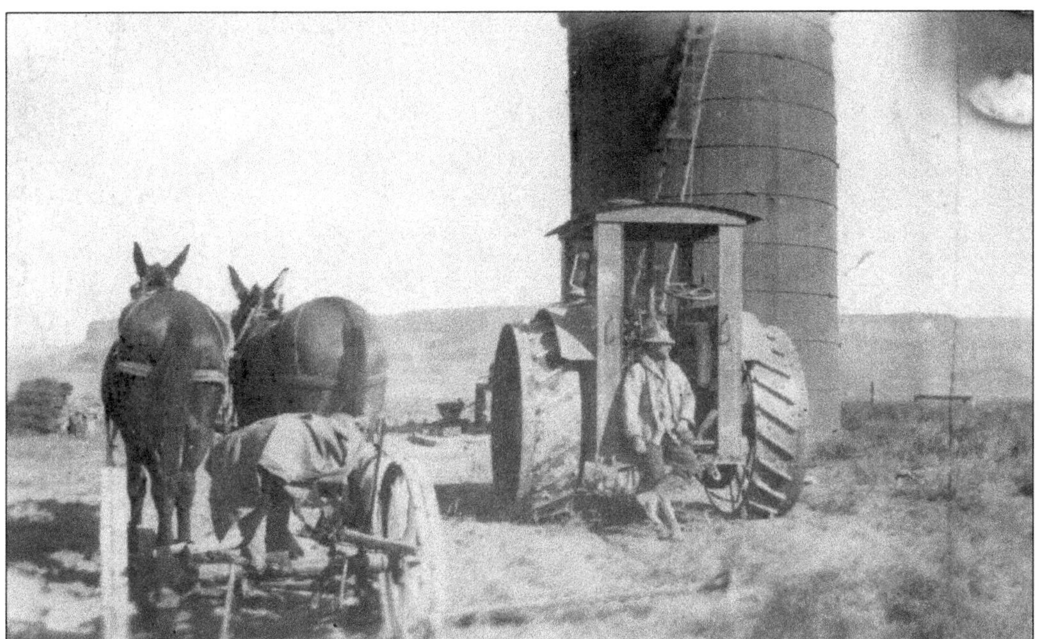

For a while, the Steamboat Rock Stock Company was able to hire people from around the community and beyond to help in the fields and with the manual labor. People would come via train from all over the country to try their luck at being a farmhand, but most would fail and be sent back to Coulee City for the next train.

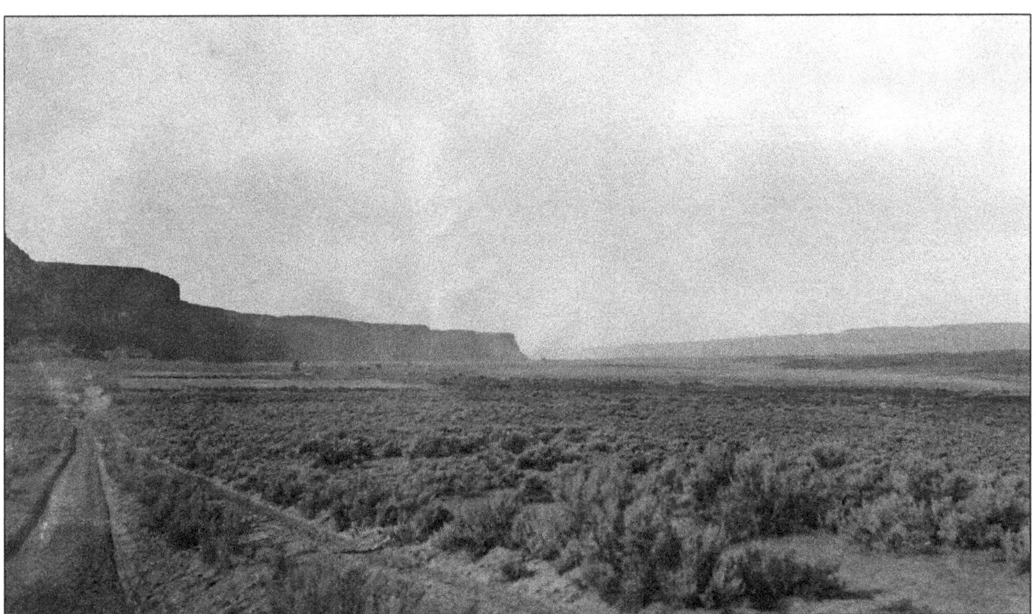

The road to Coulee City was not much more than a wagon trail in most places. Automobiles were starting to appear, and the mailman that had the route to Steamboat Rock had one of the first cars in the area. More than once, he would find his old Model T filled with fresh produce, eggs, dairy, and sometimes, fired workers making their way to the nearest town.

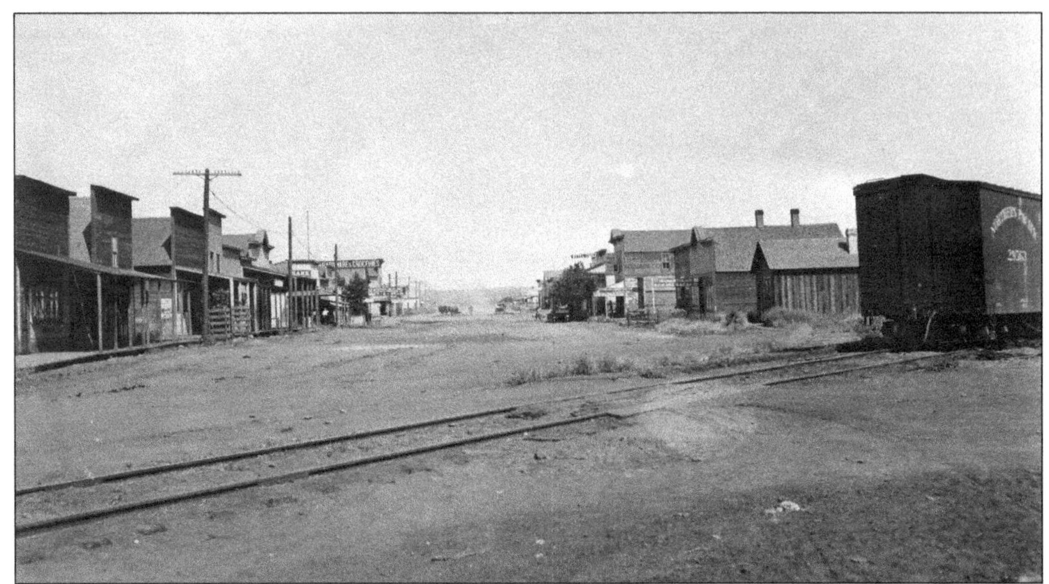

The closest town to Steamboat Rock in 1900 was Coulee City, which was a hub of activity at the turn of the 20th century. The desert town boasted a transcontinental rail line back east and was also a stage stop for people traveling on toward Waterville or Brewster. This gave rise to hotels, restaurants, and saloons, which all sat along a boardwalk lined up on the main street, next to feed and tackle stores and general mercantile.

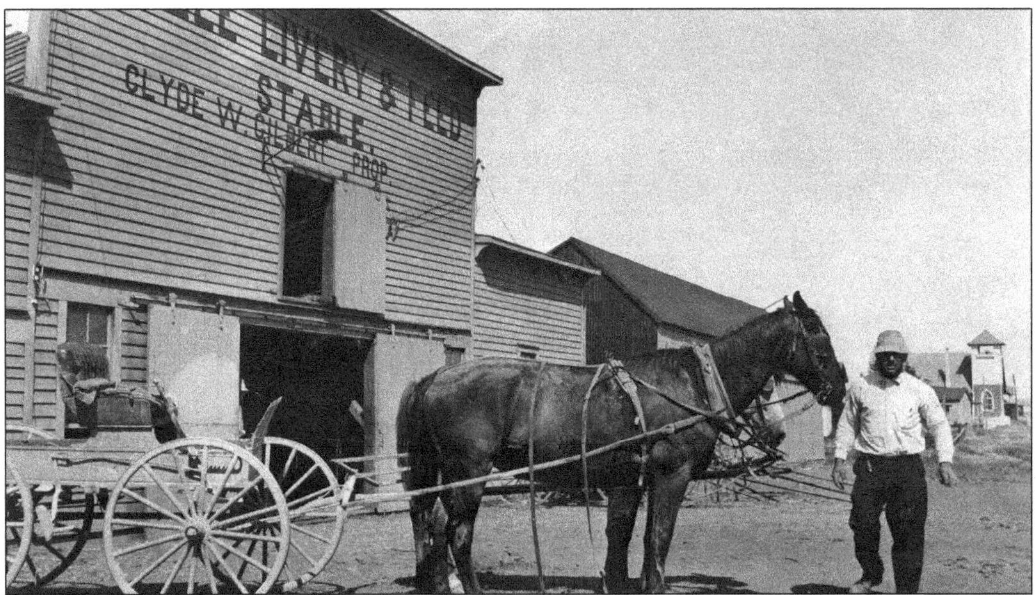

Coulee City was also the place that many of the settlers went for supplies. Often, it took a whole day to load up and travel from Steamboat Rock to Coulee City, less than 20 miles away. Until the advent of cars in the Coulee, the return trip would usually last into the night, with many choosing to spend the night.

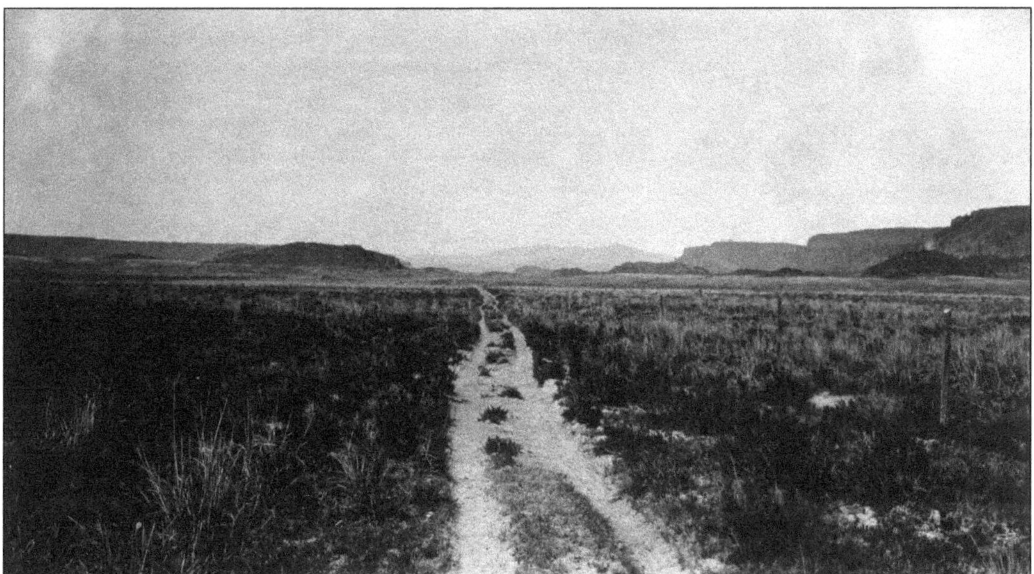

The road leading down past Steamboat Rock to the Columbia River, at the time, was called the Old Coulee Highway and was more like a dirt road. At one time, this trail was known as a military road, but its origins date back further than that to the original inhabitants of the area.

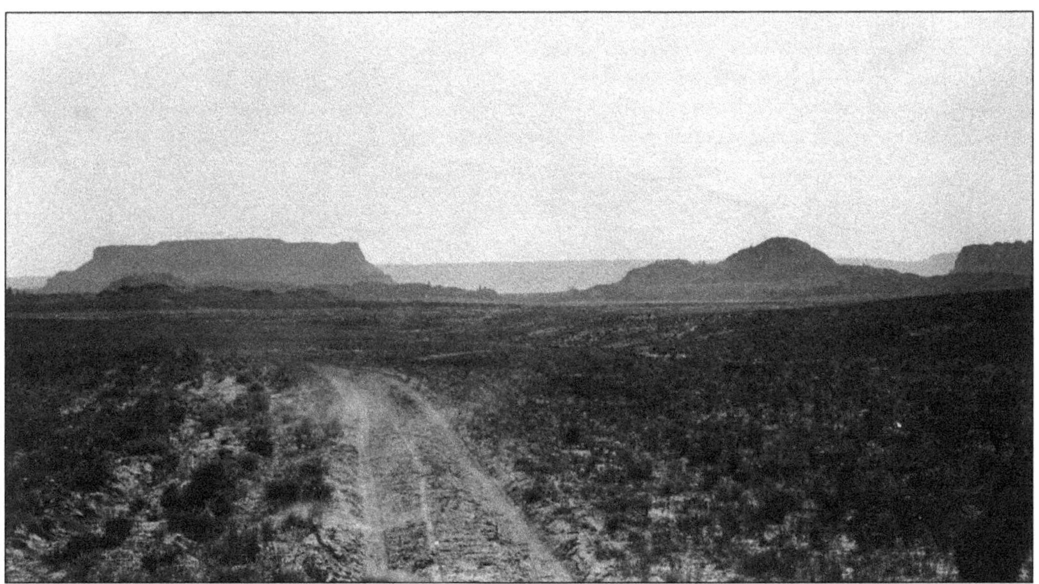

The Old Coulee Highway was used by many people traveling down from Coulee City past Steamboat Rock to either Northrup Canyon or onto Seaton's Landing, to catch the ferry. If they turned west at Pinnacle Rock, they could get on part of the Okanogan Trail and head up through Leahy Junction and onto Waterville or Brewster, following the path the stagecoaches took from Coulee City.

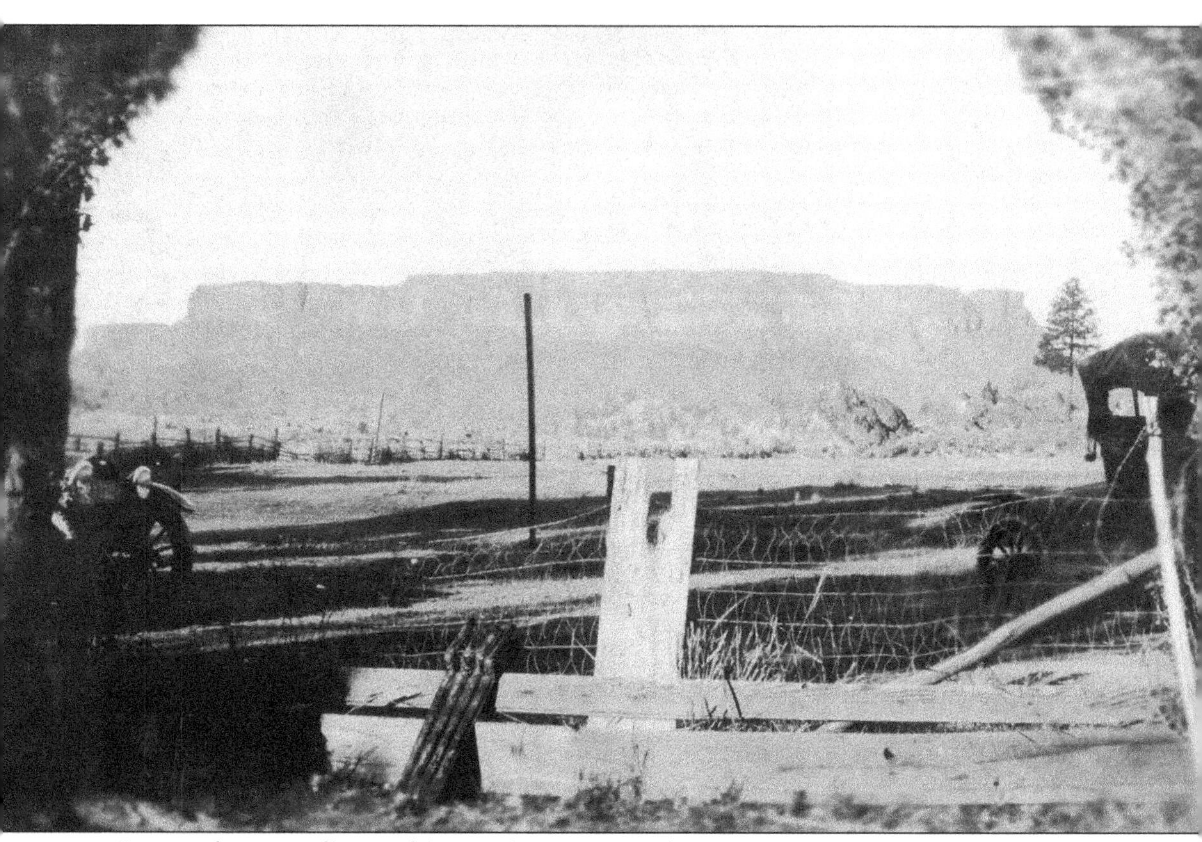

Despite the time, effort, and financial investment, the Steamboat Rock Stock Company suffered troubles. The weather always seemed to rain when the crops were down, and inexperienced hired hands often ended up being detrimental. Ranch Two, where George Baldwin and his family had been staying in Barker Canyon, burned to the ground, and finally, George's partner, Barnhizle, pulled out, leaving George in charge of the whole operation.

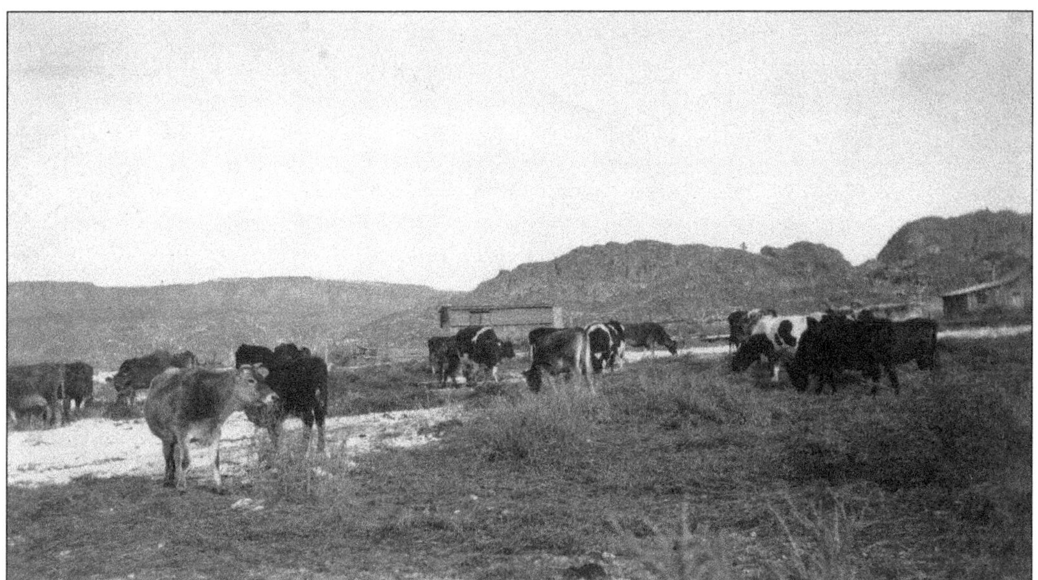

After Ranch Two was destroyed by fire, George Baldwin and his family moved into Ranch One, also known as the old Fleet/Schrock Ranch, across from Steamboat Rock and under Castle Rock. George still ran irrigation out of Devils Lake and maintained the huge ranch, even without his partner.

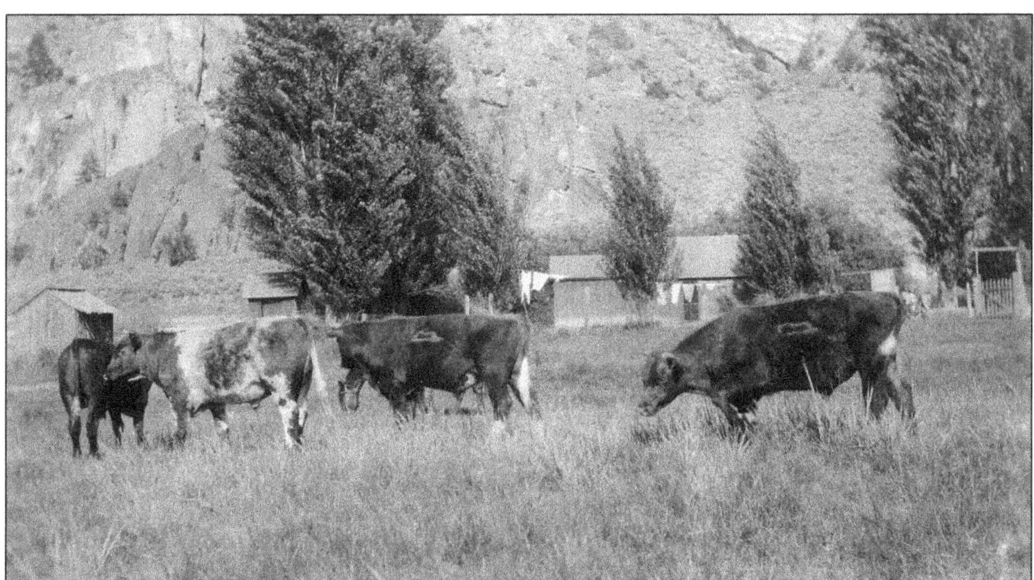

George Baldwin continued to sell and move cattle up the coulee from the Steamboat Rock Stock Company despite his hardships. Here, branded cattle can be seen grazing in front of the old Fleet/Schrock farmhouse, where George and his family resided after the fire destroyed Ranch Two.

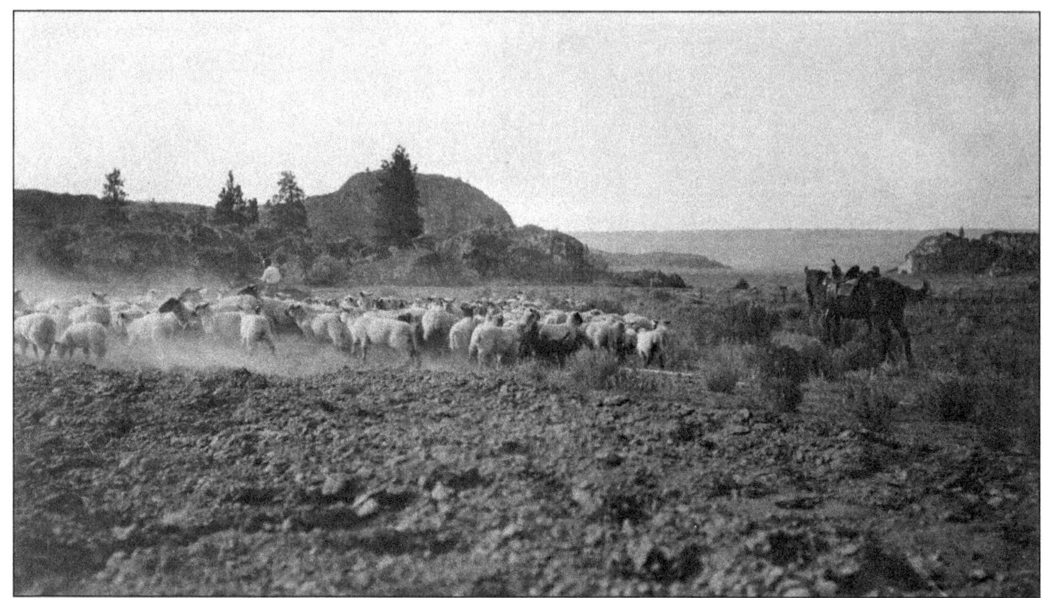

During this time, George Baldwin experimented in different types of stock. The luxuriant bunch grass had been overgrazed, and new stock and new crops meant the stock farm could stay in business for years to come. George introduced hogs and sheep into his livestock holdings.

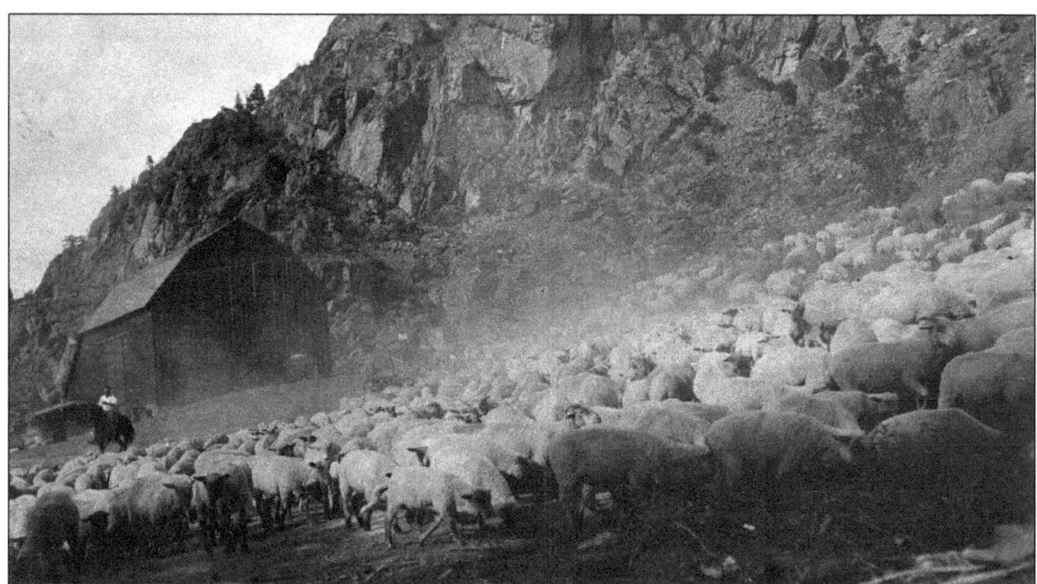

Sheep adapted and did really well in the area; they could graze the areas that cattle could not and were smaller and easier contained. Eventually, sheep became one of the main exports from the Steamboat Rock Stock Company and staple livestock in the coulee, replacing cattle.

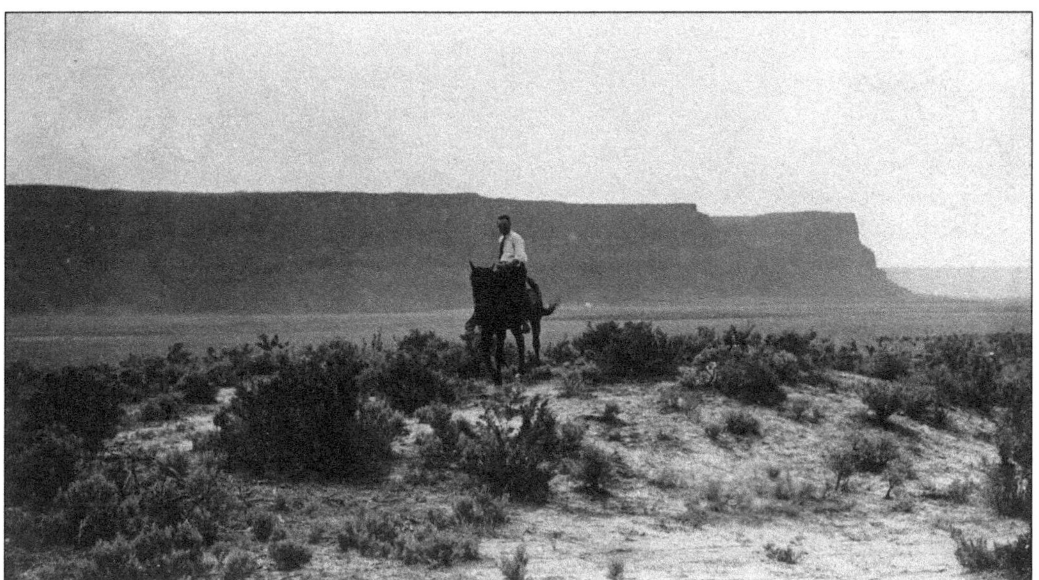

From 1886 until the first decade in 1900, the area around Steamboat Rock was really the Wild West. People moved around this lawless territory on horses, and the nearest neighbor could be miles away; however, the new century brought changes that would sweep through the coulee, changing it forever.

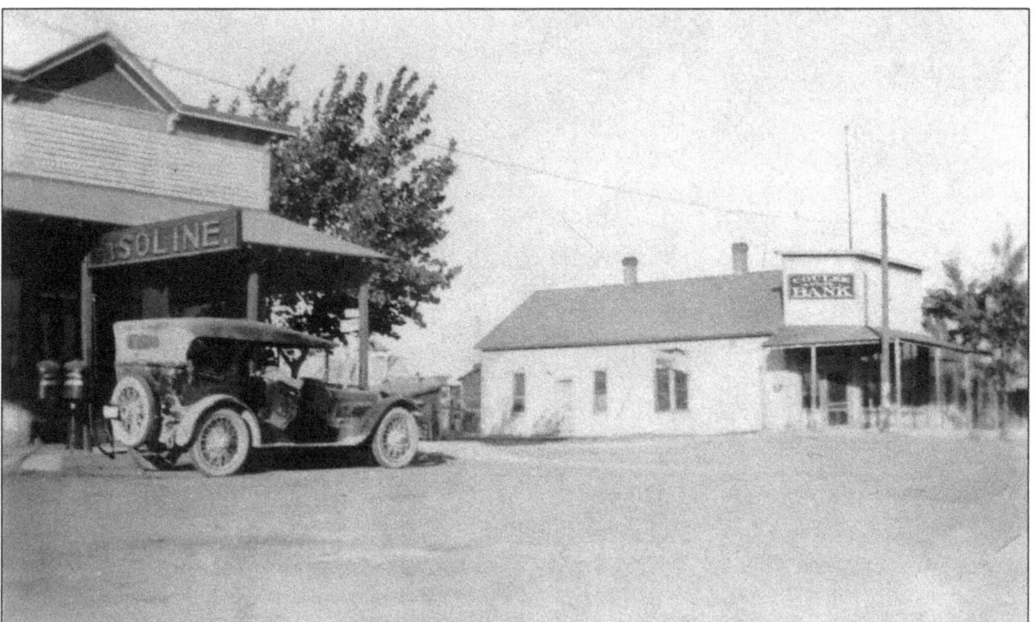

As the modern world started to move west, cars started to appear in the bigger towns like Coulee City and slowly made their way out to the Steamboat Rock community. At first, only a few people had them, but soon, everyone seemed to be fueling up. Here, a car waits to get gas across from the bank at Coulee City.

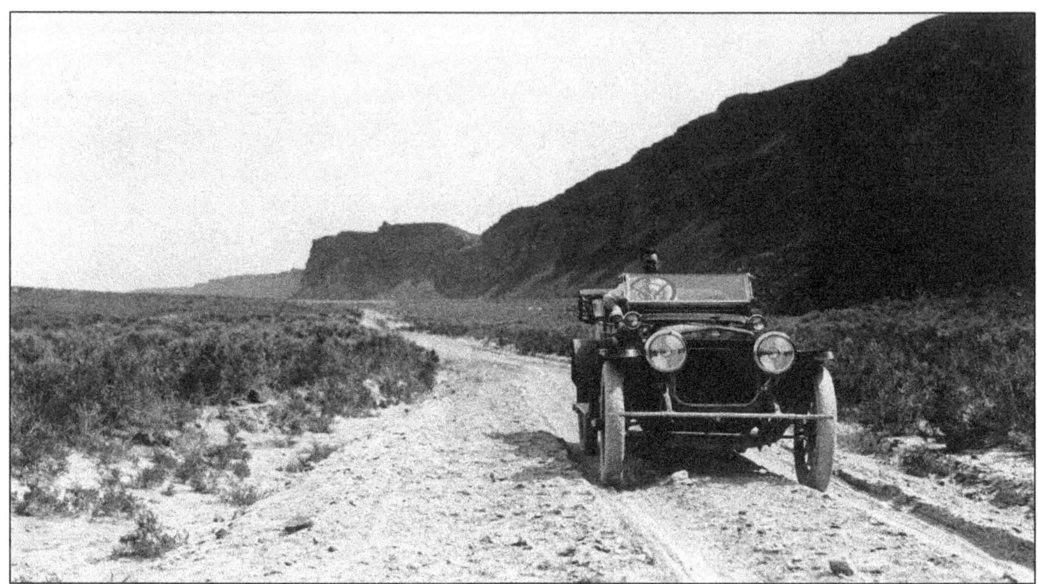

As automobiles spread west, repercussions started to spring up, with a main one being who was going to build and maintain roads. Cars were using old wagon trails to travel on, and at first this was the case in the Grand Coulee. Steamboat Rock had long been surrounded by wagon trails, but now, early cars and trucks made their way up those same old wagon roads.

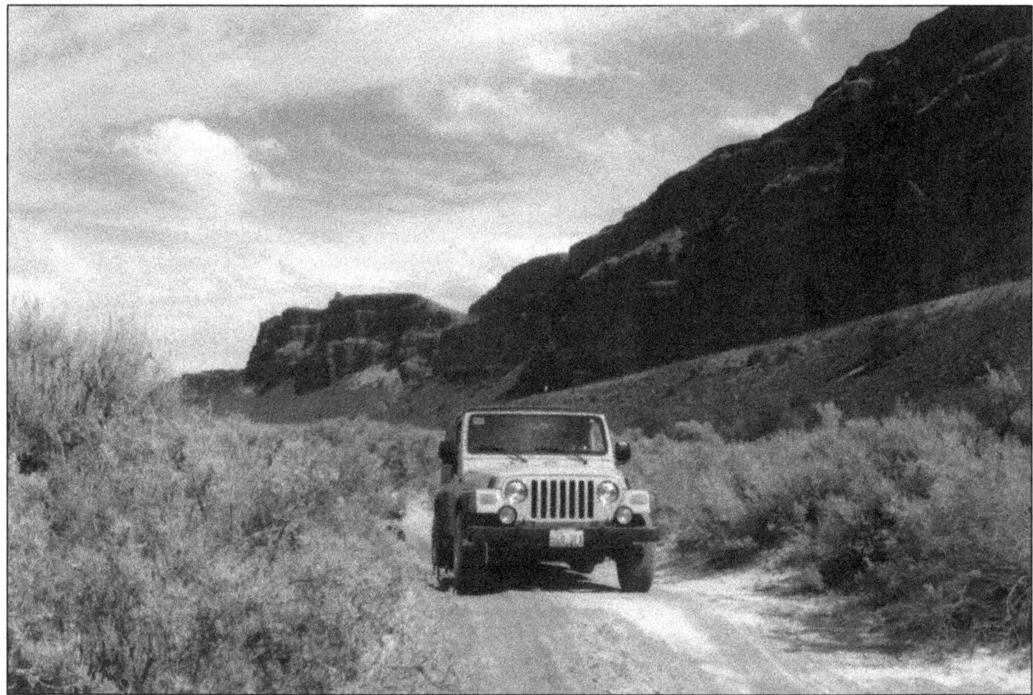

At least one part of the Old Coulee Road can still be found tucked away in the corner of Salishan Mesa under Rabbit Rock. Used by recreationalists, the remaining sliver of the very old road runs from State Road 155 down into Banks Lake on the north side of Million Dollar Mile. Other parts of old roads can still be found today as well, like the Scheibner Grade in Northrup Canyon. (Courtesy of Lowell and Birdie Hensley.)

Four

COMMUNITY

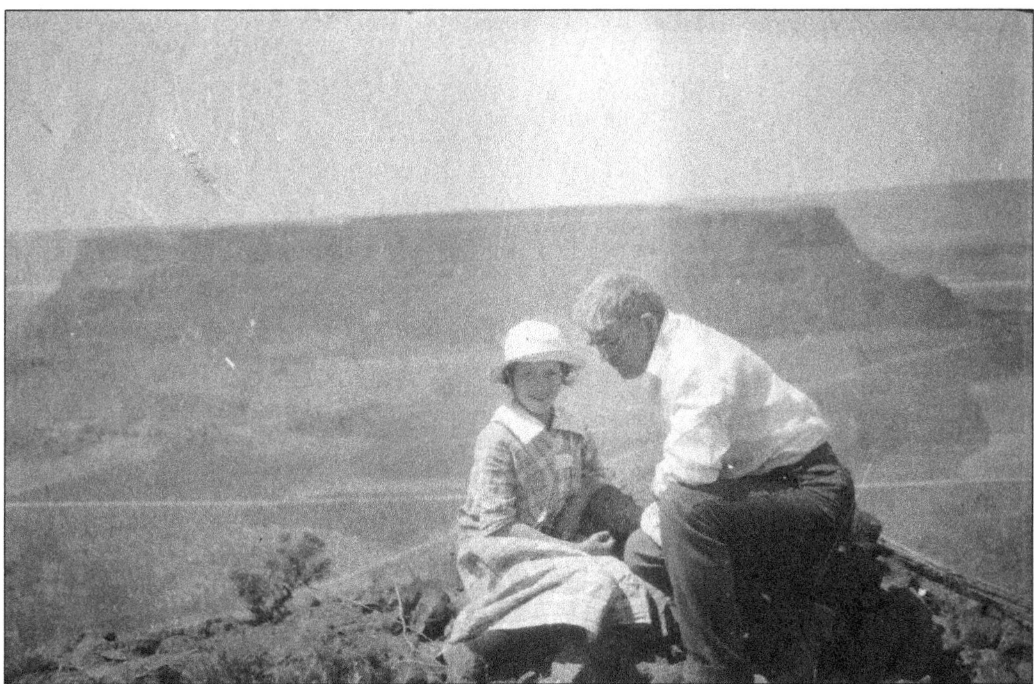

Life during the turn of the 20th century in the Grand Coulee could be an interesting place. There were still some aspects of the old Wild West hanging on as the country discovered cars and radio. In the rural area around Steamboat Rock, the farms were spaced just beyond walking distance but close enough to create a community.

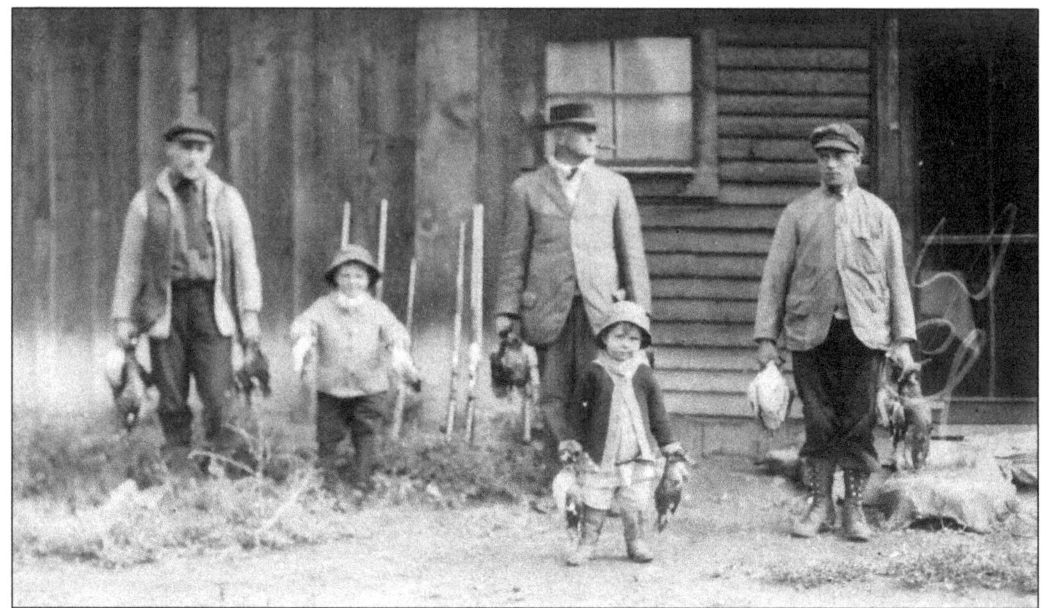

Hunting, farming, and raising a variety of livestock and crops were important. Not only did the people raise enough to barter to neighbors or sell in Coulee City, but they also fed the family. Aside from this, some ranches or farms sold enough to hire workers, while other people in the community worked as hired hands to supplement their own endeavors.

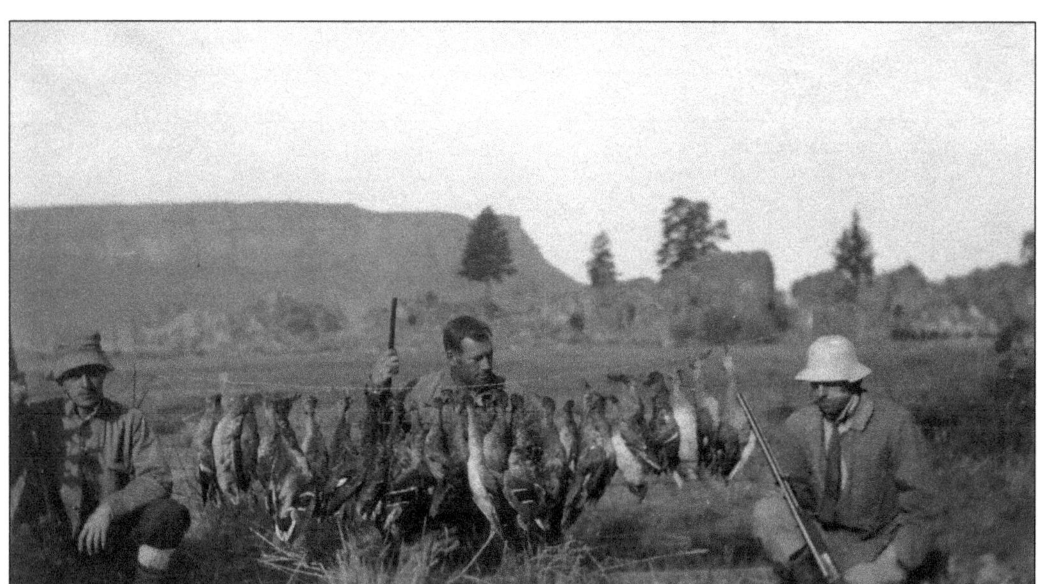

Being able to live off the land was also very important; hunting and foraging a way of life. Guns were viewed as tools, and in a place with little to no law enforcement, there was no need for regulation because people respected both the land and the other people living in the community.

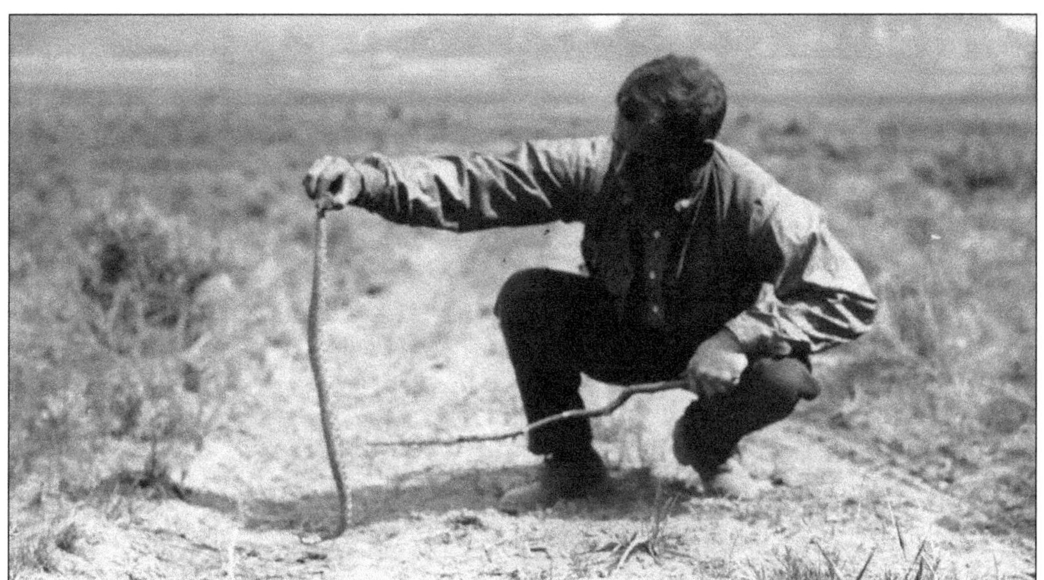

In the early 1900s, living in the Steamboat Rock area meant living closer with nature and the threats it brings. Snakes, bears, badgers, cougars, coyotes, and bobcats also call the Grand Coulee home and far outnumbered the few brave men and women homesteaders.

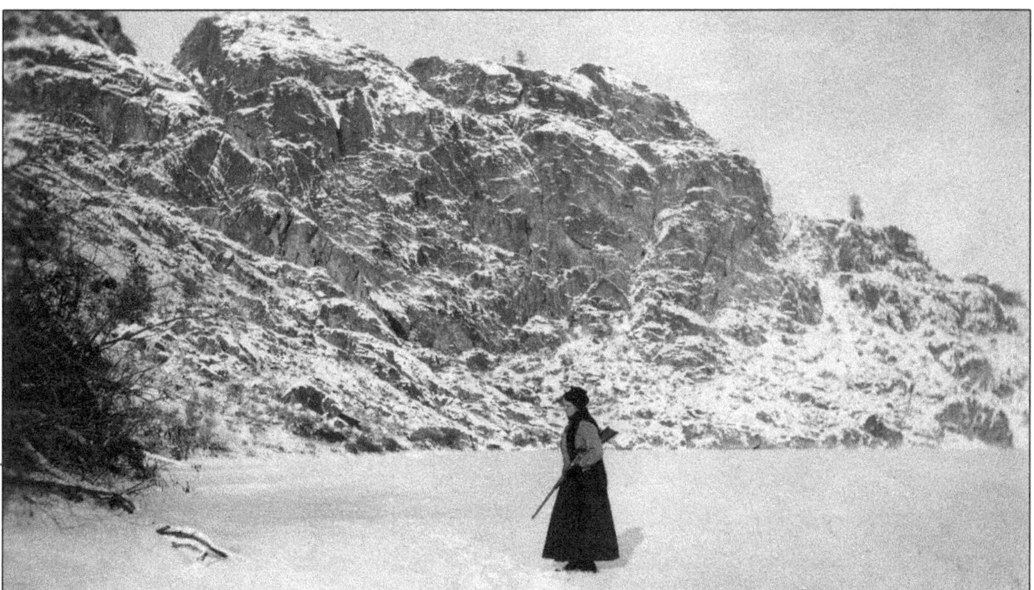

Weather is another factor that pioneers had to contend with; there were not only blistering summers in the triple digits but also winters cold enough to freeze the local lakes solid and trap people in their homesteads for months at a time under a blanket of pure, white snow.

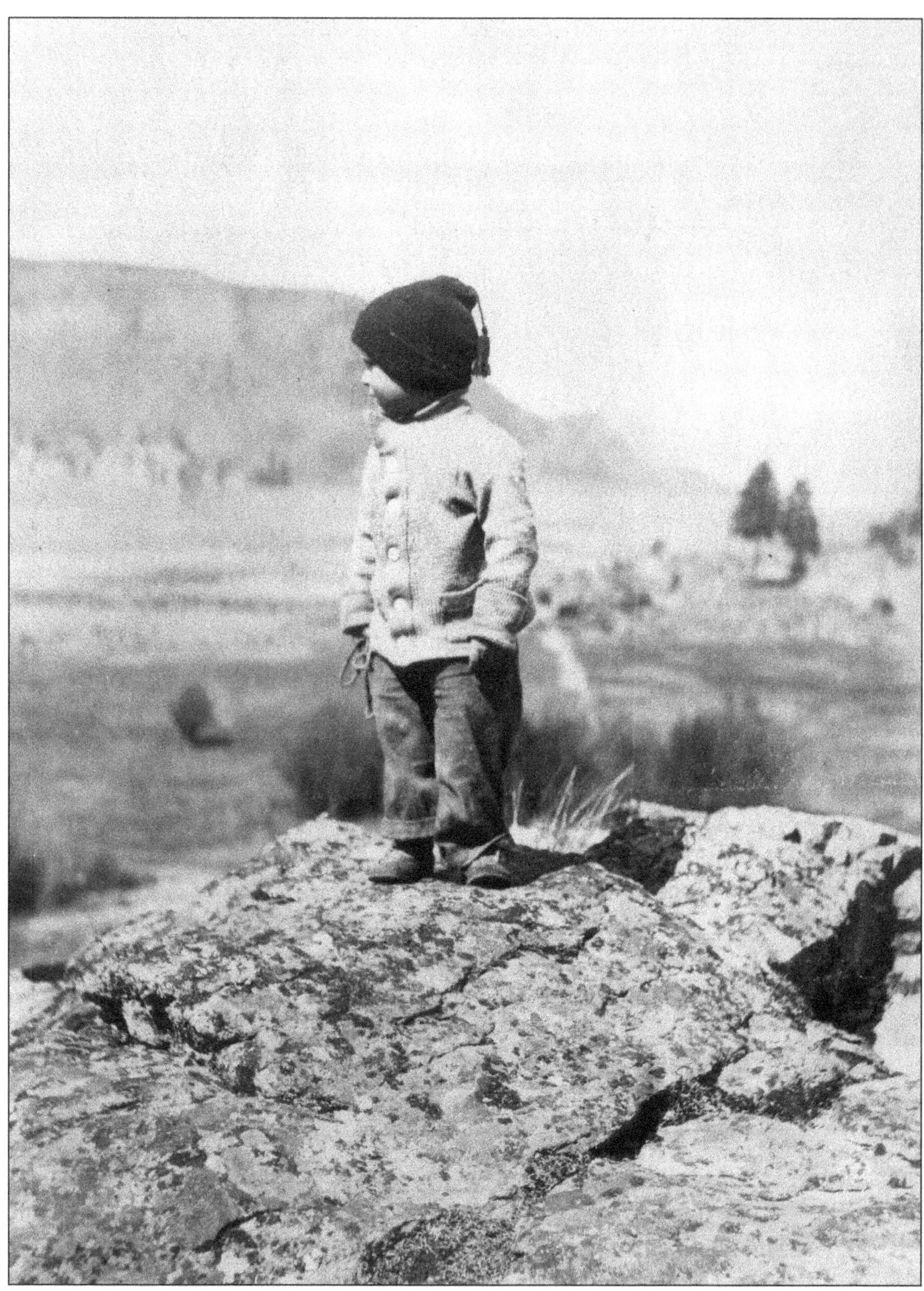

A mile and a half south of Steamboat Rock was the small, short-lived community of Lakeview. A small loose-knit community of ranchers and farmers rarely mentioned in literature, they had a baseball team that played against Leahy Junction at the Steamboat Rock County Fair in an exhibition match. Lakeview was also home to the Steamboat Rock pioneer cemetery.

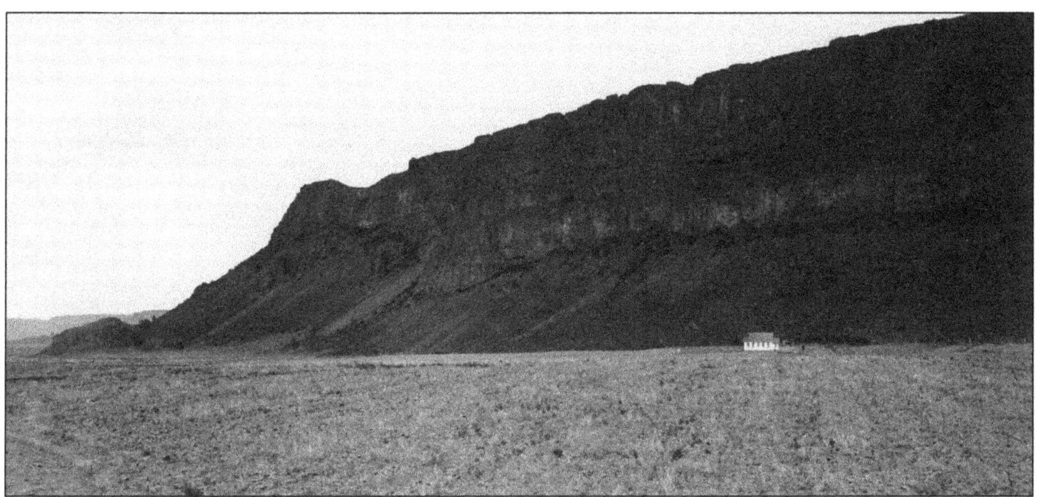

It was important for everyone in the area of Steamboat Rock to communicate and work together, creating a loose-knit community. They would gather at the local school that served as a grange, church, town hall, and center for the seasonal festivities and entertainment. The schoolhouse's location can be seen on several maps (see page 28).

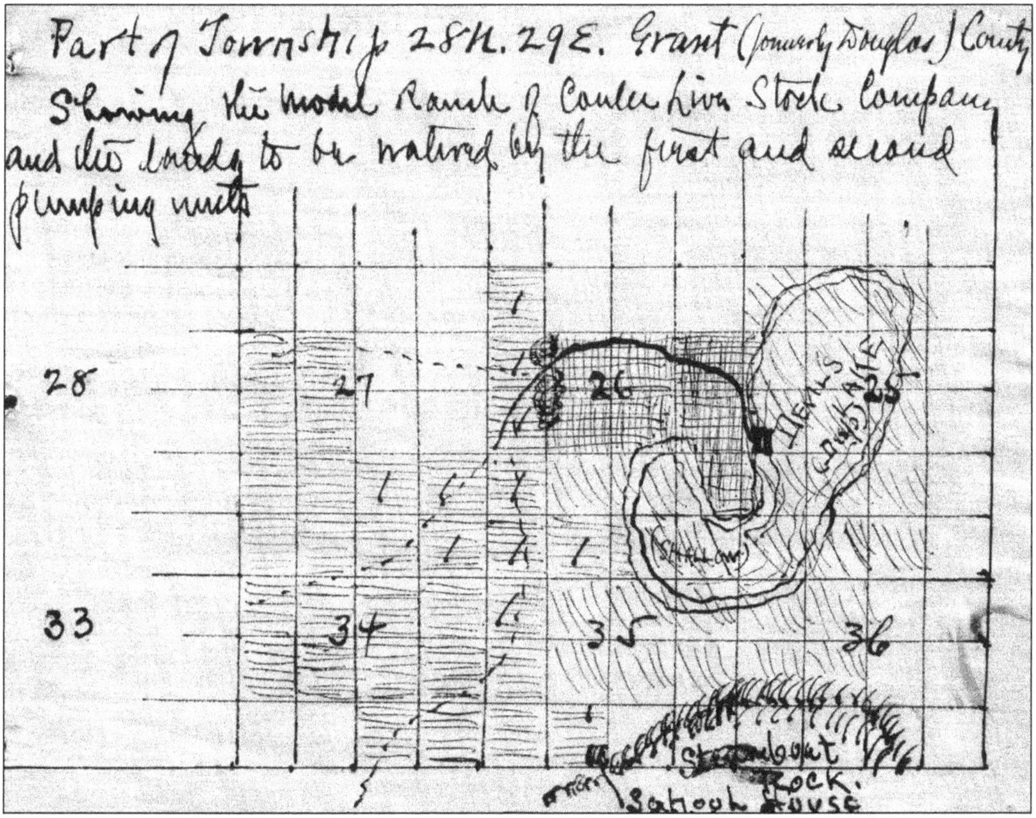

Part of Township 28N. 29E. Grant (formerly Douglas) County Showing the model Ranch of Coulee Live Stock Company and the lands to be watered by the first and second pumping units

Steamboat Rock.

School House

This township map shows the school's first location next to the shallow end of Devils Lake in the Barker Canyon area. The school sat up close to the west wall of Steamboat Rock and across the shallow end of Devils Lake from Baldwin's Ranch Two. The map also shows the location of the pumphouse in relation to the school.

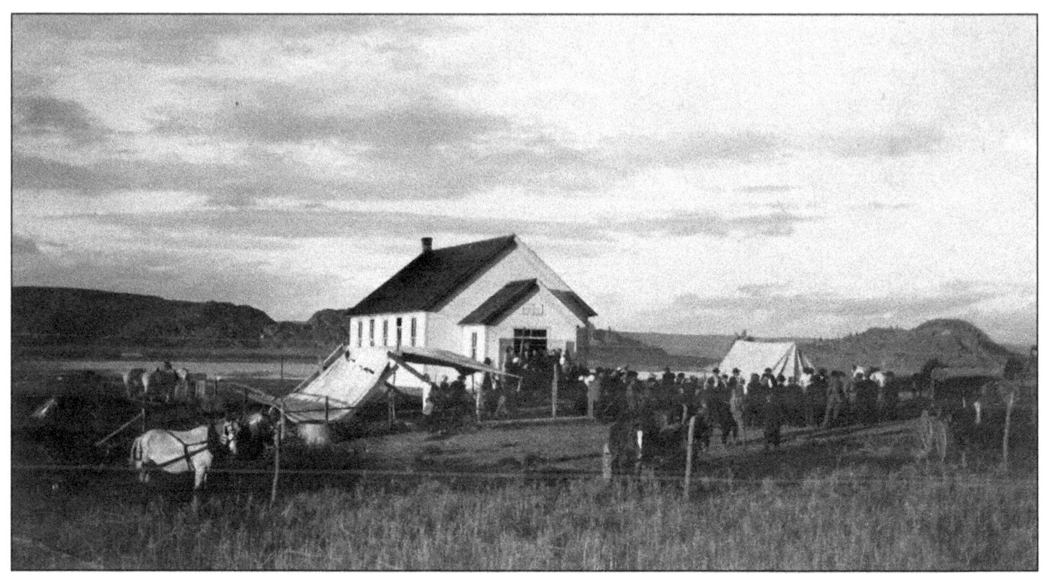

This iconic picture of Steamboat Rock school was taken by George Baldwin or a family member. This school was located close to the wall of Steamboat Rock and the shore of Devils Lake; in the background, the lake can be seen, as well as some of the Granite Hills.

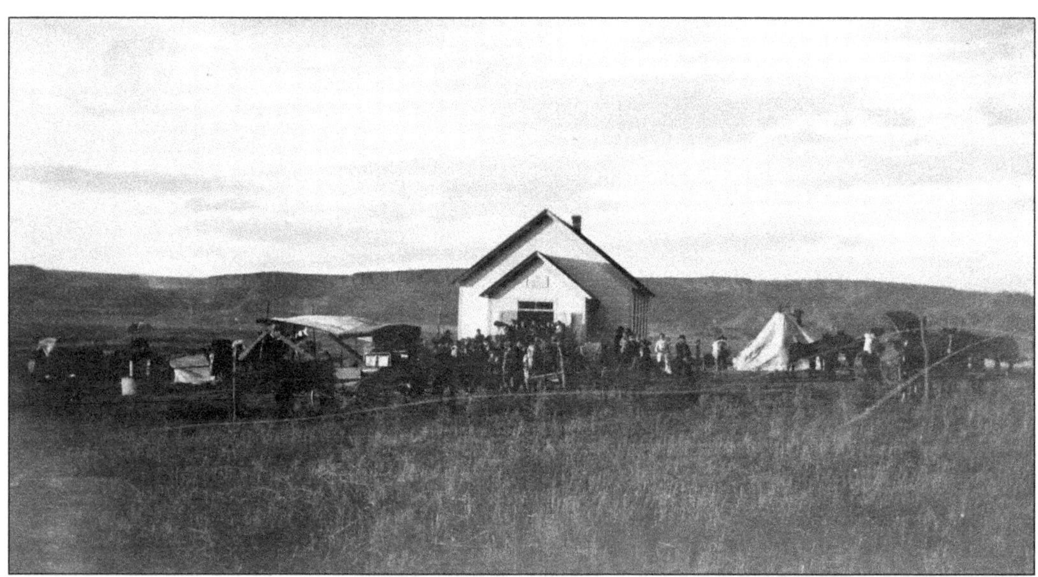

At first, the Steamboat Rock school was a basic structure made of logs and mud, but later, around 1908, a better school was created, with lumber from Charles Scheibner's sawmill on Northrup Creek. For a while, original Steamboat Rock settler William Fleet worked at the sawmill as a millwright.

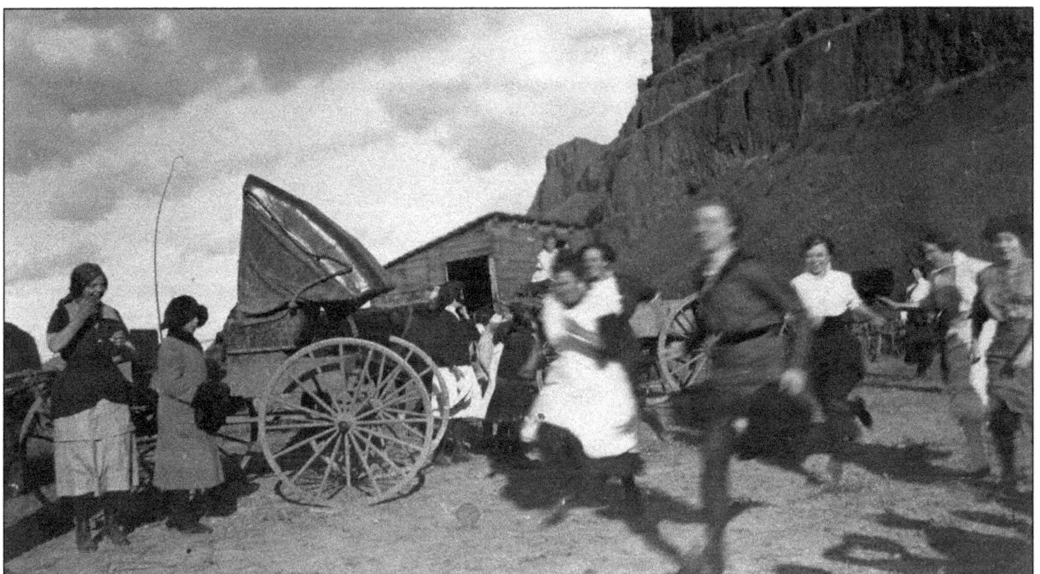

In 1916, a Grant County agricultural agent helped the community organize a fair that was held at the Steamboat Rock school and included events such as horse races, foot races, and wild bronco busting, as well as the usual cornucopia of fruits and vegetables grown in the coulee.

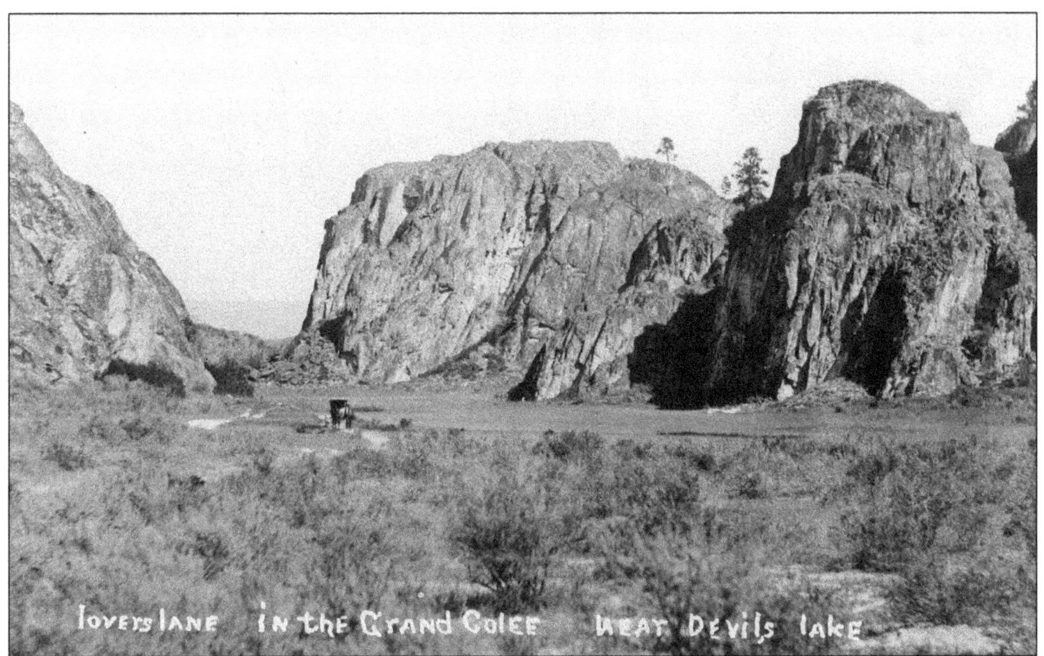

There was also an exhibition game of baseball between Leahy and Lakeview. Baseball was a big sport, and several of the communities had teams, including Steamboat Rock. In the age before cars in the coulee, the Steamboat Rock team would load up on a wagon and head up the Okanogan Trail to play their closest rivals at Leahy Junction.

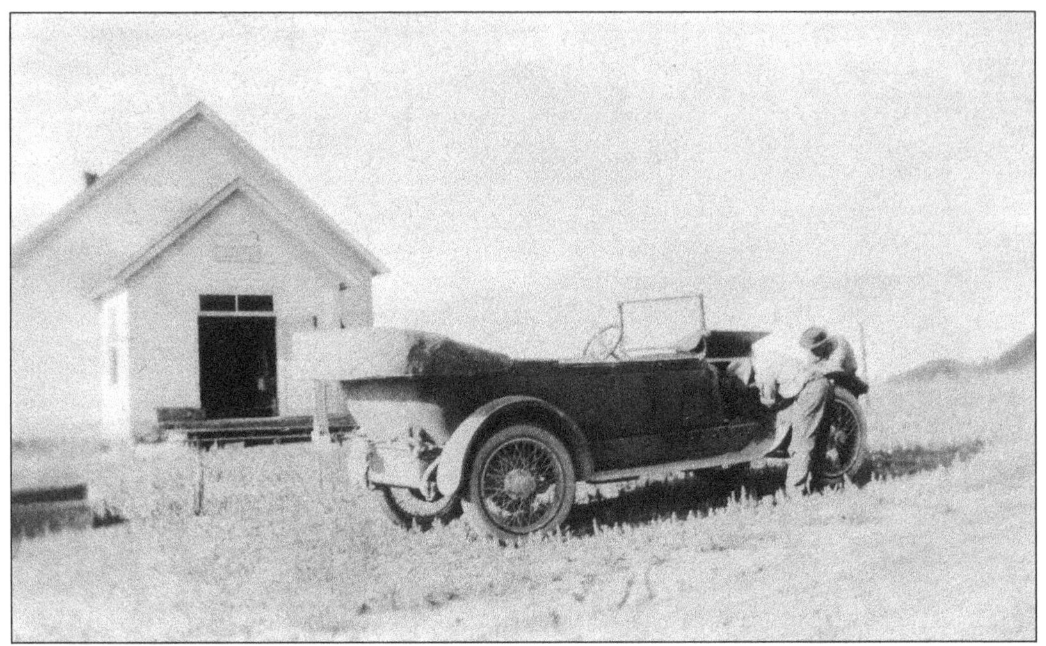

With the help of the community, the school eventually moved around to the north end of Steamboat Rock but never stopped being the center of the community and is fondly remembered by many. The school became the meeting place for local politics, and many civic issues were resolved within its walls.

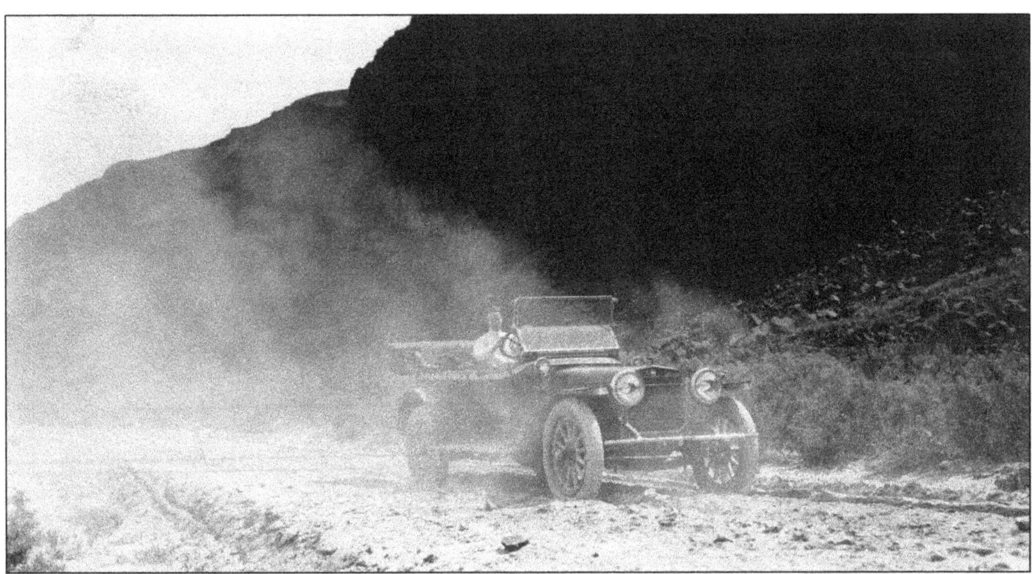

There were a couple of ways by car into Steamboat Rock, depending on which direction one was coming from. The Old Coulee Highway, also known as the Old Coulee Road, was used for decades by travelers coming from Coulee City into the Steamboat Rock area; it remained dusty in summer and muddy in winter, filled with deep holes and sharp rocks.

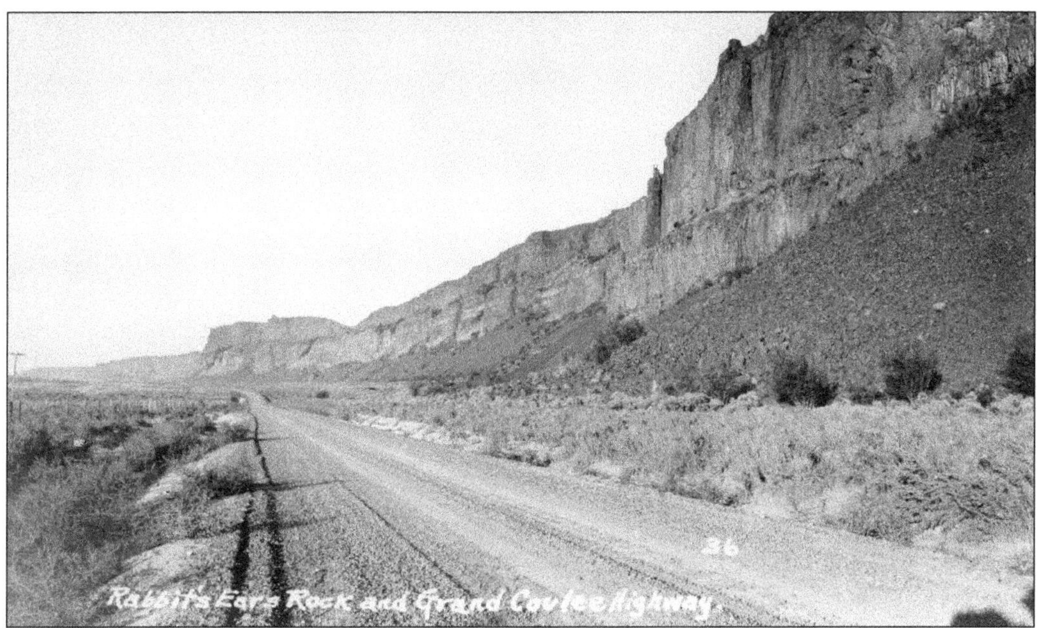

As time progressed and more cars made their way into the coulee, the roads were improved, usually by being graded, graveled, and sometimes watered or oiled to keep the dust down. In this picture, the Old Coulee Road runs under Rabbit Rock, labeled "Rabbit's Ears Rock." Rabbit Rock is a natural basalt formation that is said to be Rabbit from the Steamboat Rock creation story (see page 13).

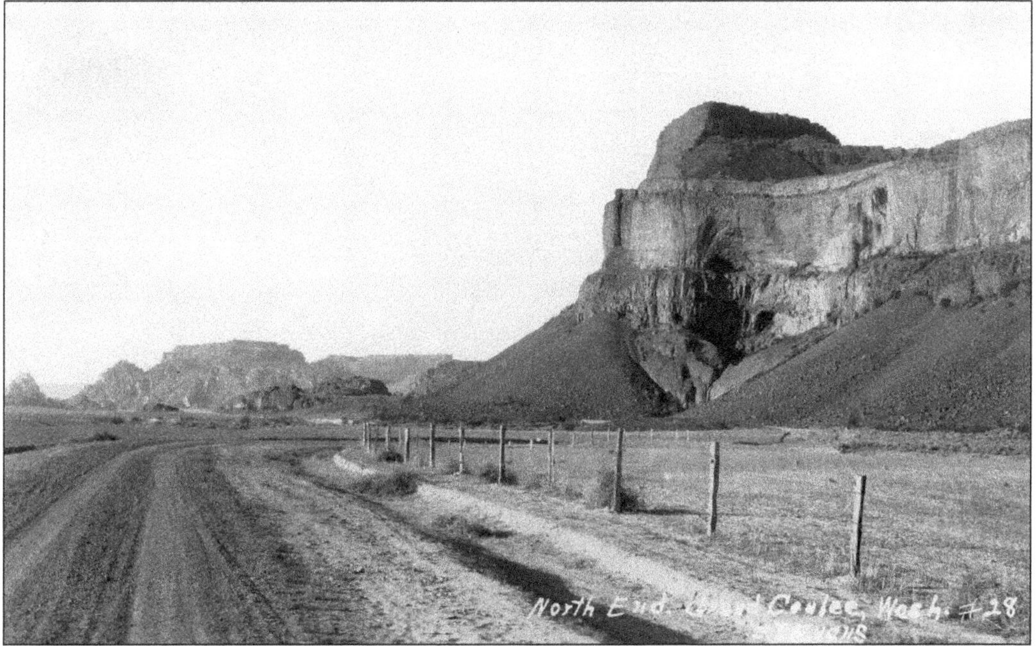

In this picture, the graveled and grated Old Coulee Road meanders by Martin Falls/Devil's Punchbowl. The falls were a common stopping place, especially in spring during the runoff when the water thundered over the coulee wall. In the distance, Pinnacle and Castle Rock loom and the long-missing bridge can be seen in front of the falls.

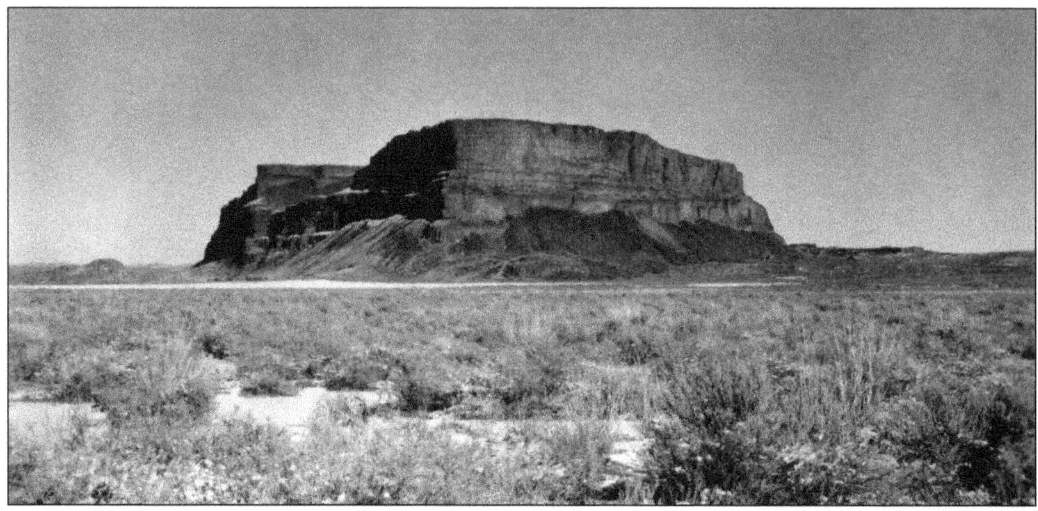

By 1910, the Steamboat Rock area was a community, even if a very small, scattered one. With the newly upgraded roads and nearby Northrup Canyon orchards, people traveled up and down the coulee with more frequency in their automobiles. The area around Steamboat Rock, with its fields of wheat and spread-out orchards, dairy, produce, and livestock, soon became the center of the upper coulee.

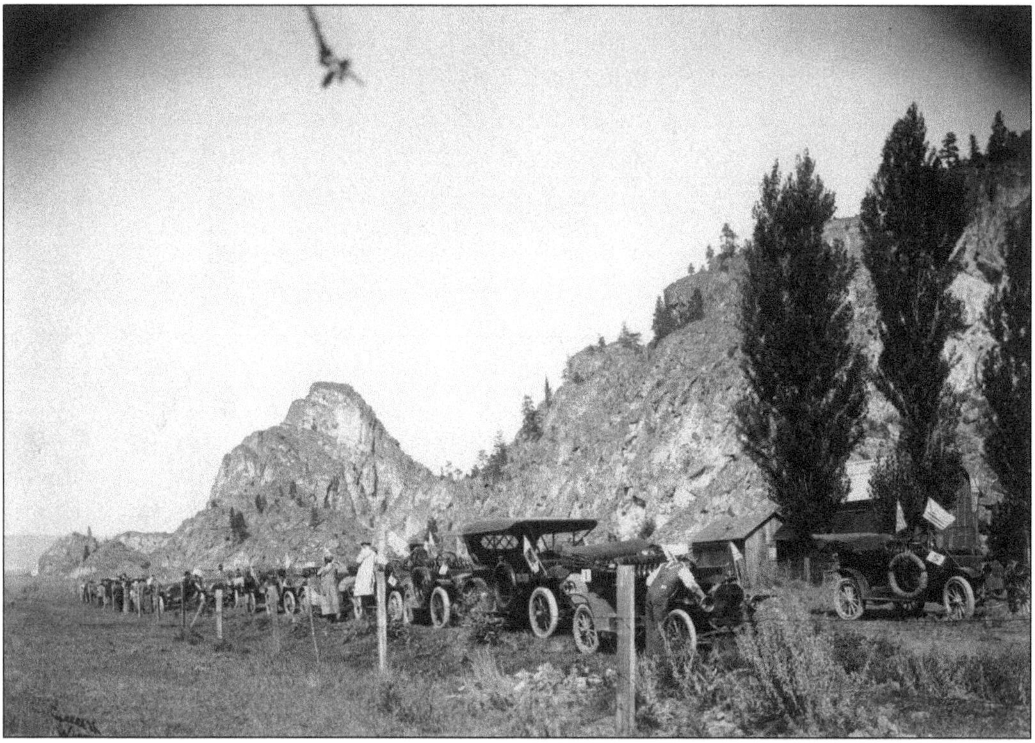

One hot day in September 1912, a ragtag assemblage of cars arrived at the old Fleet/Schrock Ranch, where George Baldwin and his family resided. It was the National Geographic Society's transcontinental excursion of 1912, a tour group of people from all over the world comprised of scientists, geologists, artists, and photographers. They had ventured into the coulee to study the effects of dry-land farming in the Steamboat Rock region.

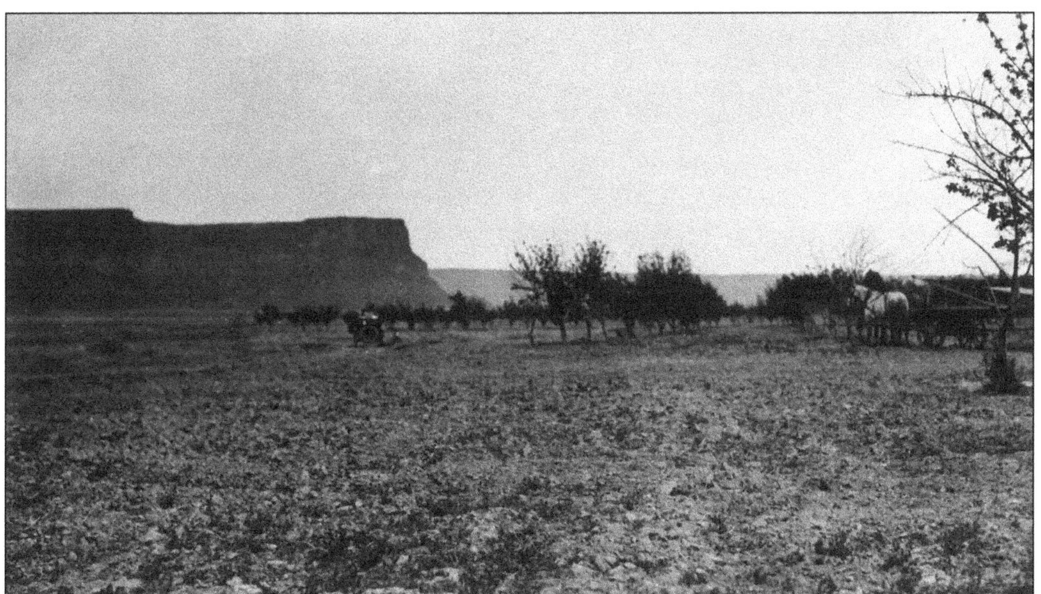

The Baldwins fed the group and then took them to a nearby orchard, explaining the effects of dry-land farming to the inquisitive visitors. The orchard shown in this picture was to the southwest of Steamboat Rock. It was acquired in a land purchase by George Baldwin in later years and irrigated with water pumped from Devils Lake. Before the land was acquired, the orchard was not irrigated at all.

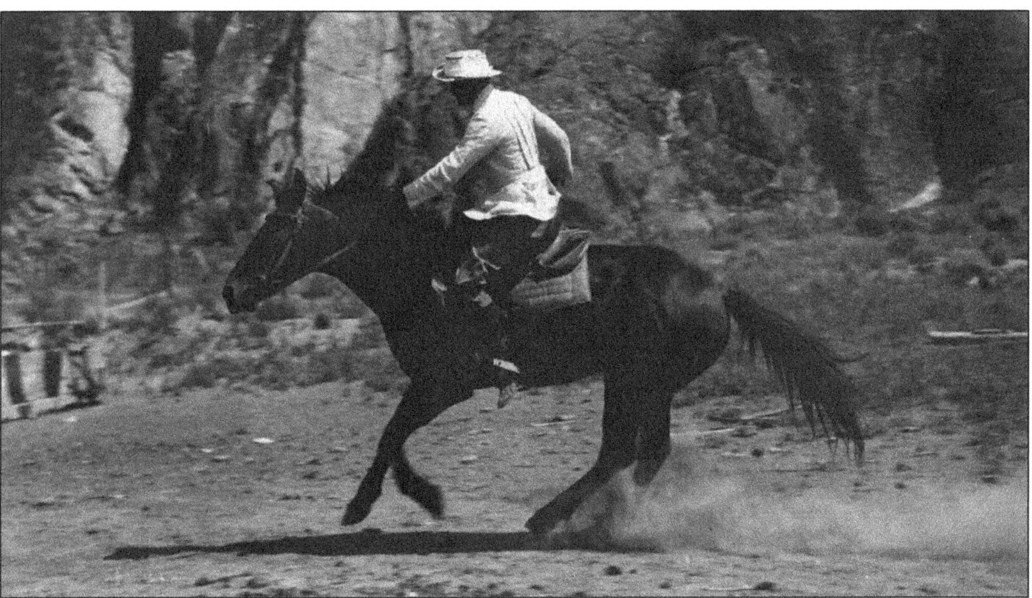

Back at Ranch One, the Baldwin family and neighbors had prepared a meal for everyone and entertained them with authentic bronco busting. The society's itinerary included New York, Niagara Falls, Chicago, St. Paul, Yellowstone Park, Spokane, Coulee City (Steamboat Rock), Yakima Valley, Seattle, San Francisco, Yosemite Valley, Los Angles, the Grand Canyon, Albuquerque, Colorado Springs, Rio Grande, Salt Lake City, Kansas City, Memphis, Mississippi, Cincinnati, Pittsburgh, Washington DC, and Delaware in 50 days.

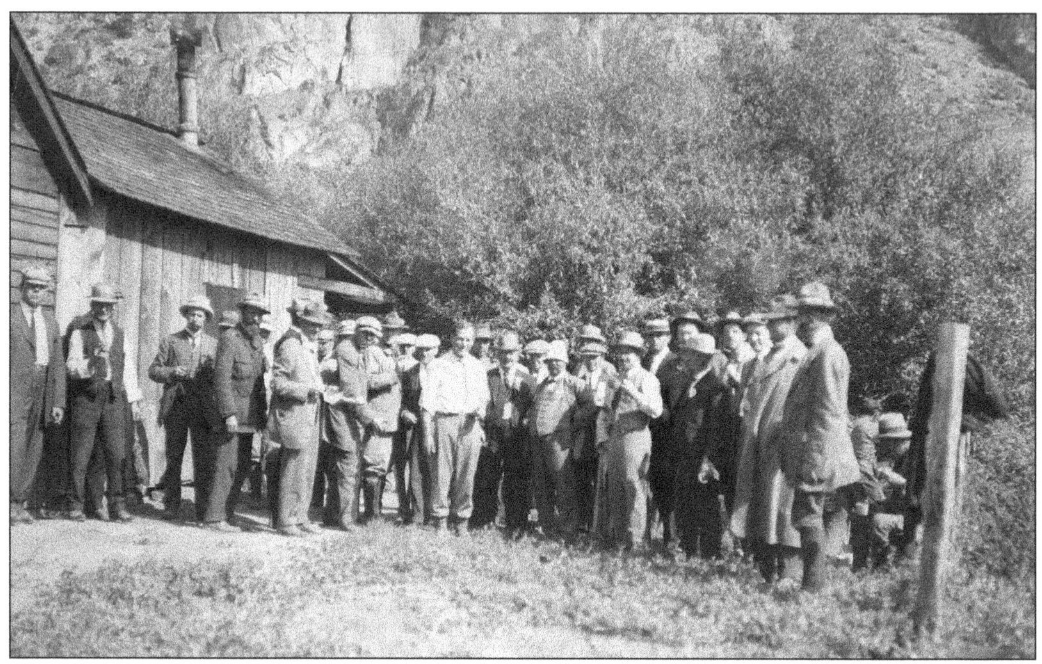

The National Geographic Society posed for this picture outside of the Baldwin home in 1912. Many of them traveled for weeks overseas, and it was their first time in America. The travelers included people from Austria, Belgium, Denmark, France, Germany, Great Britain, Hungary, the Netherlands, Norway, Russia, Sweden, and Switzerland. The transcontinental excursion later drove its caravan down the dusty Old Coulee Road and into Coulee City.

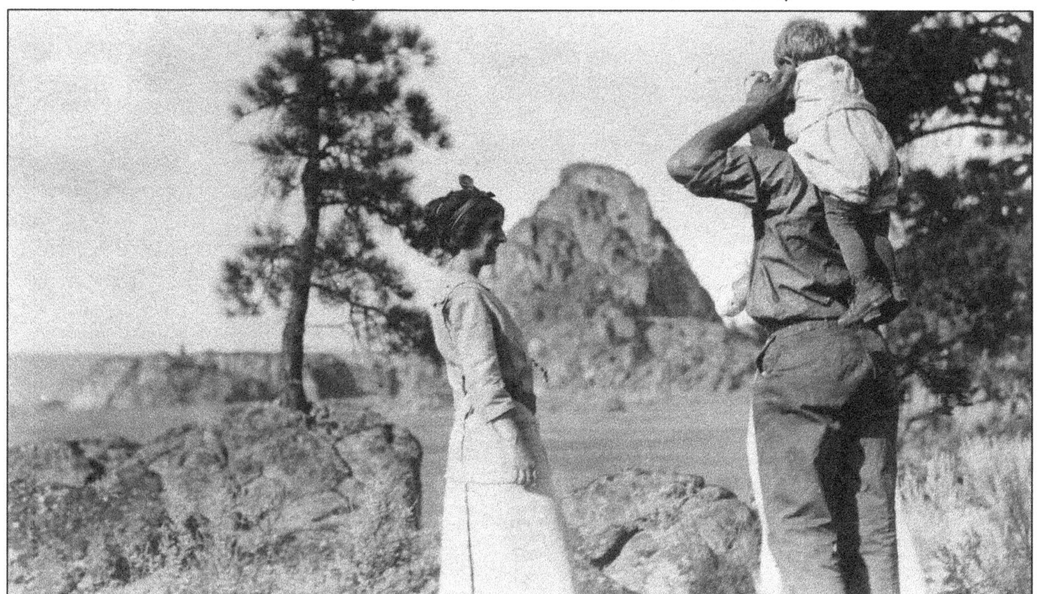

George Baldwin left the coulee in 1917, selling the Steamboat Rock Stock Company to a couple of investors from Spokane who hired Otis J. Martin to manage the land. Despite the accounts of mismanagement, the Steamboat Rock Stock Company introduced mechanized irrigation to the dry land and, using turn-of-the-century technology, were able to raise a family in the rugged environment of the coulee.

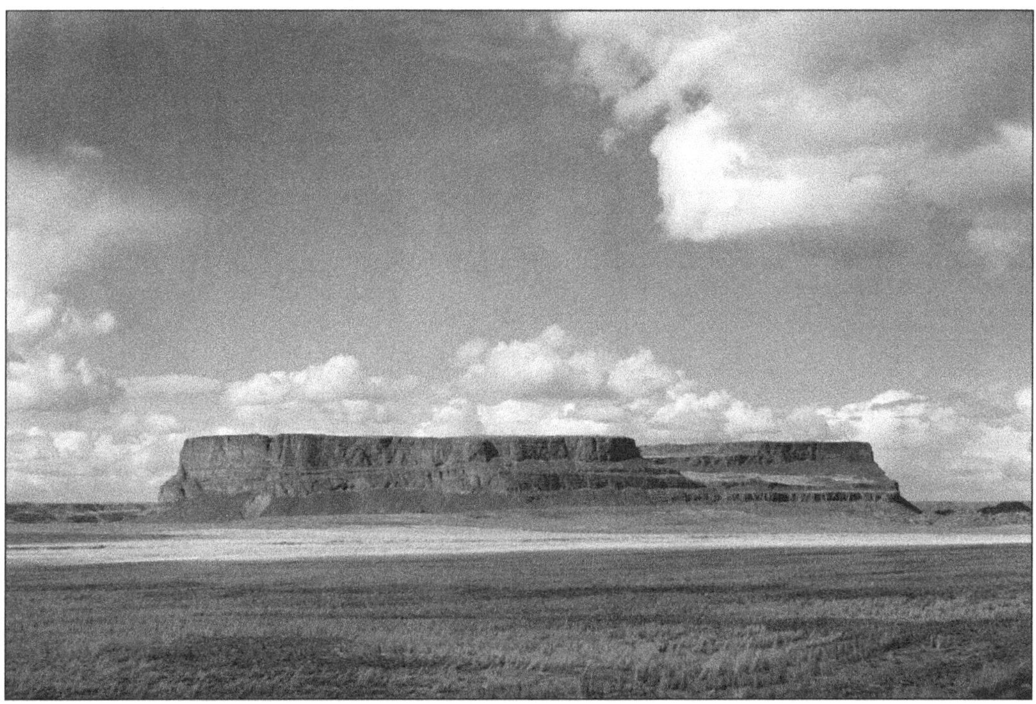

Under new leadership, the Steamboat Rock Stock Company became the Lincoln Stock Farm. The farm branched out and started raising hogs for market, as well as sheep. Under Otis Martin's leadership, the Lincoln Stock Farm flourished. Martin was able to hire on help and, because of this, soon became well known, liked, and respected by the community.

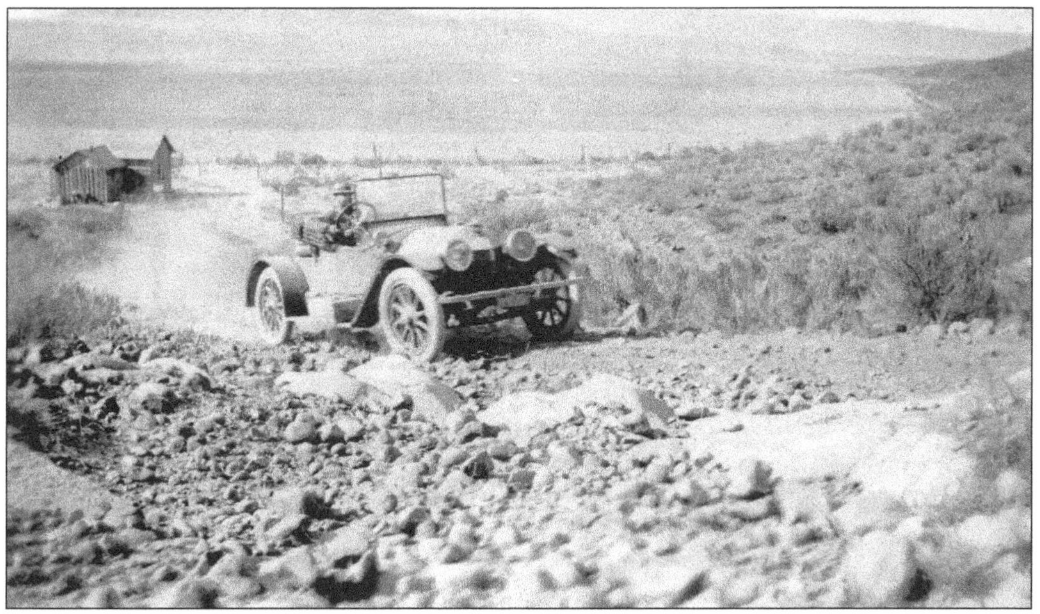

Otis Martin fixed up and expanded Ranch Three on the west side of Steamboat Rock in Barker Canyon with a new bunkhouse, mess hall, and manager's house, which his family moved into. Otis hired a crew of men who lived on the property, and drinking water was piped in from a nearby natural spring.

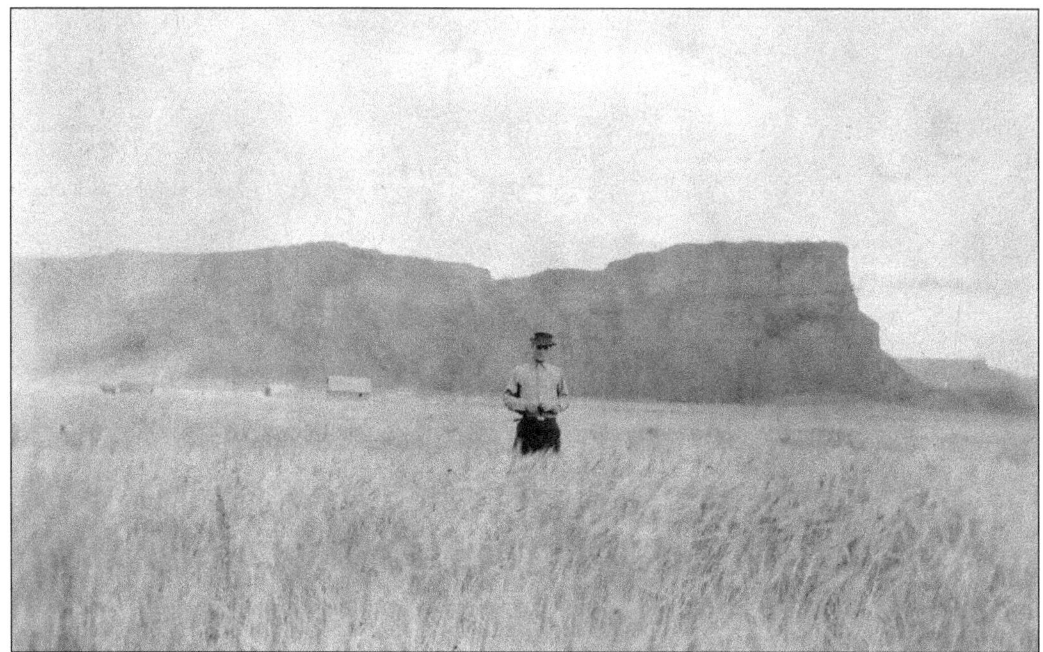

The pump from Devils Lake was again expanded on, and wheat and alfalfa crops were planted and thrived under the new, improved irrigation. The area boomed in huge wheat harvests and hayfields. One old-timer from the area was reported as saying the area was nothing more than "wheat, heat, and rattlesnakes."

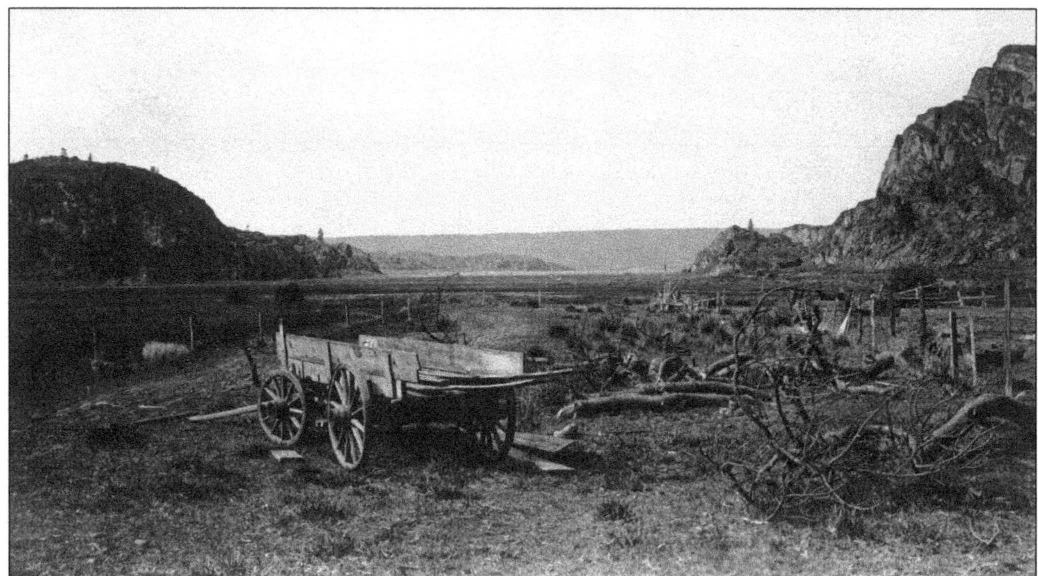

In 1919, unusually hot and dry summers turned into an almost decade-long drought. Lakes and springs dried up, and so did the topsoil, as it started to literally blow away in the wind. It was hard enough to breathe in the hot blowing mess, so planting a crop and feeding a family became impossible. Many families lost everything and left the coulee, as parts of it turned into a huge dustbowl.

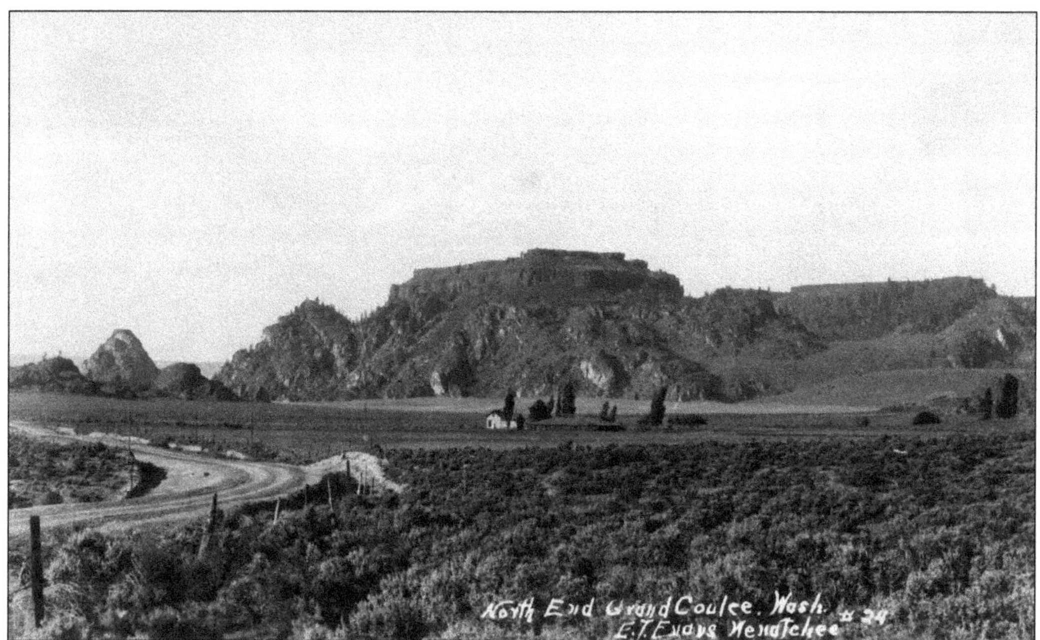

The fertile land they left behind soon turned to a wasteland, and abandoned farms dotted the landscape. The few families who decided to stay around Steamboat Rock and tough it out struggled through while looking out for each other and pulling together as a tighter community.

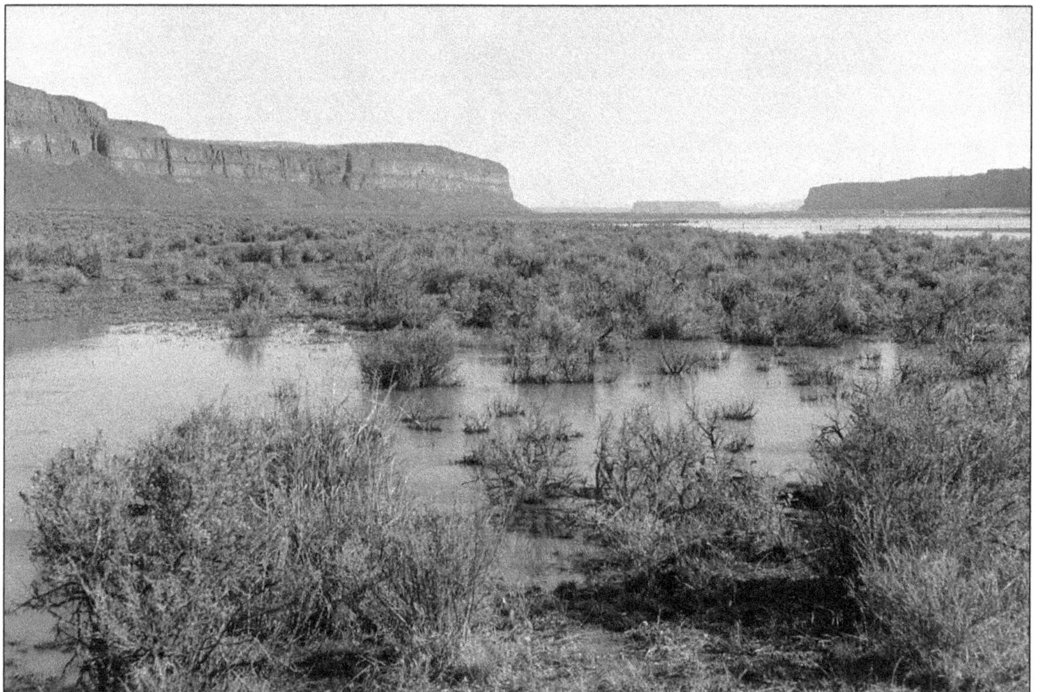

Then, in 1929, just when it looked like things were starting to turn around and the water table was picking up, the Great Depression struck, and the coulee began an economic downward spiral. The Coulee City bank collapsed during the Great Depression, and many more farmers followed it into ruin, with even more leaving the region. (Courtesy of Dan Bolyard.)

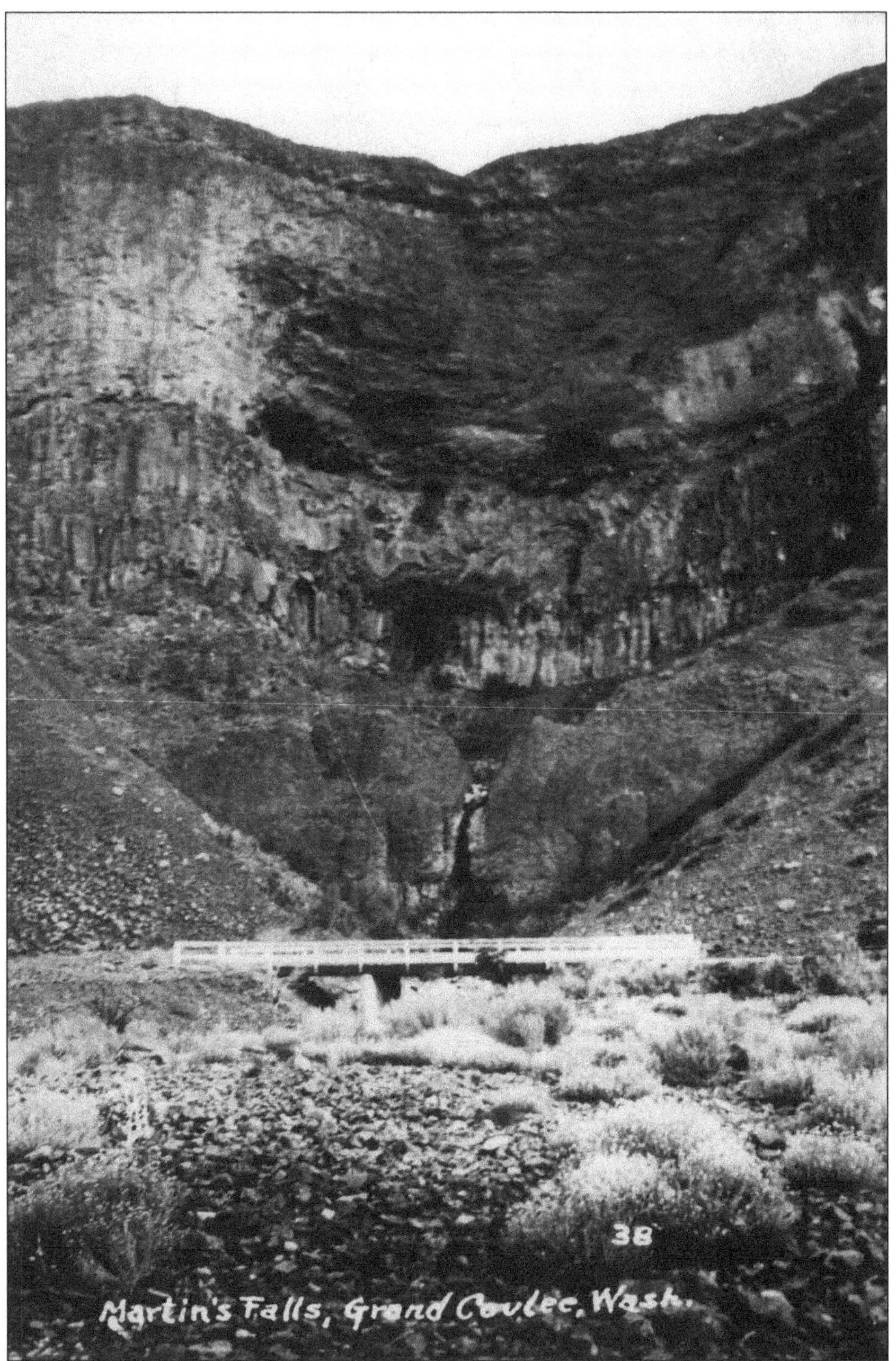

Through drought, the Great Depression, and an exodus from the coulee, the Lincoln Stock Farm was able to employ even during hard times, making Otis Martin a well-known and remembered person around the Steamboat Rock region. The Lincoln Stock Farm continued to operate from 1917 up until 1942, when the land was condemned to make way for a huge artificial reservoir.

Five

Grand Coulee Dam

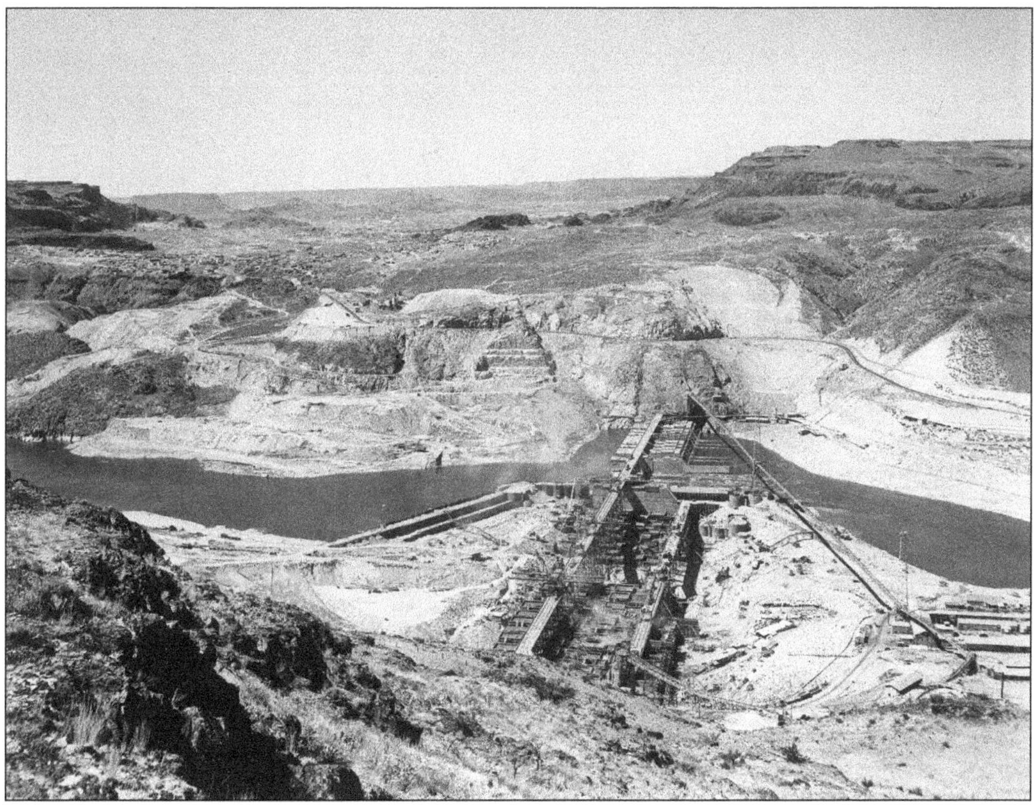

Dry-land farming was not only an issue in the coulee but also in the Columbia Basin, and soon, plans were coming that would change everything in the Steamboat Rock community forever. By the early 1930s, the political fight to build a dam across the Columbia River, about 15 miles away, was over, and work began on the Grand Coulee Dam.

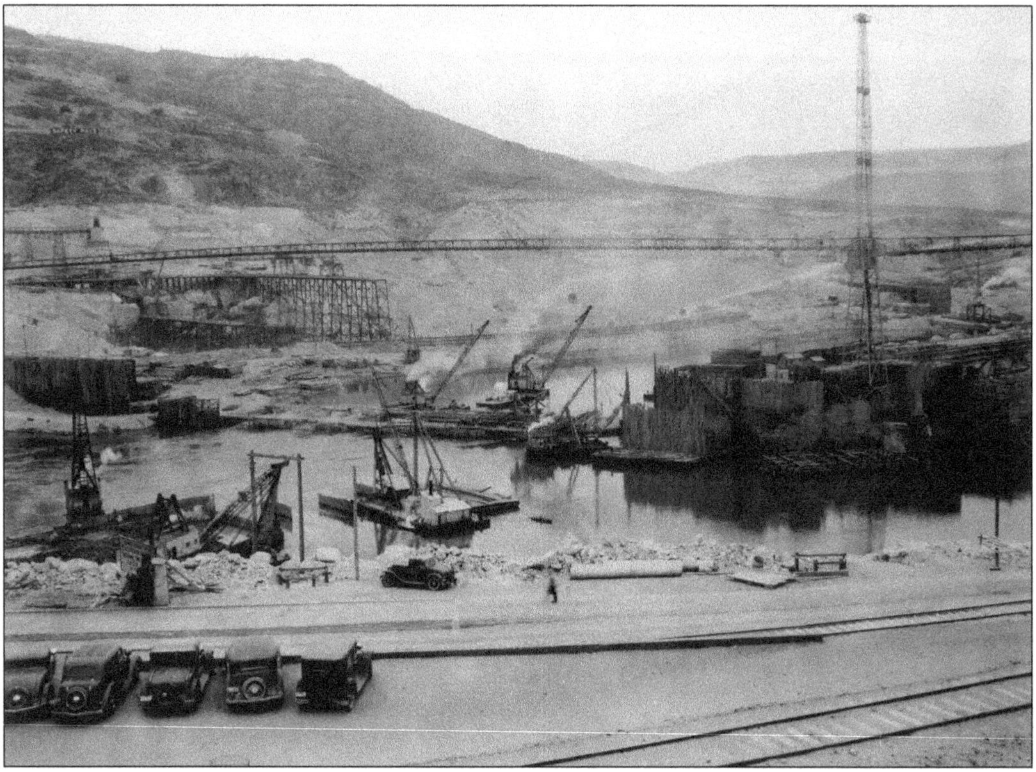

The construction of Grand Coulee Dam had a major impact on Steamboat Rock and the community of ranchers and farmers located in the coulee. People came from all over during the Great Depression in hopes of finding work in the Grand Coulee, either on the dam construction or in support of the dam workers.

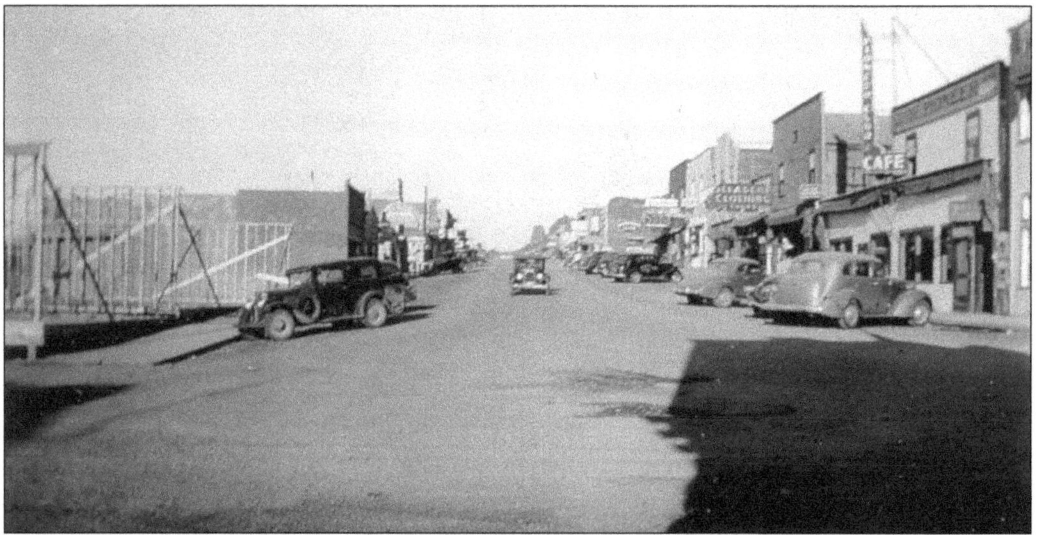

The start of the Grand Coulee Dam brought a flood of people into the coulee, but not all wanted to work for the dam. Boomtowns full of dreams and aspirations sprung up overnight around the construction site as people continued to pour into the coulee. The most infamous of all was arguably B Street in old Grand Coulee.

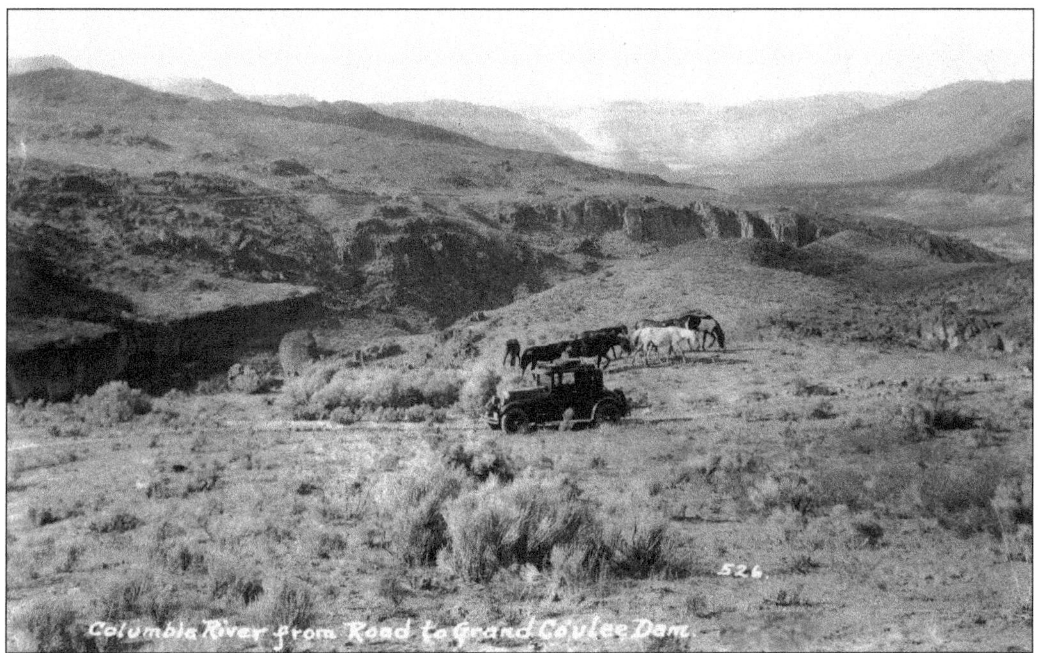

The people already in the coulee living around Steamboat Rock watched as a new wave of pioneer arrived, just like they had been watched decades earlier by the indigenous people. In the same fashion, as the earlier settlers, these new pioneers brought change with them.

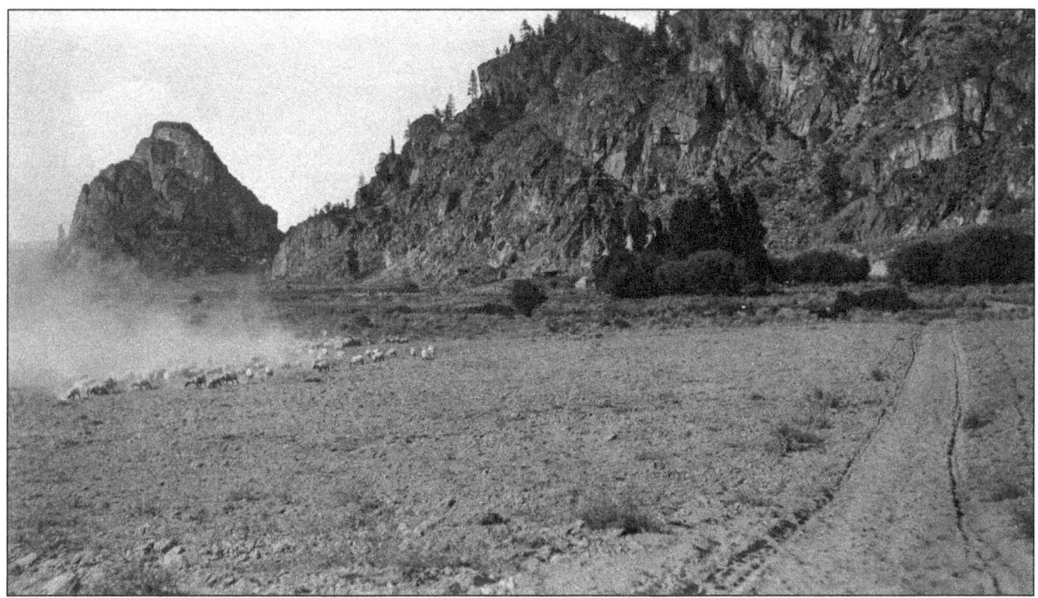

Farming around Steamboat Rock was in an economic slump; few families managed to stay in the coulee and, despite hard times, move ahead and grow their operations or at least survive. Some locals entered politics and worked for irrigation and better roads.

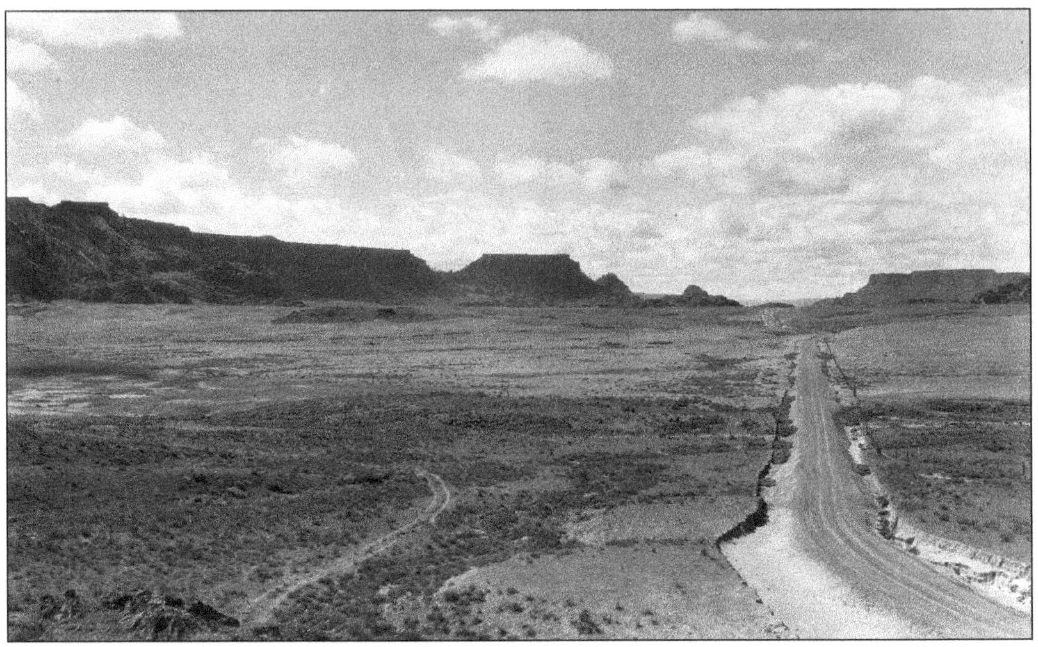

When construction began, people headed to the dam site were urged not to use the Old Coulee Road. This set off a dispute between Wilbur and Almira over who would be the "Gateway to the Dam." The United States Bureau of Reclamation (USBR) had other plans for where the gateway would be. (Courtesy of Spokane Public Library.)

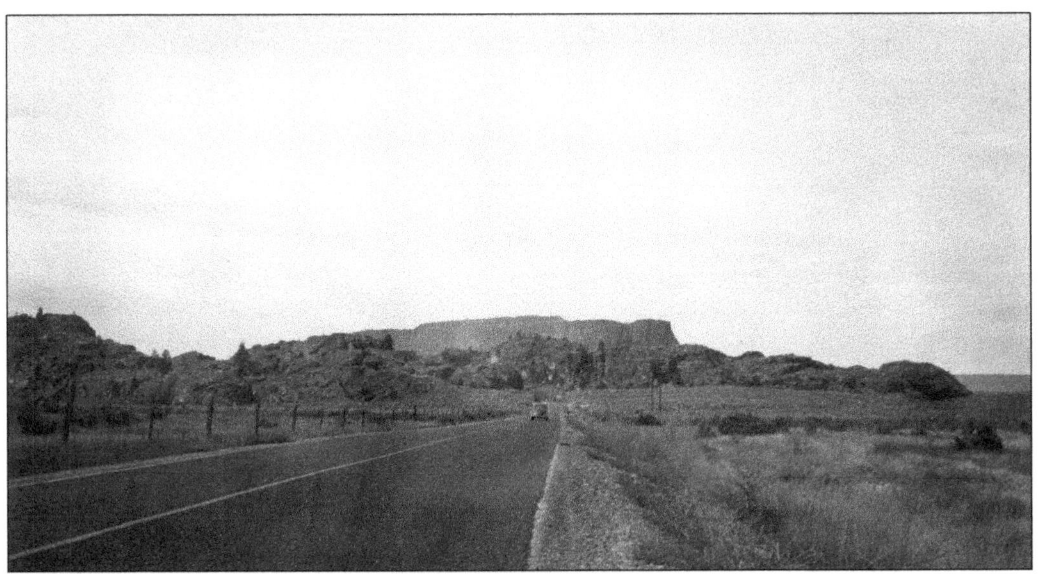

In 1934, the Department of Highways, under the direction of Lacey Marrow, appointed by Gov. Clarence Martin, created the State Highway 7A as an alternative and straightforward route down the coulee from Coulee City, past Steamboat Rock, and on to the Grand Coulee Dam construction site. The highway was created in record time, opening the same year. To save time, the new highway was built over parts of the graveled and grated Old Coulee Road.

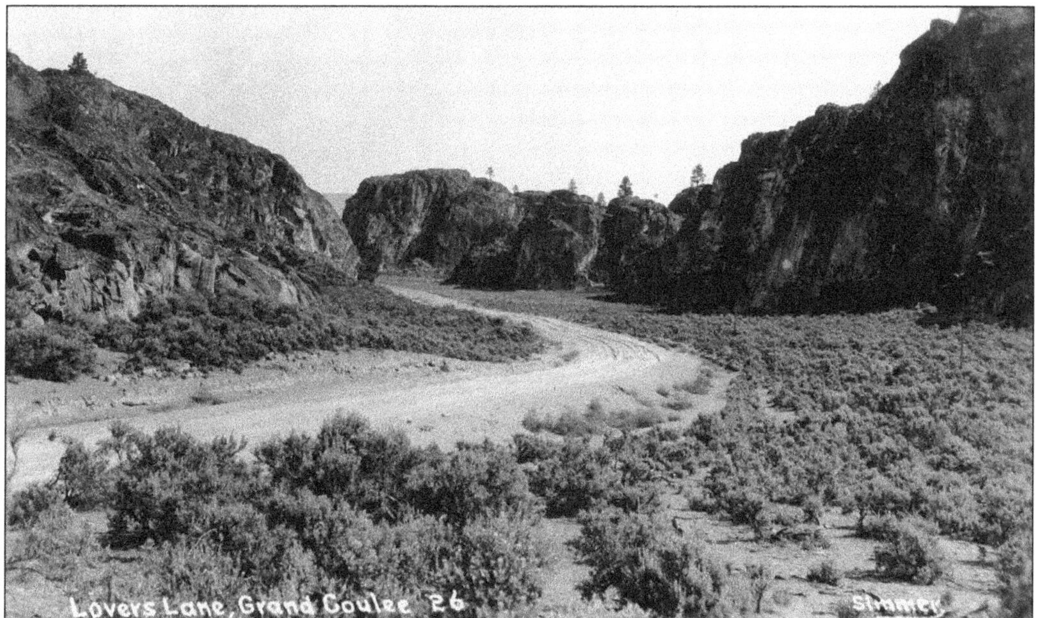

Just to the northeast of Steamboat Rock is a place where the Missoula floodwaters stripped the basalt away, leaving huge granite hills. Known as the Granite Hills, there was a natural path that ran for a quarter mile through while the rocks towered overhead; it was known as "Lover's Lane." At first, the path was a wagon trail, and later, improvements were made.

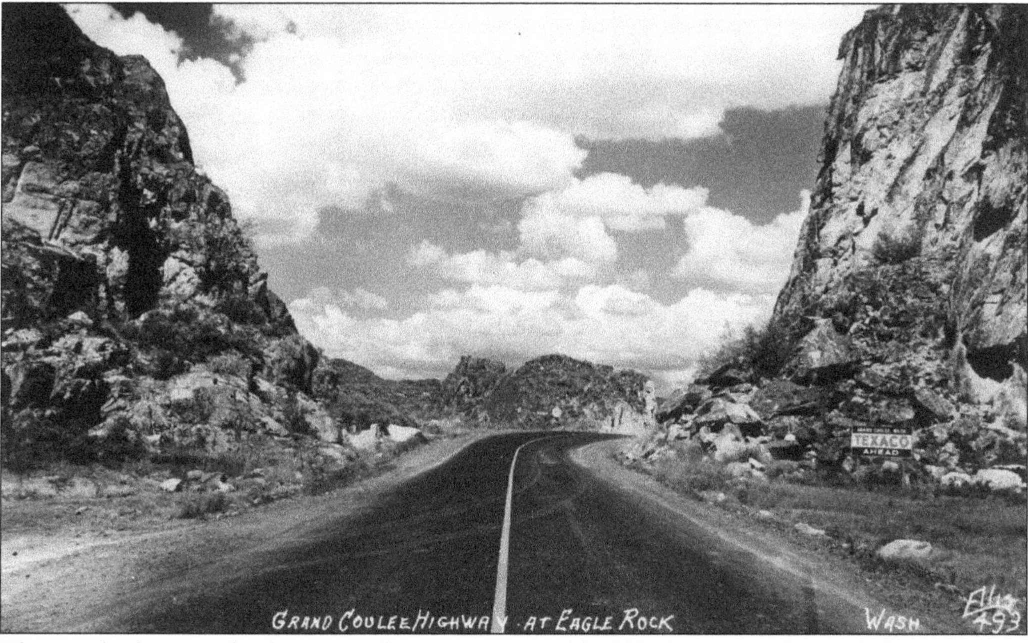

The new highway took advantage of Lover's Lane and laid blacktop over the graded and graveled cut. This was quicker than blasting through the solid granite and saved both time and money. Nothing was slow about the new road, and soon after its creation, Highway 7A earned a name that would stick with it throughout its use: "the Speedball Highway." Eagle Rock was a pull-off on the northeast end of Lover's Lane.

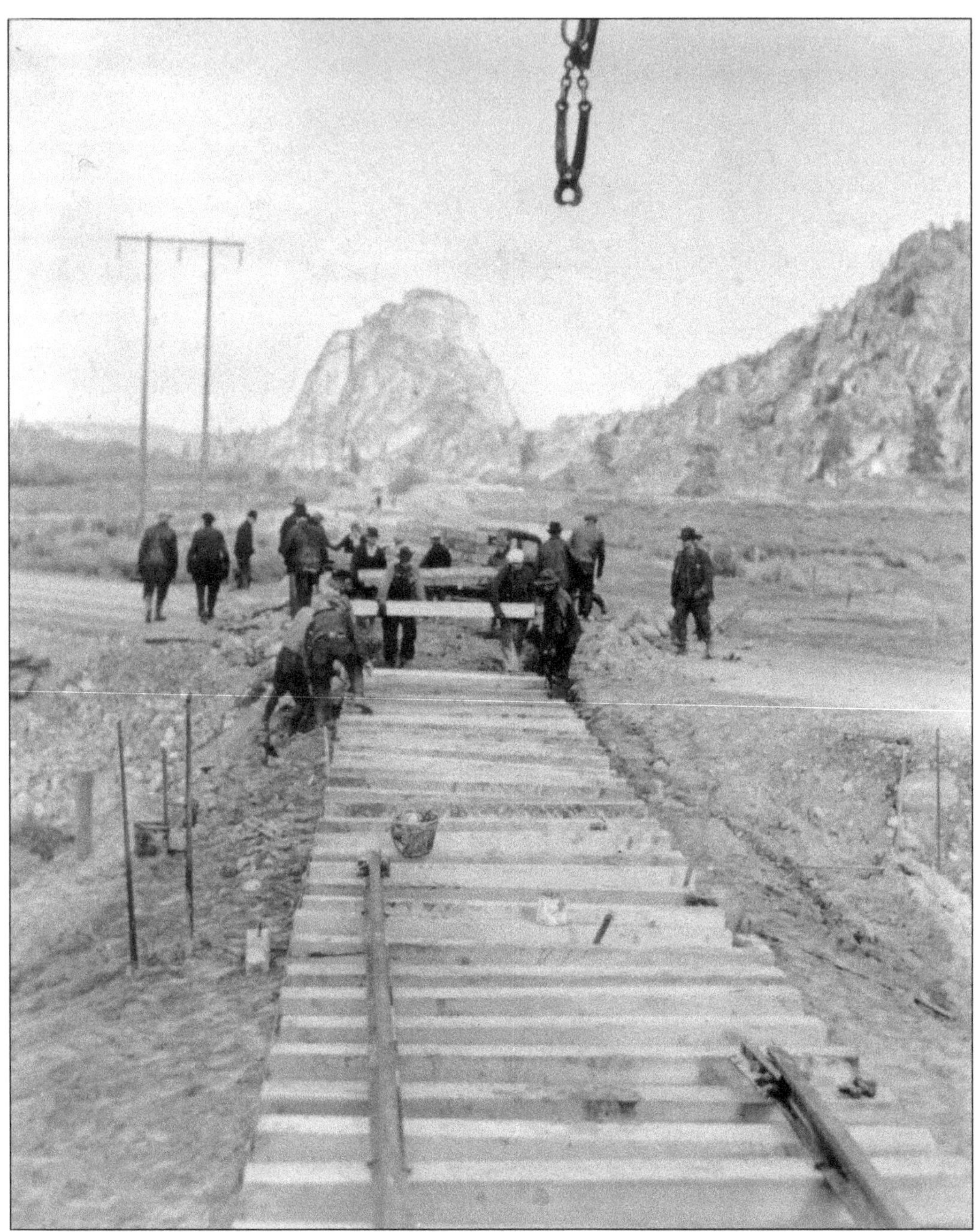

With a controversial government contract, David H. Ryan began work on the US Construction Railroad between Odair, outside Coulee City, and the Grand Coulee Dam. This rail line ran parallel to the Speedball Highway in most places, but it took longer to open the line due mostly to red tape and accusations of corruption.

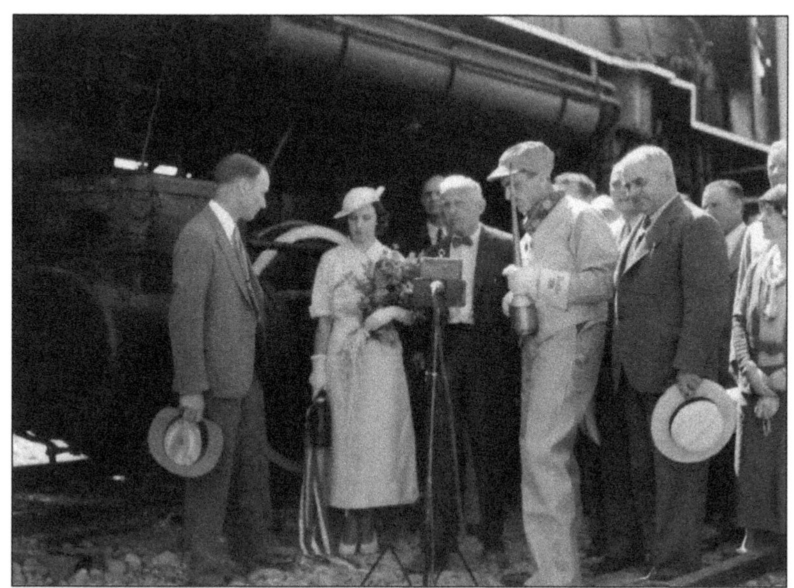

David H. Ryan's US Construction Railroad opened to much fanfare, with a golden spike ceremony in January 1935, followed by a maiden voyage in July of the same year piloted by Gov. Clarence Martin and a collection of specially selected passengers. Also pictured is the editor-in-chief of the *Wenatchee Daily World*, Rufus Woods.

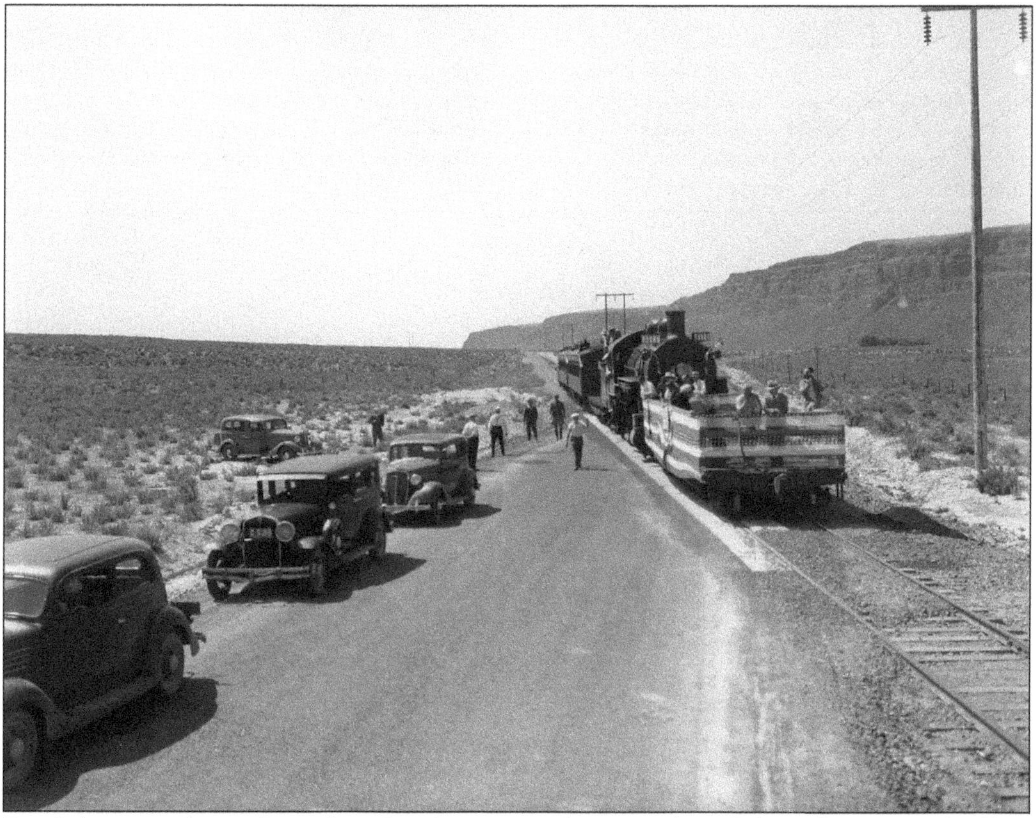

People living in the coulee gathered as the train made its way from Odair, whooping and calling out as it passed. The US Construction Railroad only officially carried a select list of VIP passengers on its initial trip. The US Construction Railroad, sometimes referred to as "the Gopher Chaser" or "the Sagebrush Express," was the first train to run down the coulee and was only officially used to haul material to the dam site except on its maiden voyage. (Courtesy of Dan Bolyard.)

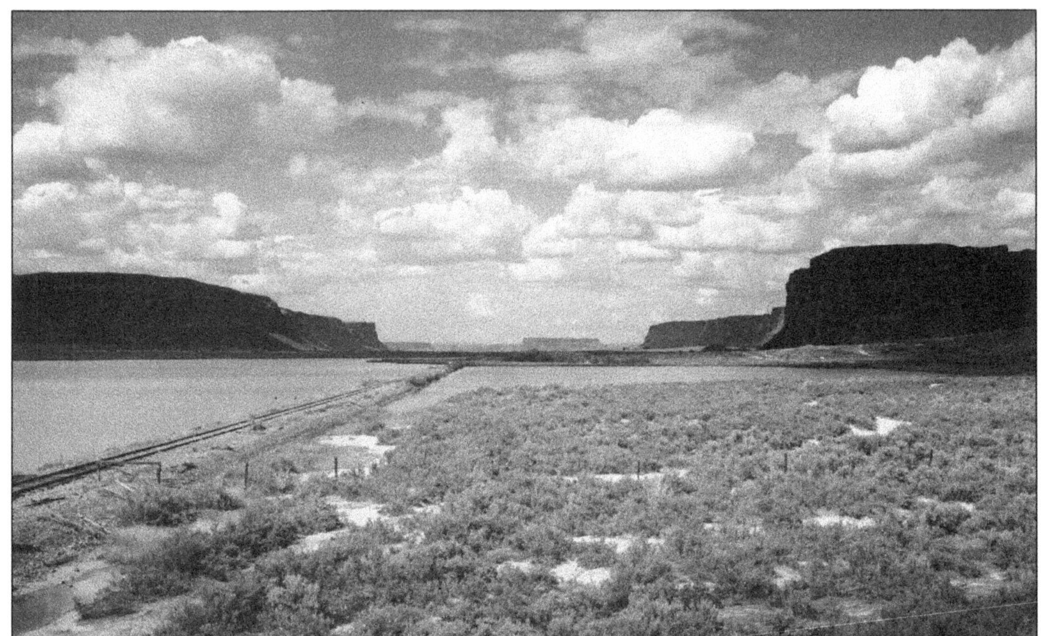

Here, the US Construction Railroad runs across Alkali or Alkali Sinks Lake. David H. Ryan was warned not to build the tracks over the west end of the lake due to flooding, but several consecutive "dry" years had led him to believe the land was solid enough to be used. In the spring of 1936, a torrential runoff occurred, flooding the railroad and forcing Ryan to move the tracks. (Courtesy of Dan Bolyard.)

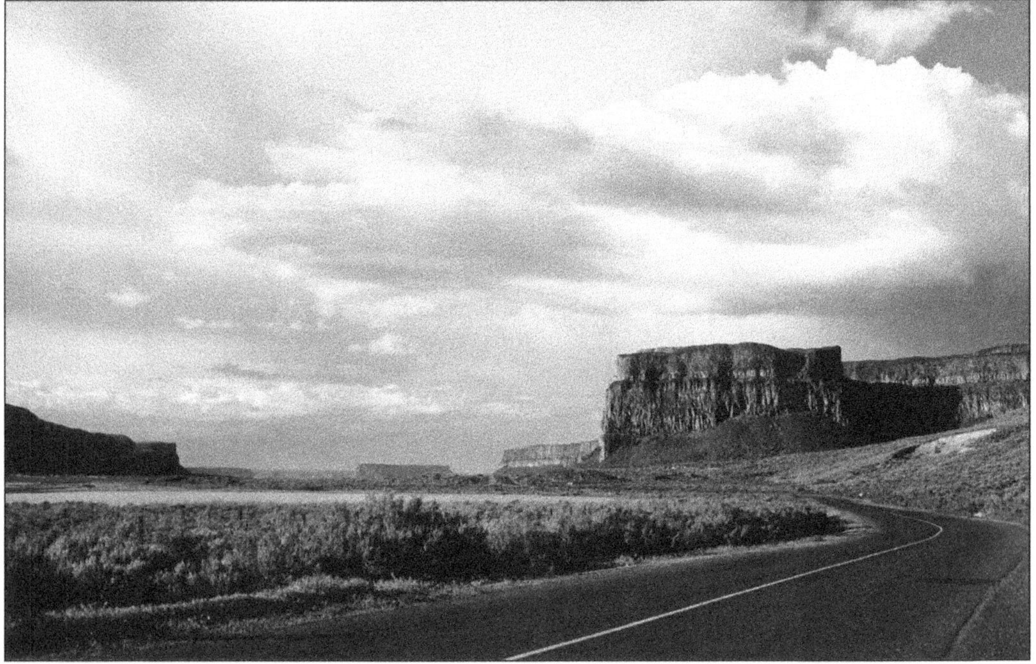

The Speedball Highway was also flooded, but it did not sustain any real damage and was soon reopened. Here, the Speedball Highway travels between Alkali Sinks Lake and Salishan Mesa, with Steamboat Rock in the center. (Courtesy of Washington State Digital Archive.)

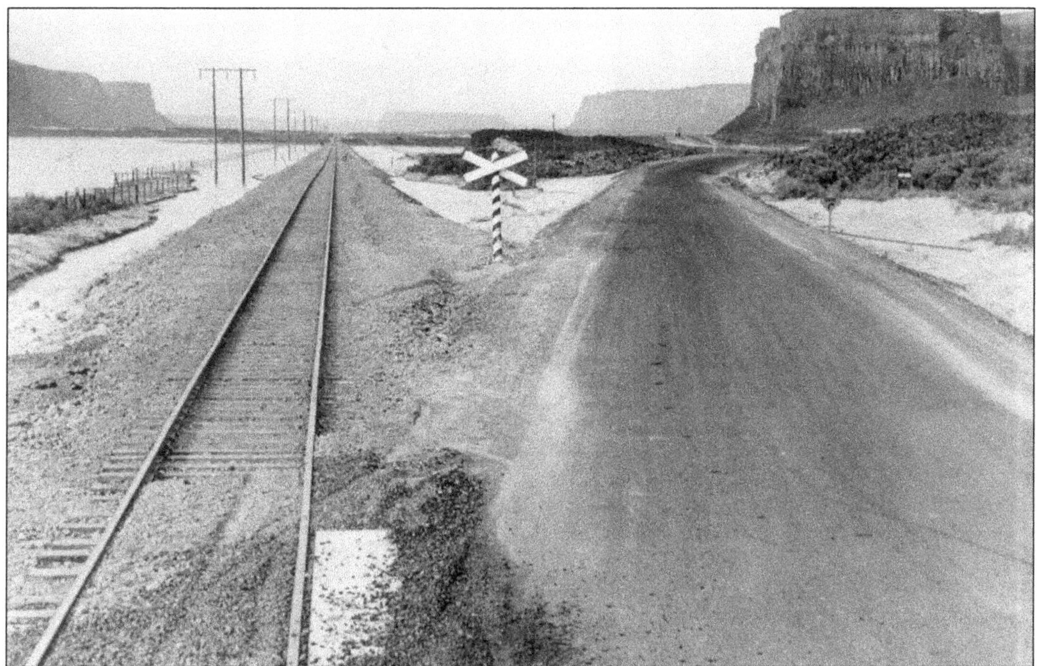

The Speedball Highway and the US Construction Railroad crossed five times as they made their way down the coulee, often side by side. There are many stories about people racing the train down the coulee to the crossings. It was a decadent time; people who never had money now drove their first car while the rest of the country suffered through the Great Depression.

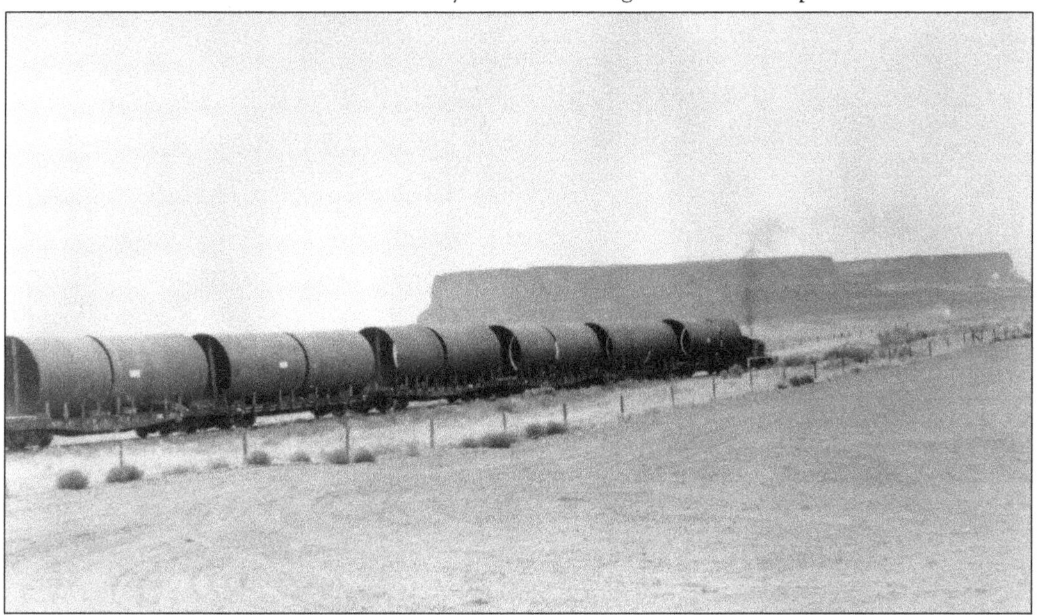

Although David H. Ryan's US Construction Railroad never officially hauled people except on its maiden voyage, there are rumors and stories to the contrary about an occasional guest. The railroad was built cheaply, with plans of removing the track when its use in the construction of the Grand Coulee Dam had ended. The train is pictured here, loaded with 12-foot-diameter steel pipes for the skip car at the Grand Coulee Dam.

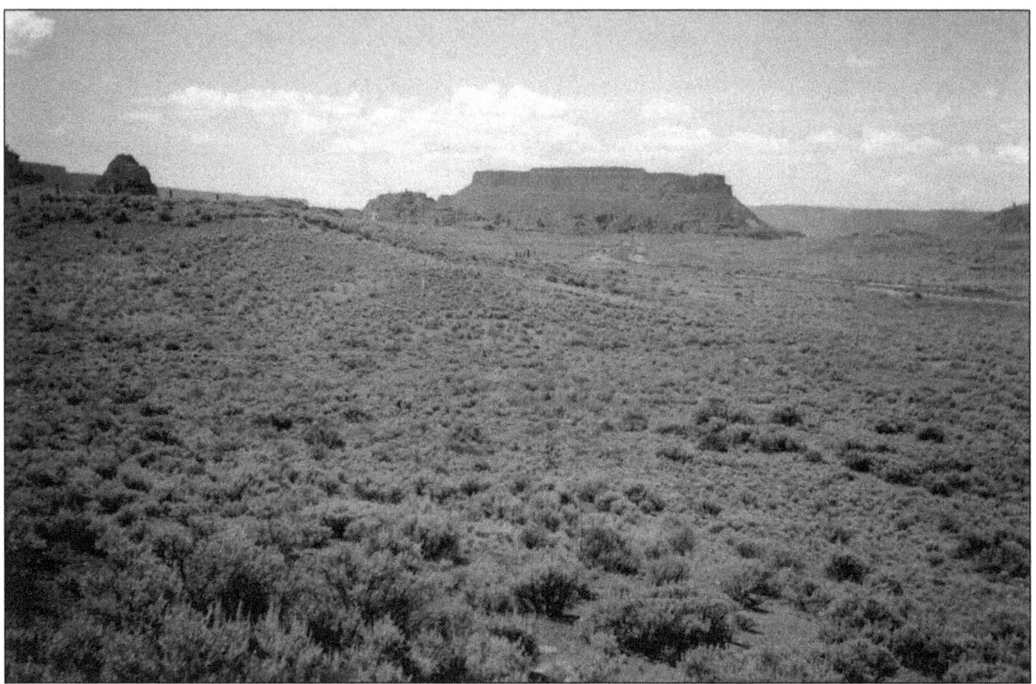

By the end of 1936, the new highway and railroad traveled side by side down the coulee from Coulee City in the south to the Grand Coulee Dam construction site in the north. People and products traveled down the coulee all hours of the day and night past Steamboat Rock, which stood firm, almost in the center of all the hustle and bustle. (Courtesy of the *Star*.)

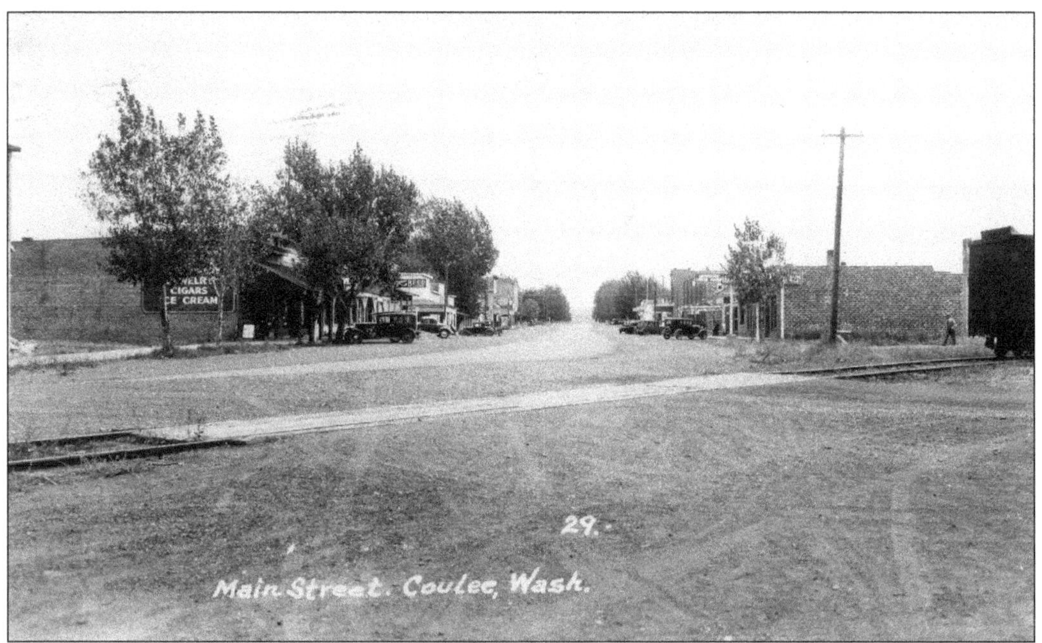

Coulee City, which for generations had been the closest and biggest town at the railhead, also started to rapidly grow, becoming a stop for people headed to the dam or making their way back out of the coulee. It was literally the other end of the tracks from the Grand Coulee Dam.

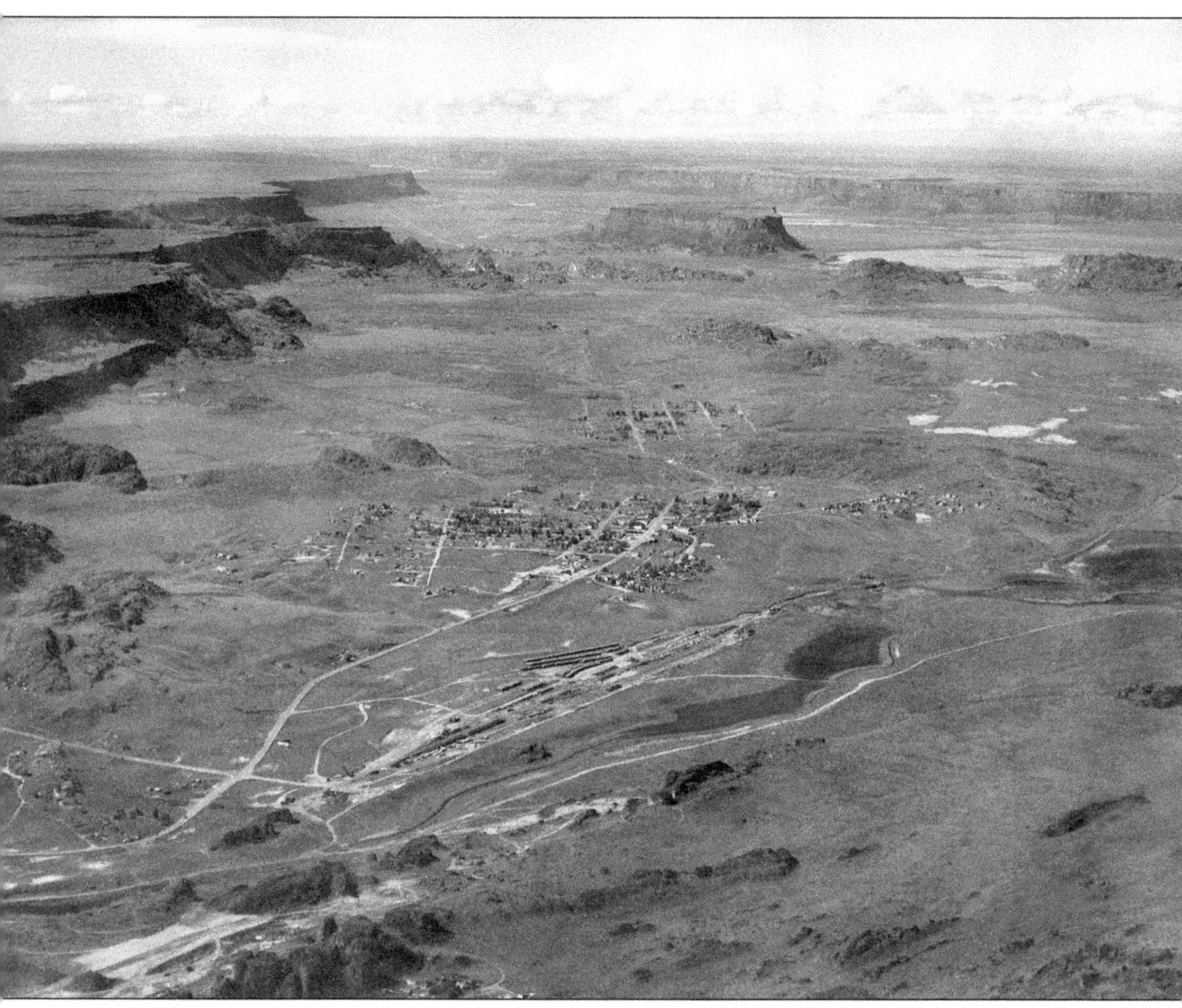

As the land around the Grand Coulee Dam construction site became a prime commodity, small towns—some no larger than a gas station and house—began to mushroom down the coulee along the Speedball Highway from the Columbia River to Steamboat Rock, bringing the next wave of settlers to the region. It also brought life back to the community, as money followed the Speedball Highway south from the Grand Coulee Dam. (Courtesy of Dennis King Photography.)

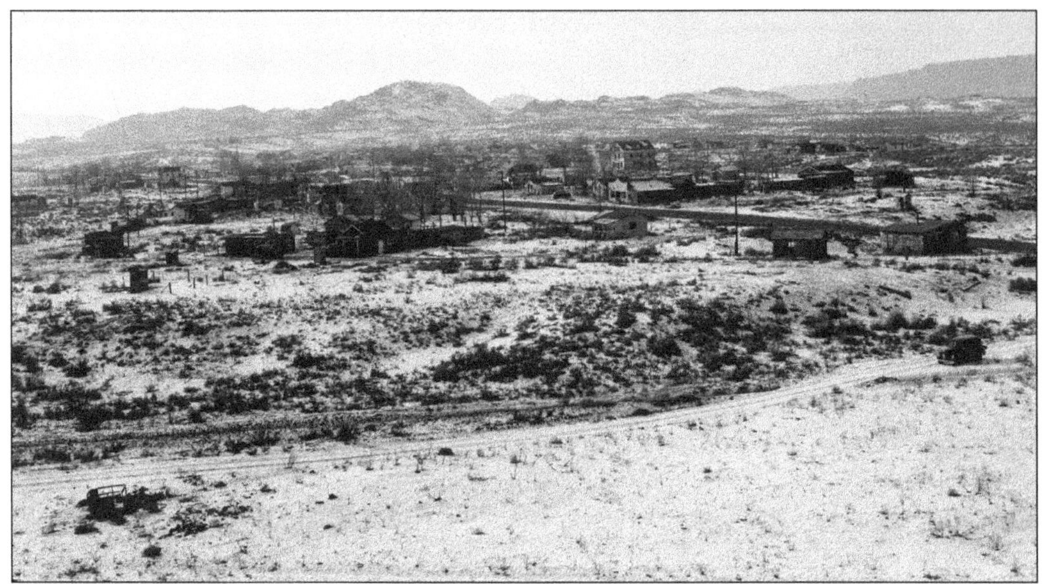

Several townships bloomed almost overnight: Electric City, Franklin, Osborne, Basin City, and Rim Rock. It was a lot easier to create a town back in the 1930s; it was almost as easy as buying a piece of land, subdividing it into plots, and then selling the plots. Some of these towns lasted a year or two, and others a bit longer, but only Electric City remains today. Shown here is Osborne in winter.

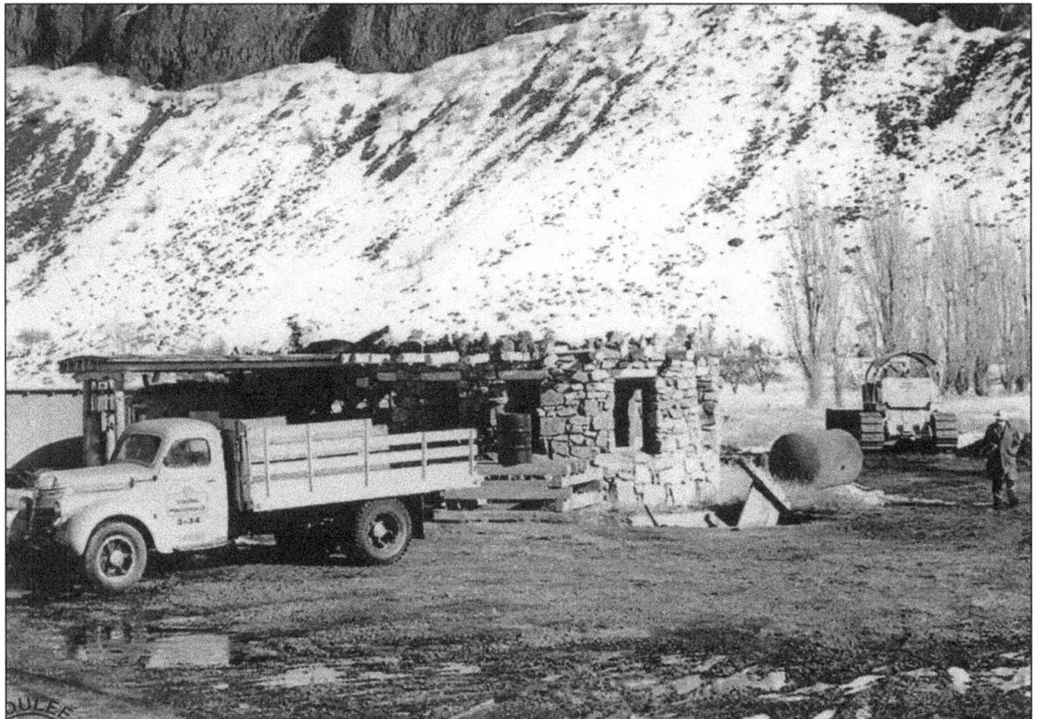

The small towns of Rim Rock and Basin City sprung up in "the shadow of Steamboat Rock" and continued to grow throughout the 1930s. Eventually, the old Steamboat Rock School was moved over closer to Rim Rock under the shade of the well-known line of poplar trees.

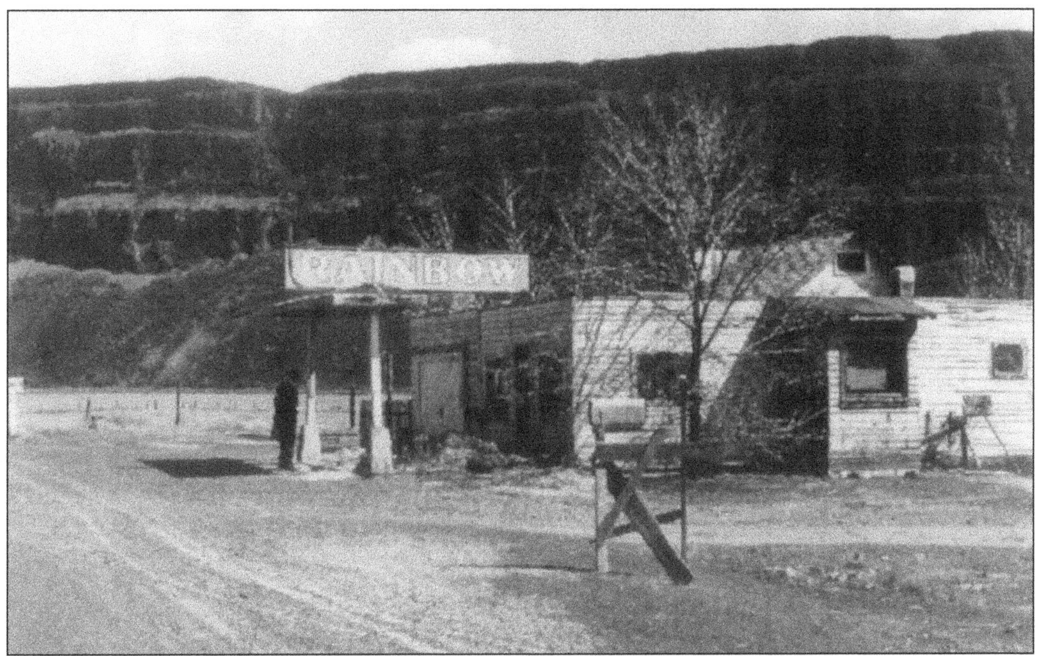

At its heights, the township of Rim Rock boasted a café, gas station, grocery store, and cottages. Ed "Happy" Lord managed a large dance hall one mile southwest of Rim Rock that held standing room–only dances and live bands. Pictured here is Harry and Golda Fulton's Rainbow Gas Station, which also had a café inside. For a while, the Fultons also owned and operated the Shamrock Café in Rim Rock. (Courtesy of Grant County Museum.)

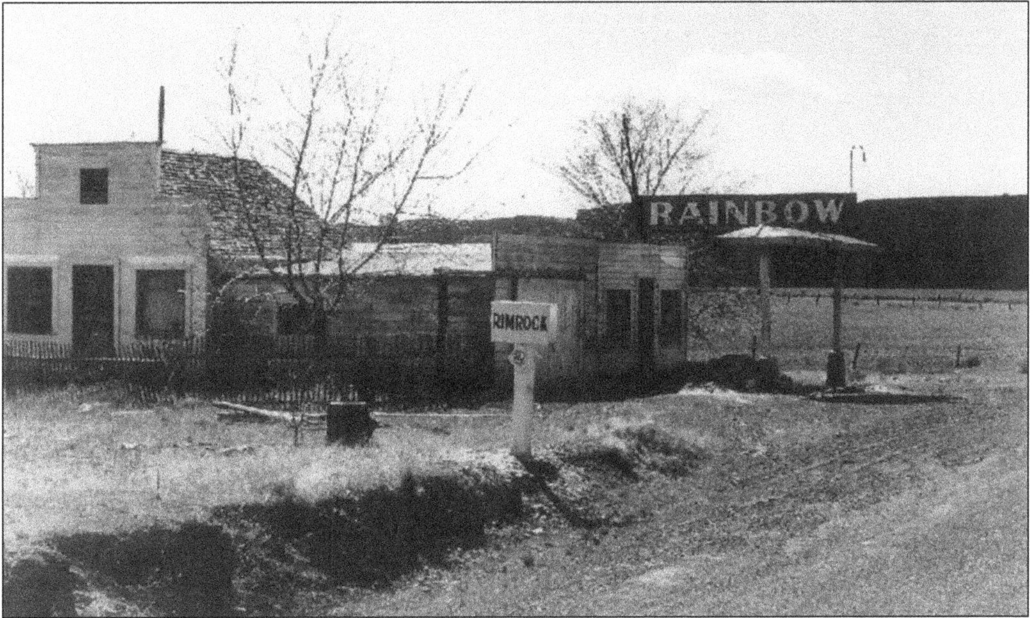

The infusion of stores, stations, trains, roads, and people had brought the Steamboat Rock community to life again. Now, old farmers and ranchers had a place to gather and talk, and the community started to come together more as a second generation raised in the coulee began to get involved and come of age. (Courtesy of Grant County Museum.)

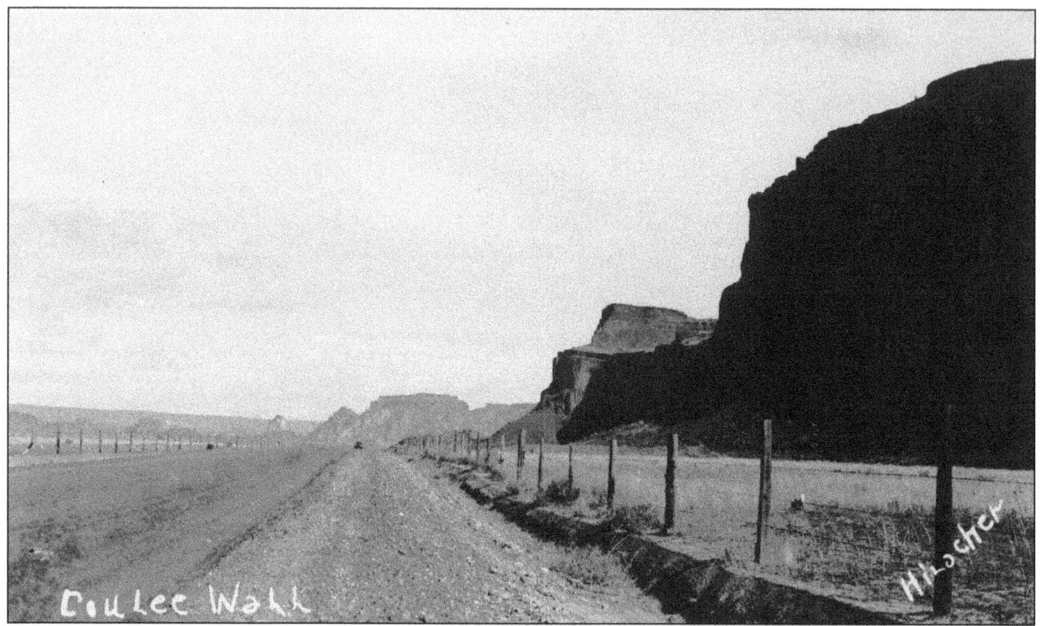

Outside the immediate community, people had money and started to move around. Probably for the first time ever, Steamboat Rock became a destination spot for recreation, rather than a place to try to make a living amid the giant sagebrush.

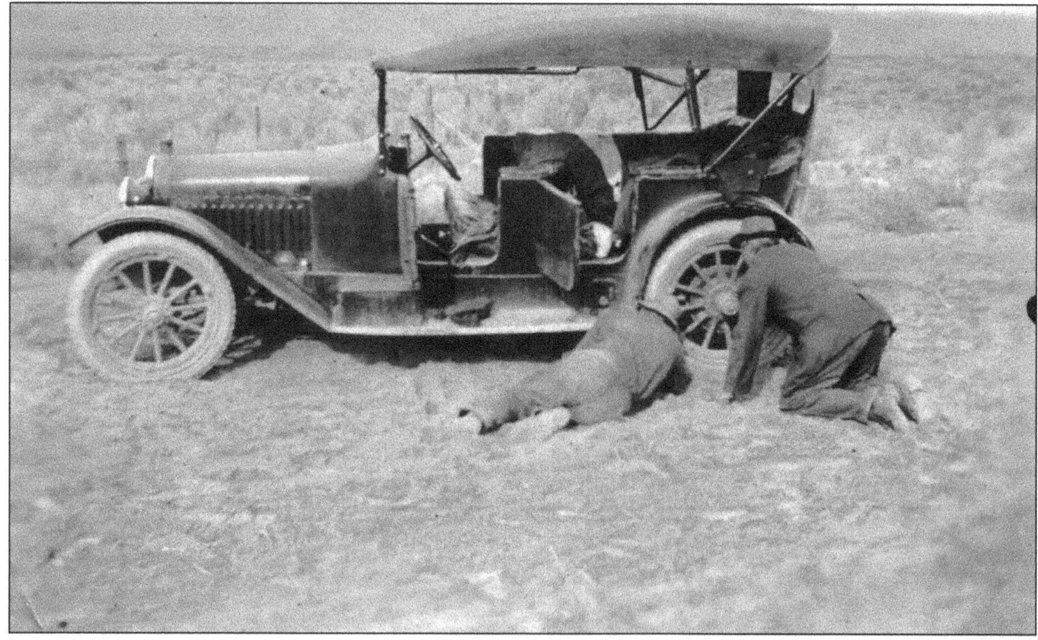

Hunting, hiking, camping, and rock hounding are just a few of the activities taken up by people traveling through the area. Searching for fossils and artifacts was made popular in the area when J Harlen Bretz released his controversial 1932 book, *The Grand Coulee*, attracting geologists and rock hounds of all stature into the coulee.

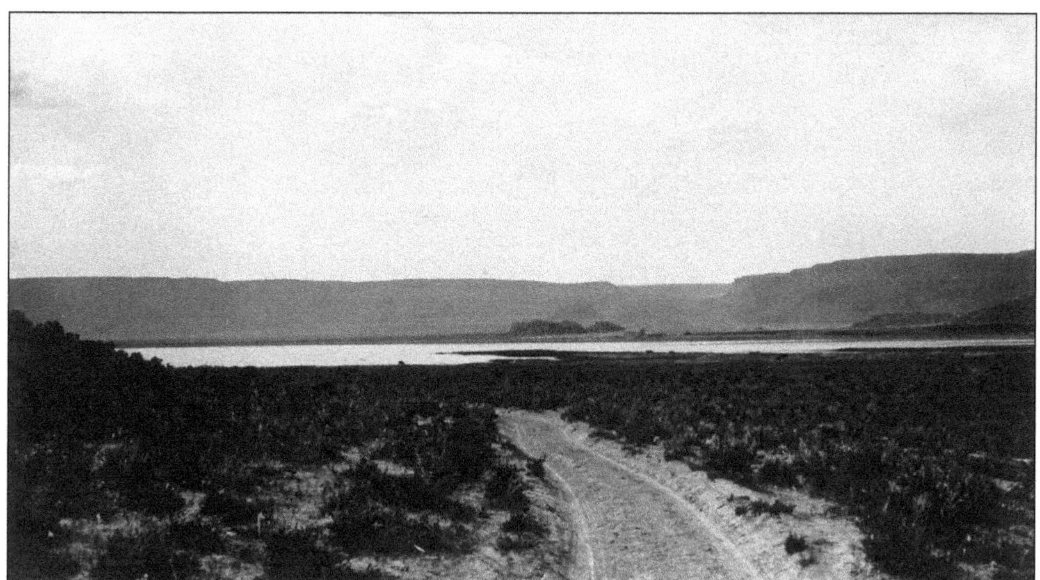

This dirt road led to Devils Lake, which was becoming a favorite fishing place for locals. Gone were the old pumps on the lake and pump house. The lake could be accessed by the public and was a great local getaway that was just off the beaten path enough to discourage the casual explorer.

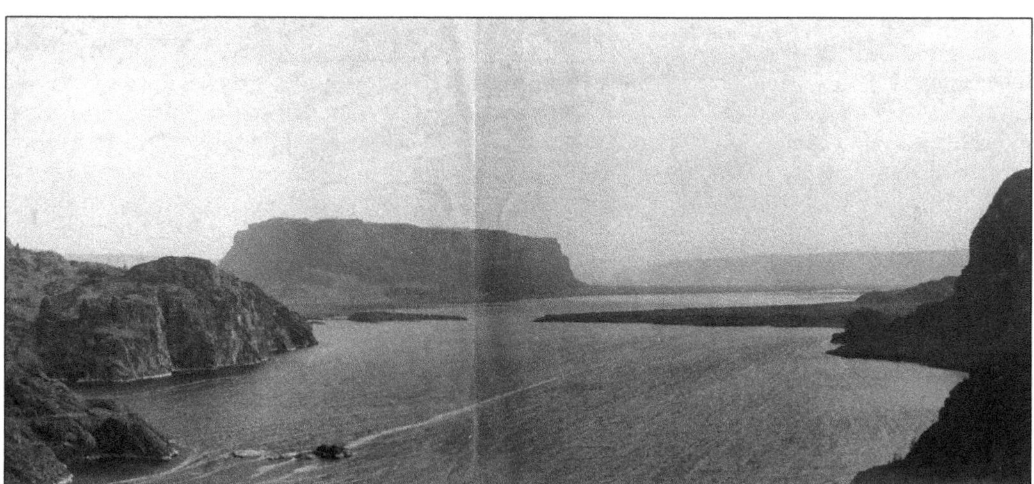

Devils Lake itself has had a long, noteworthy history. Before the first pioneers, it was a sacred place visited by indigenous people. Travelers on the Okanogan Trail would also visit it for water and easy hunting. Later, irrigation from Devils Lake helped define dry-land farming in the early 1900s, and by 1940, it was a favorite fishing spot for locals and rumored to be bottomless.

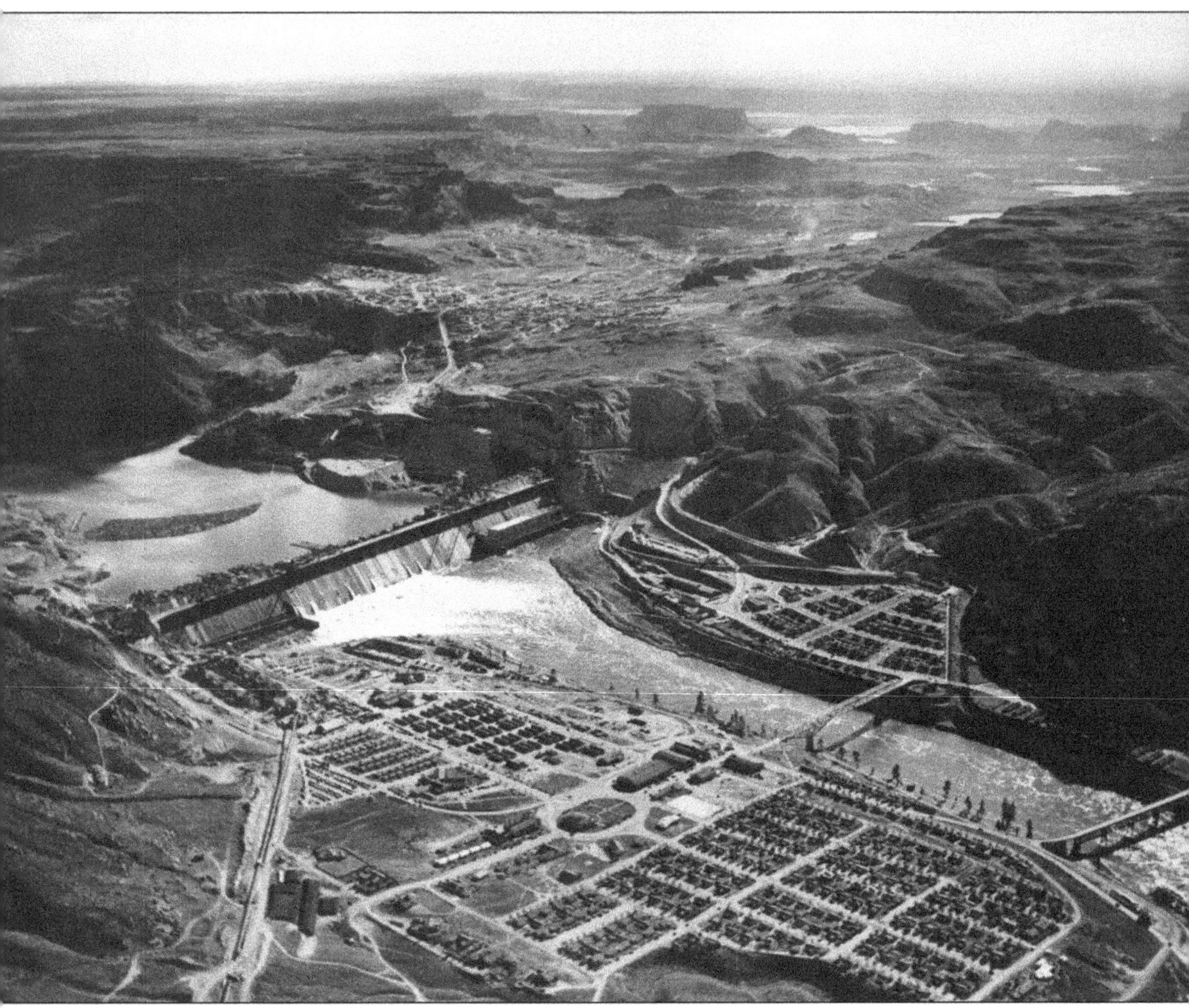

The creation of the Grand Coulee Dam not only bought thousands of workers, but it also brought thousands of curious sightseers from all over, anxious to see the construction of the "Eighth Wonder of the Modern World." Soon, the area was full of tourists, and with Steamboat Rock less than 20 miles away on the Speedball Highway, it also started to receive an influx of visitors.

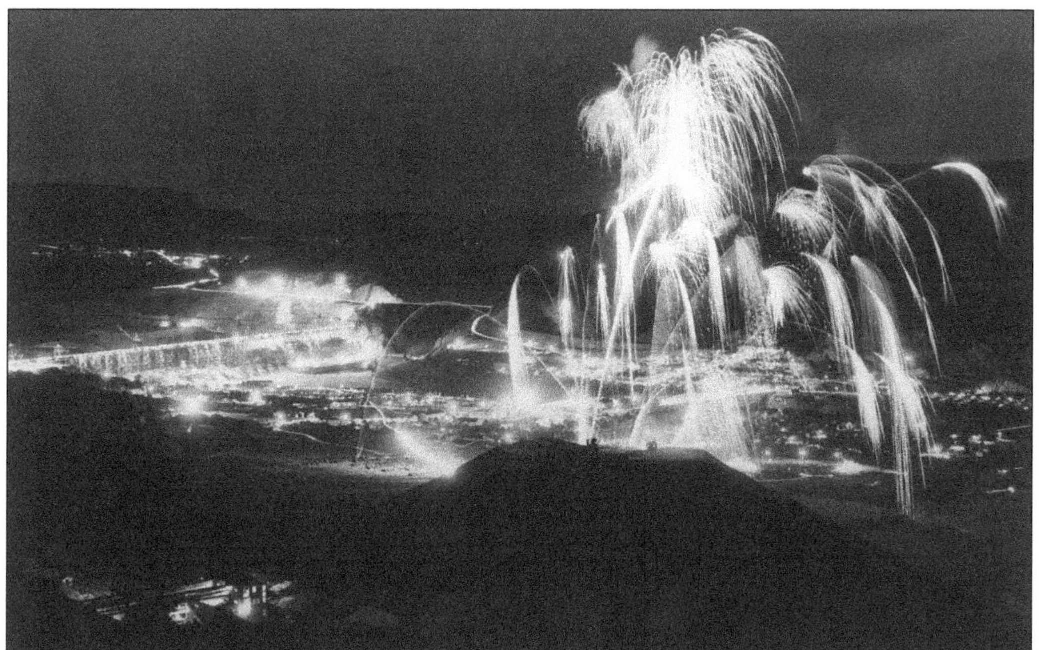

It was not long before the cities around the dam started to hold their own celebrations, which drew even more people down the coulee past Steamboat Rock. Here, fireworks can be seen on the Fourth of July in 1939, launching off the sand pile over Mason City, with the dam lit up in the background.

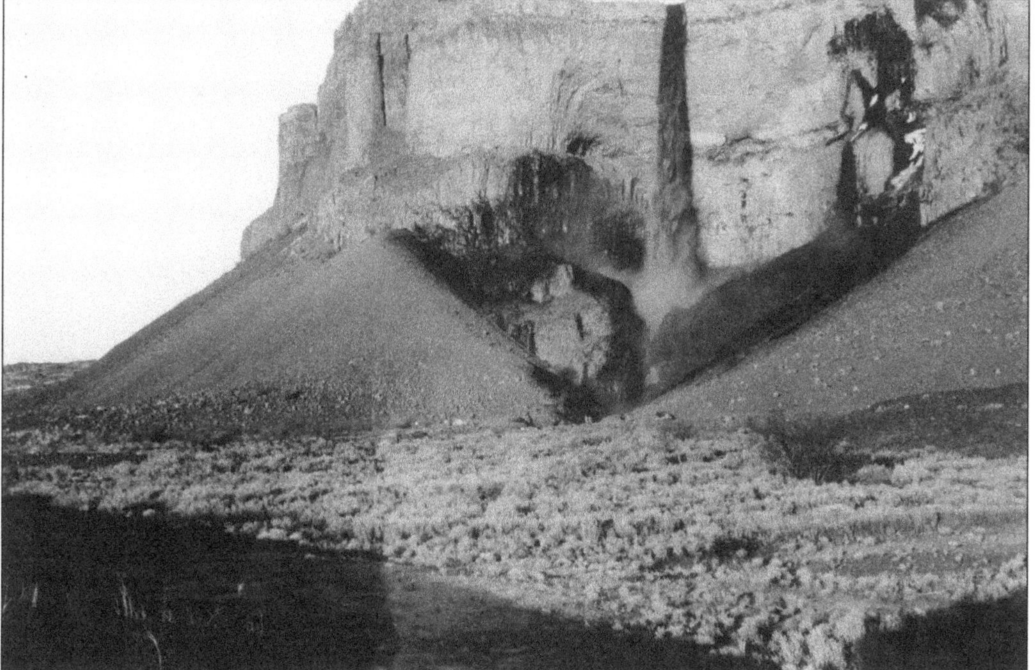

Directly across from Steamboat Rock, Martin Falls / Devil's Punchbowl, with its dramatic spring runoff, started to become a popular place for tourists to pull over for a quick snapshot, leg stretch, or picnic.

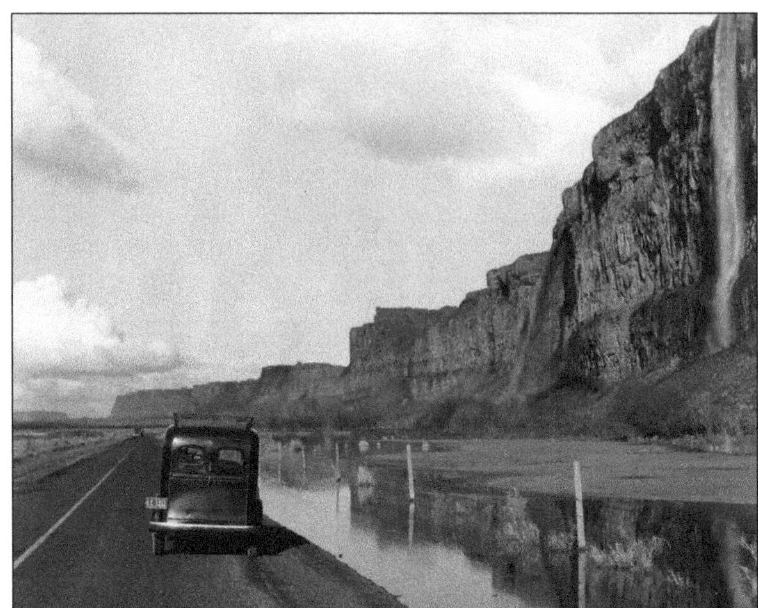

The coming of the age of automobiles created great changes around the whole country despite the Great Depression. Now, people could easily move longer distances than the first pioneers; the trip from Coulee City to Grand Coulee could be accomplished in an hour or so, as opposed to a whole day.

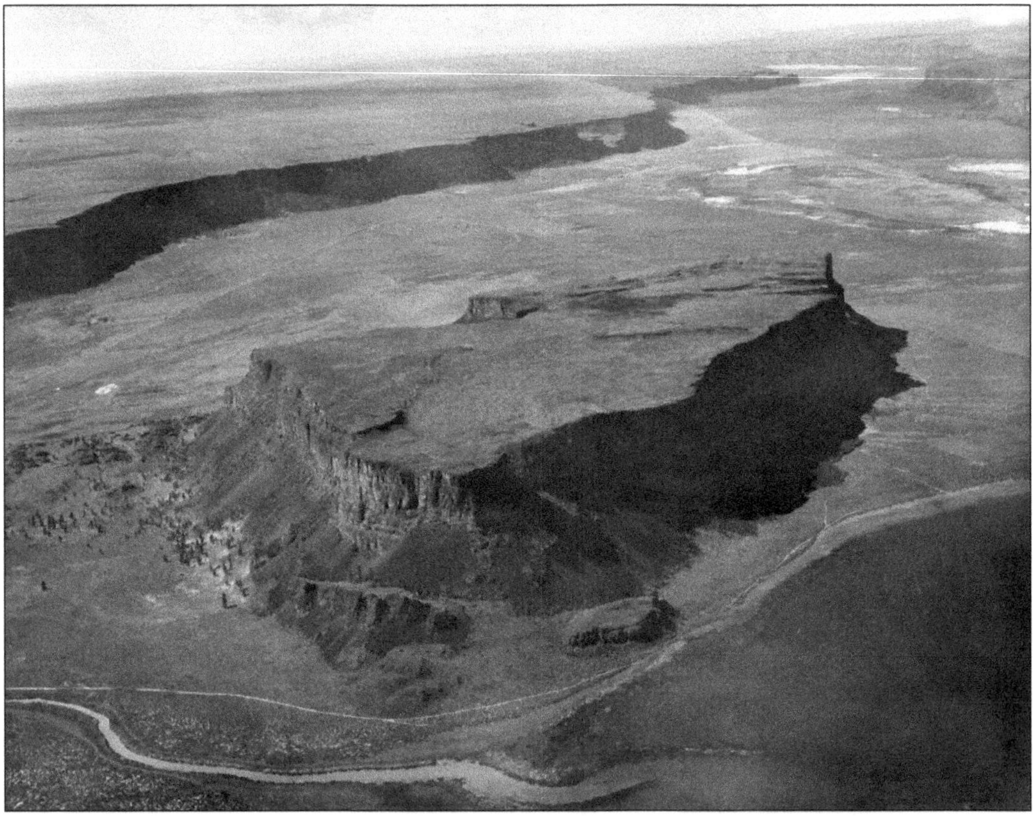

Newspaper articles challenged people, "Have you ever seen the top of Steamboat Rock?" and a new type of photography was being developed: aerial photography. Back in the 1930s, when private aviation and regulations were also new, all this meant was someone leaning out of a traveling airplane taking pictures while trying not to drop the camera or fall out.

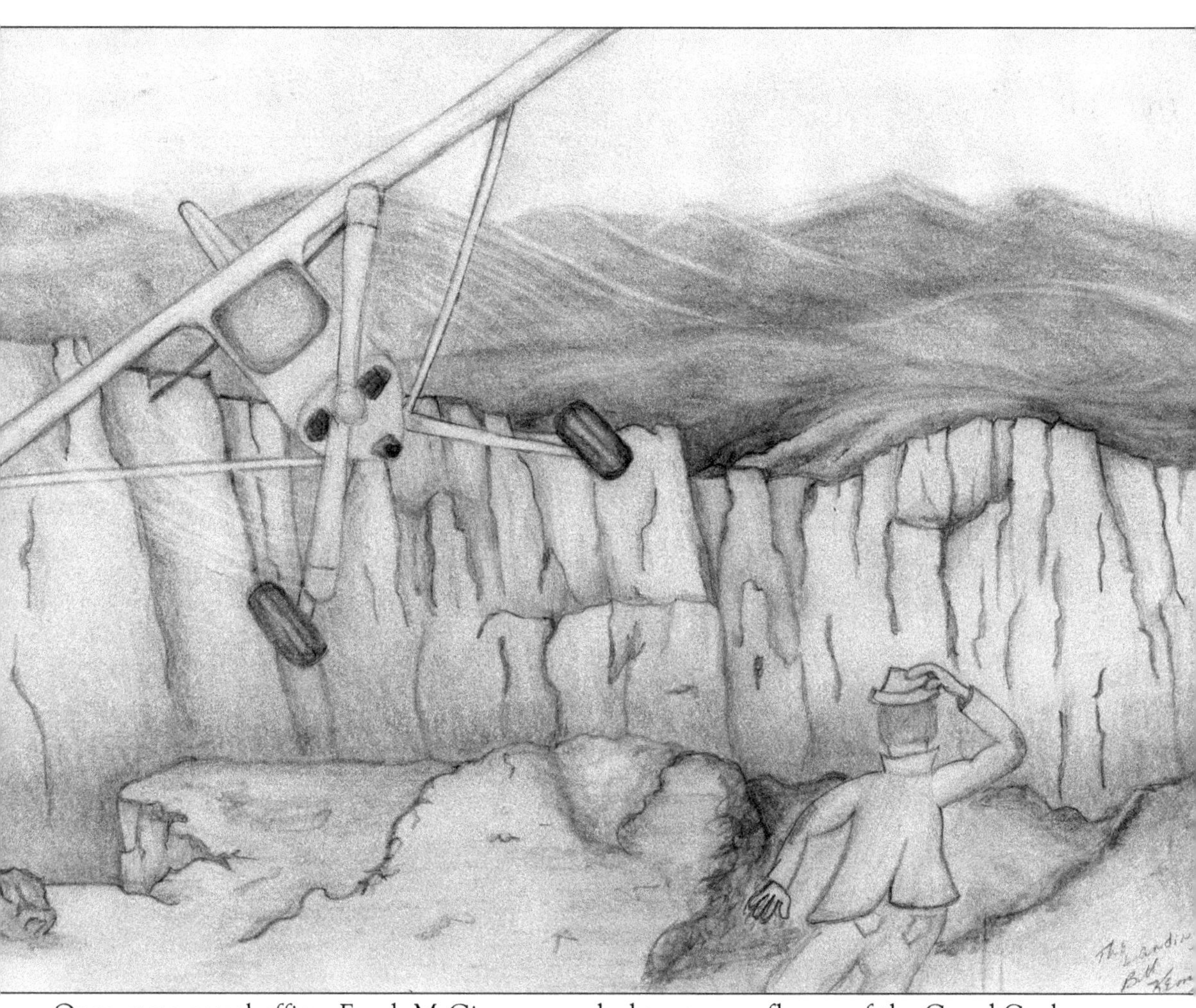

Once, state patrol officer Frank McGinns was asked to go on a flyover of the Grand Coulee and Steamboat Rock in a small private, two-person plane. The pilot successfully flew over but decided to attempt a landing on top of Steamboat Rock. Both the pilot and passenger survived in what amounted to a very rough landing, but the fate of the plane is unknown. The plane was a lightweight Taylor Cub, which was common in those days when aviation was still in its fledgling stage. (Courtesy of Bill Kemble.)

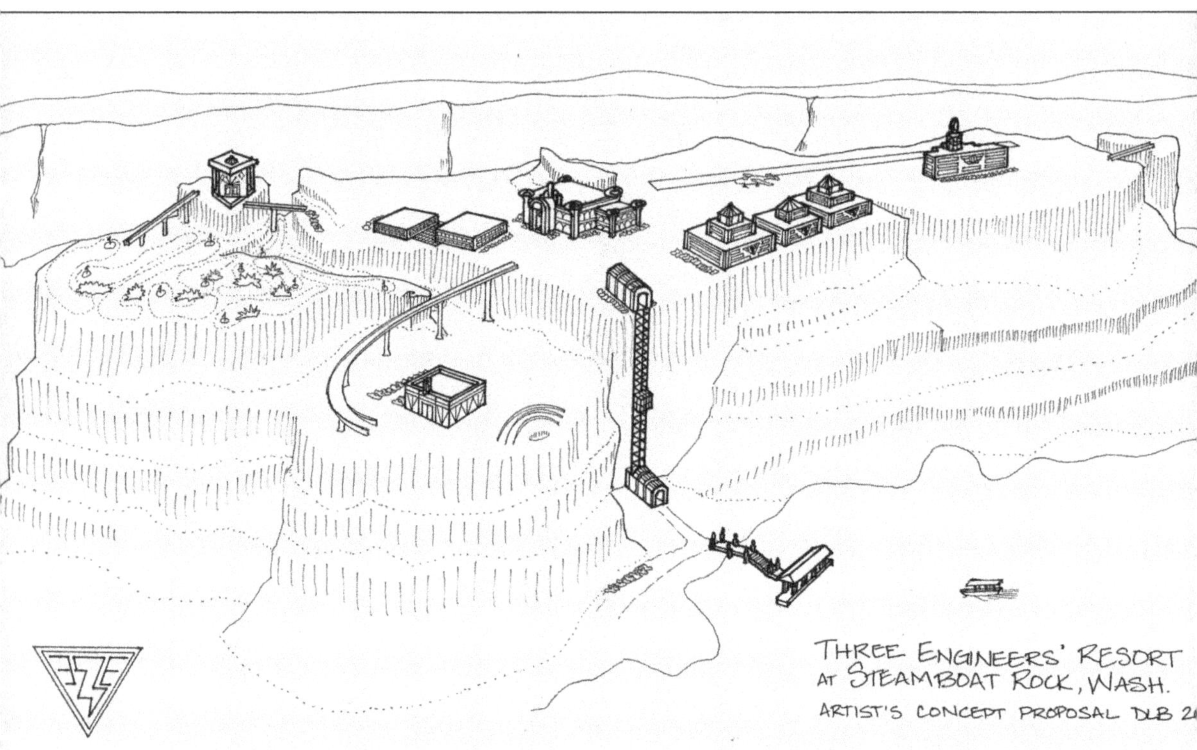

Around 1934, a rumor started to circulate around Grand Coulee, and the papers picked up on it pretty quickly. A group called the Three Engineers had been supplying power to B Street via generators, and when asked what they were going to do when the dam was completed, the senior member replied they had plans to buy Steamboat Rock and put a luxurious hotel on top, complete with a hotel, golf course, private airstrip, and elevator. Clients would either arrive by plane or be ferried in via private boat. The story, as it turned out, was a publicity stunt, and none of the Three Engineers ever planned on buying Steamboat Rock. (Courtesy of Dani Bolyard.)

The Three Engineers might have started rumors with big decadent plans for Steamboat Rock, fabricated for publicity, but one well-to-do fellow on the Hanford Nuclear project almost became the second private owner of Steamboat Rock after Steamboat Bill. He viewed the paperwork to purchase the whole mesa, but when he learned it was going to be surrounded by a huge reservoir, he decided it would be worthless and never pursued the purchase any further.

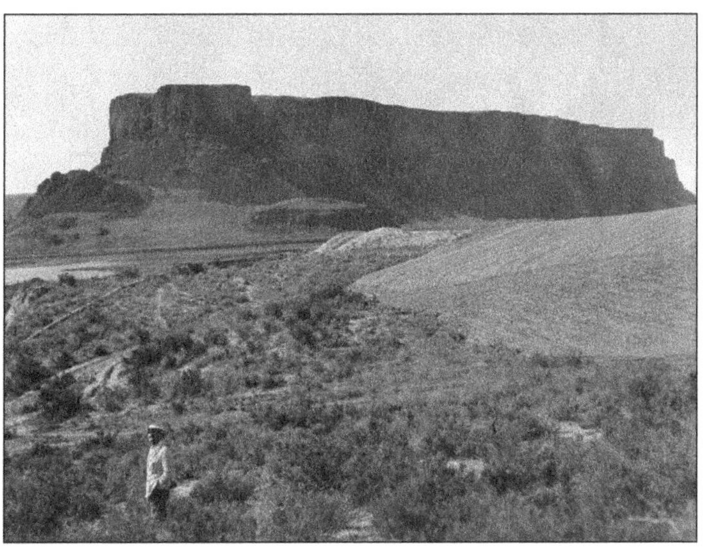

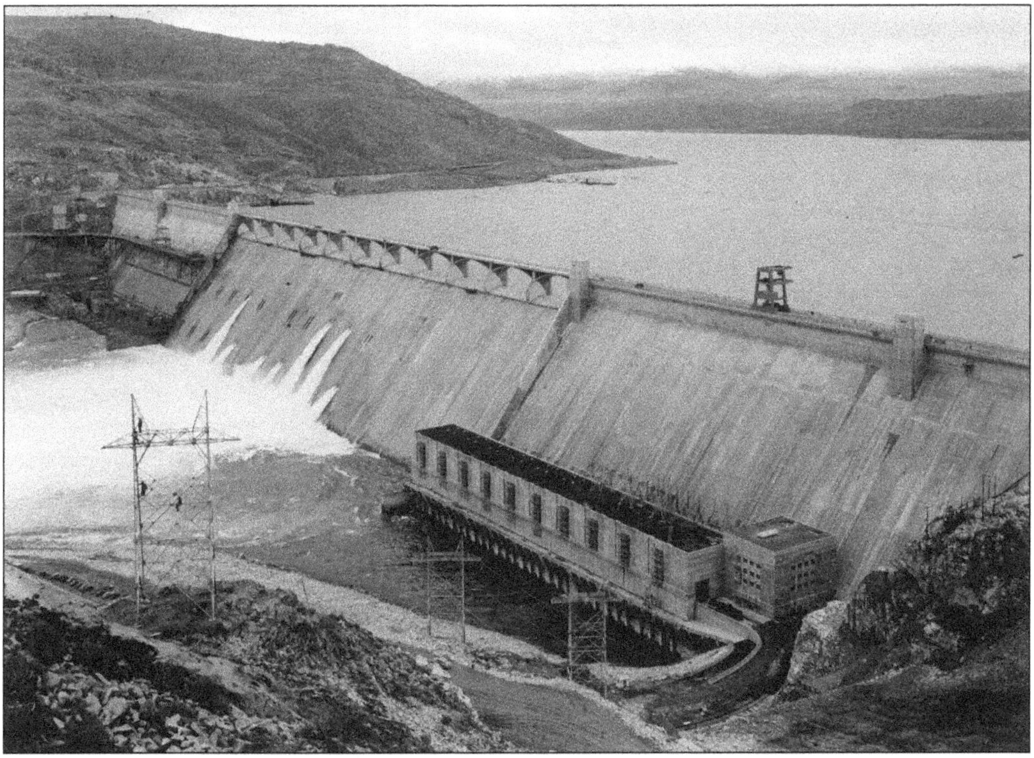

Just as the first phase of the Grand Coulee Dam was about to be completed, America entered World War II. The start of the war diverted the Grand Coulee Dam from being primarily for irrigation and flood control to making its first priority the production of electricity. When the war was over, the US Bureau of Reclamation was once more ready to focus on the creation of the Columbia Basin Irrigation Project.

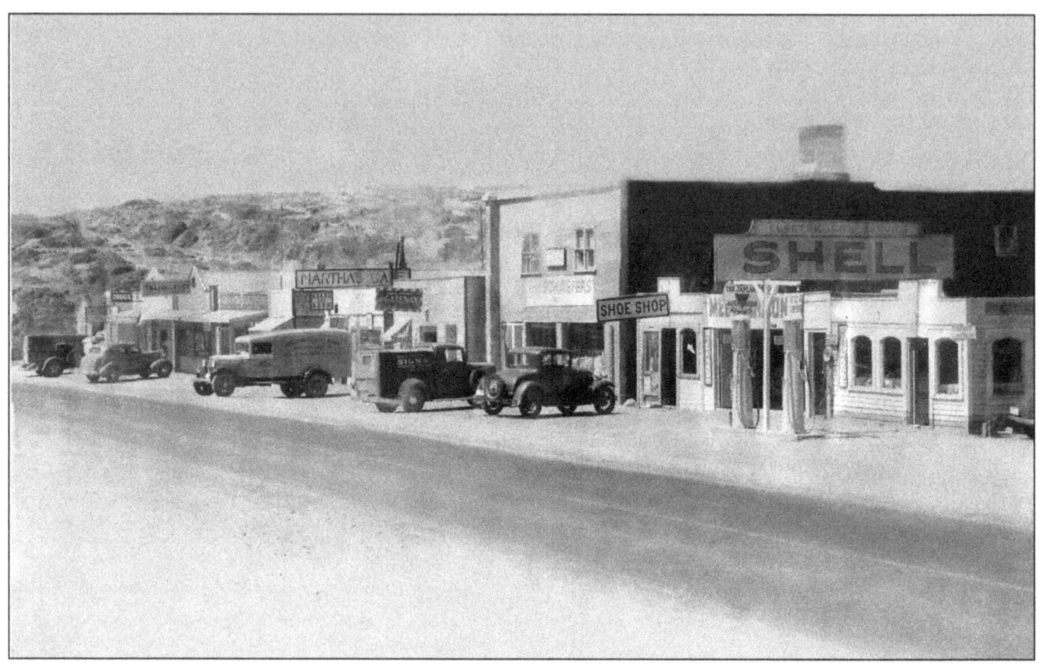

During the war, the population in the coulee started to decline as workers left for war, and production changed focus. The small townships that sprung up along the Speedball felt the crunch, with towns like Franklin and Basin City fading into obscurity. Other towns like Rim Rock, Osborne, and Electric City managed to stay in business. Shown here is Electric City in the 1940s. (Courtesy Dennis King Photography.)

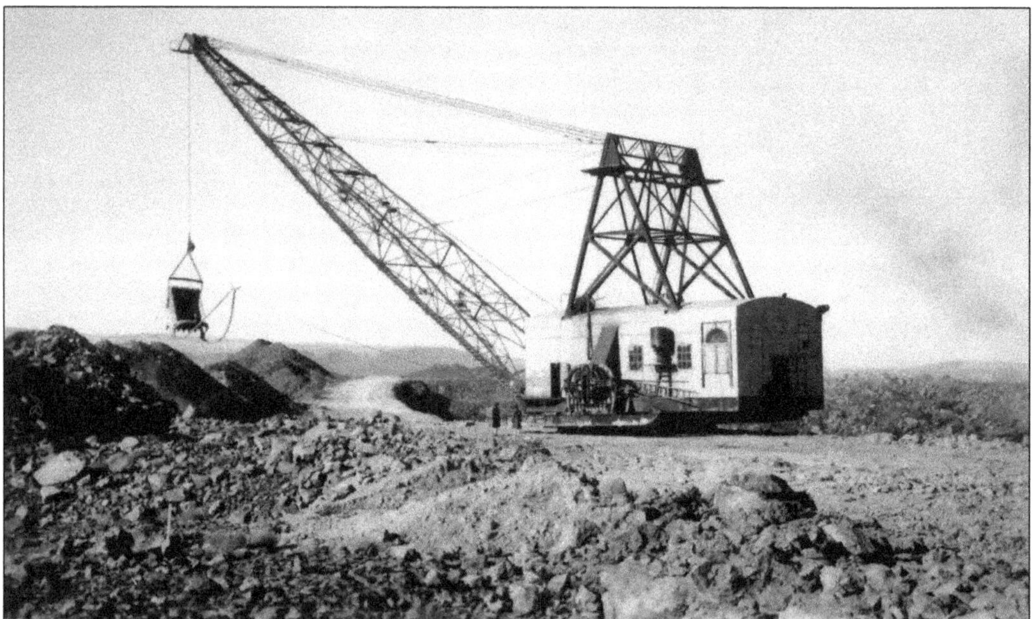

After World War II, some of the soldiers returned to the coulee, and the Bureau of Reclamation got to work on the second part of its plan: building dams at either end of the Grand Coulee and flooding it with water to create a huge 27-mile reservoir. The project was green-lighted in 1943 but sidelined by the war. (Courtesy of Gaylene [Pryor] Green.)

Six

Columbia Basin Project

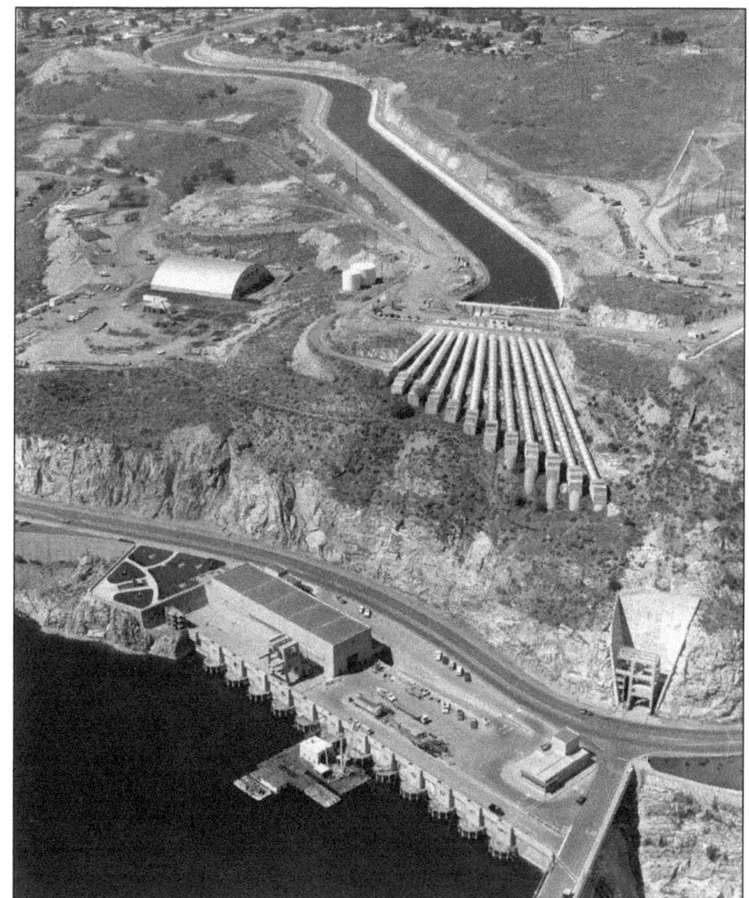

A major part of the irrigation goal was to divert the waters of the Columbia River back into the dry riverbed of the Upper Coulee, creating a 27-mile artificial reservoir. The water would then use a series of canals to irrigate 670,000 acres between Ephrata and Pasco, 120 miles away from the dam. Here, the pump that pulls water from Lake Roosevelt and pumps it into Banks Lake through the main canal can be seen.

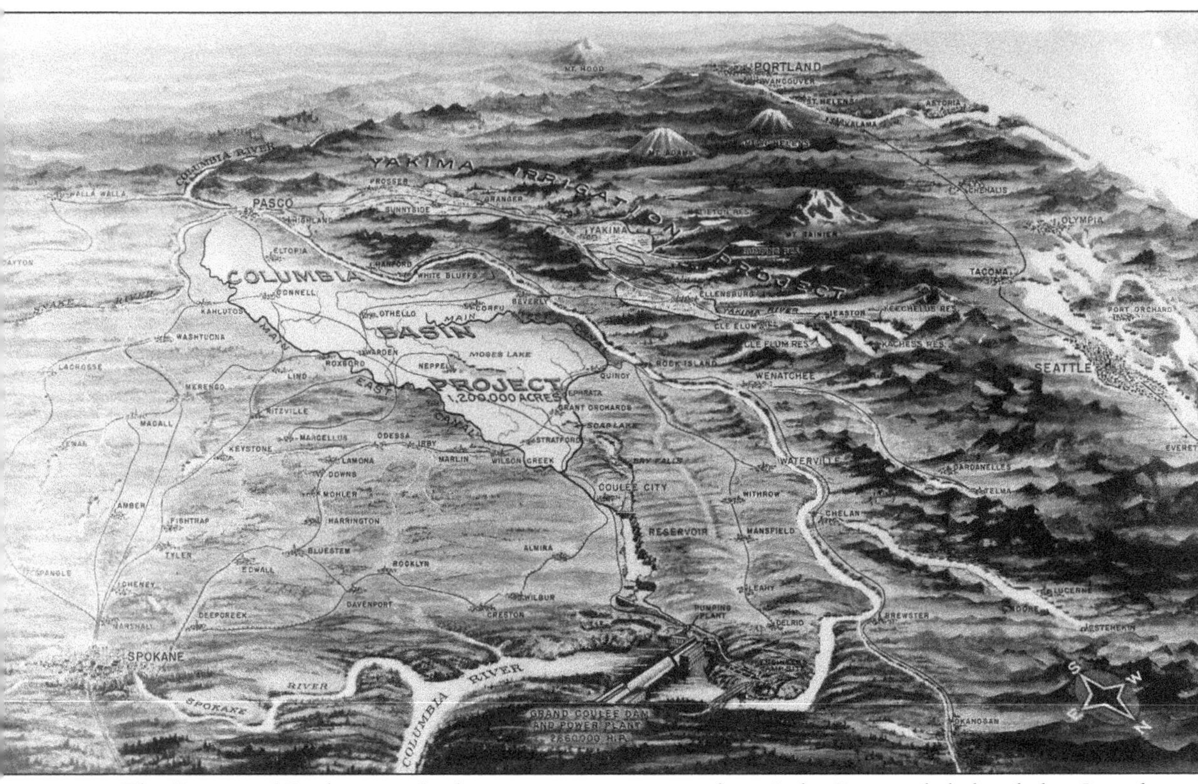

The Bureau of Reclamation's plan was to pump water from Lake Roosevelt behind the Grand Coulee Dam up into canals, where it could be distributed as irrigation for 1.2 million dry farmlands from Wilson Creek to Pasco. To hold the water, the upper coulee around Steamboat Rock would be converted into a 27-mile-long reservoir. (Courtesy of the United States Bureau of Reclamation.)

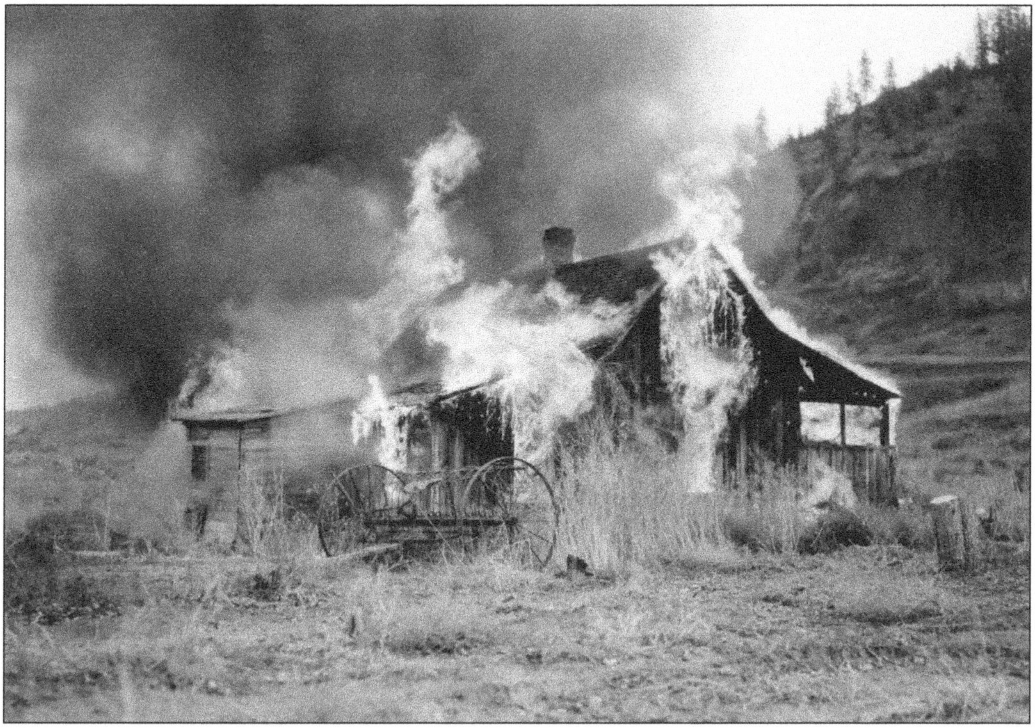

The land acquisitions began early on and slowly, due to lengthy court sessions and voting procedures, but in 1948 land clearing in the upper coulee began. Most old abandoned buildings were burned, as was common in those days for land clearing. This picture is from the clearing of the Lake Roosevelt reservoir. (Courtesy of Gaylene [Pryor] Green.)

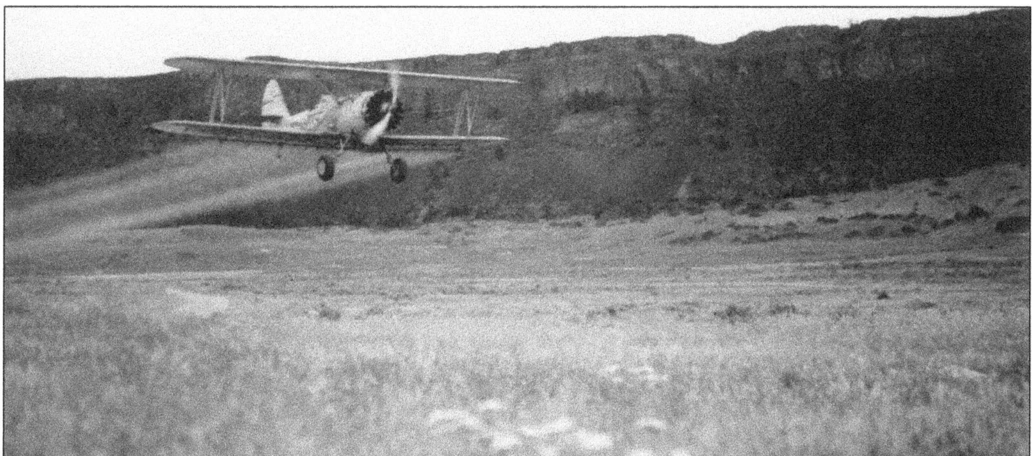

When the coulee around Steamboat Rock was cleared, the Bureau of Reclamation tried a new technique. Using crop dusters, the bureau sprayed the sage and vegetation with herbicide, in hopes of killing everything, and then burning it all off a few days later when it died out. The technique is listed as being "somewhat successful." (Courtesy of Gaylene [Pryor] Green.)

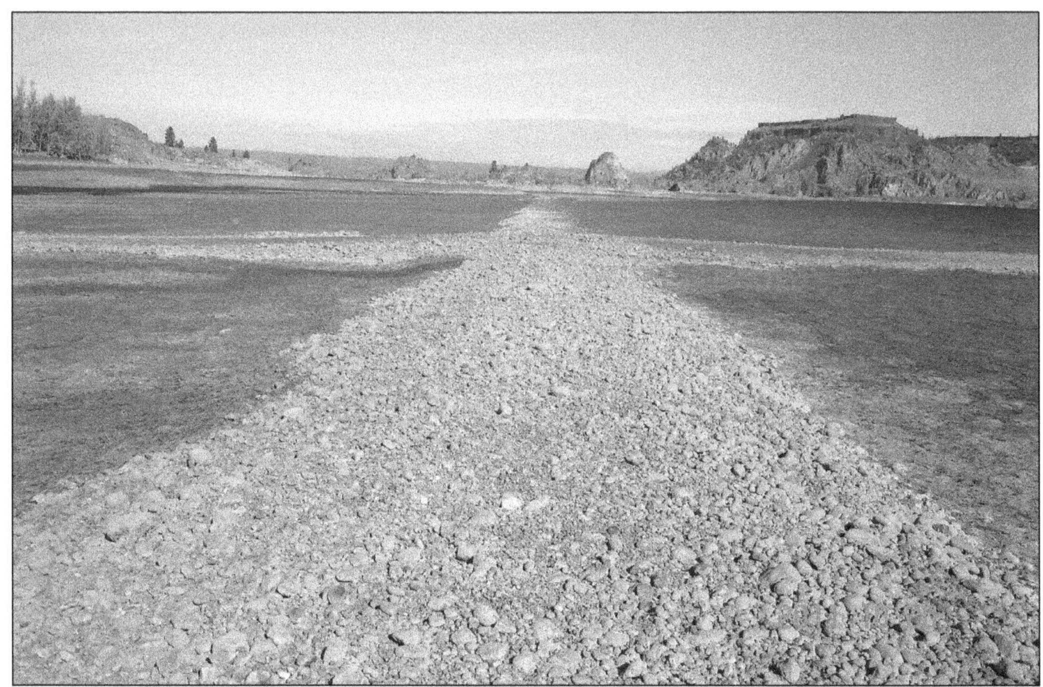

One of the steps taken to prepare the coulee for flooding was the removing of the US Construction Railroad. The first train that ran up the Grand Coulee past Steamboat Rock would now be the last. The rails were pulled up, and the spikes and wood were removed, leaving only the graded pathways to mark the passing of the train down the coulee. Here, the old railroad grade can be seen during the 2011 drawdown. (Courtesy of George Kuzminsky.)

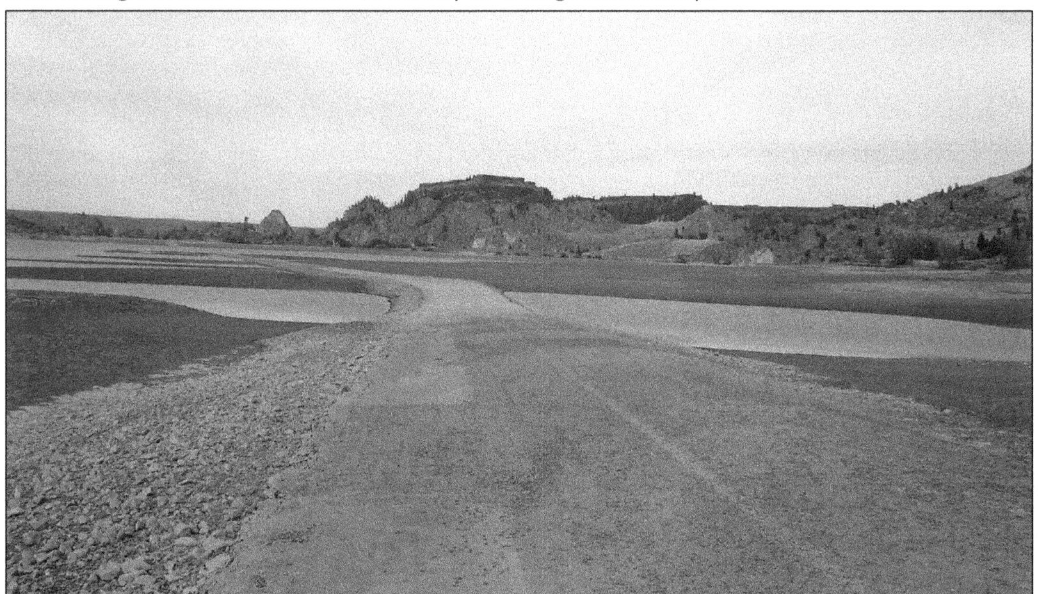

The Speedball Highway did not receive the same fate as the US Construction Railway; rather than being dissembled carefully and recycled or burned, it was largely ignored. Parts of it were gated and closed to the public, while other parts were renamed and repurposed. (Courtesy of George Kuzminsky.)

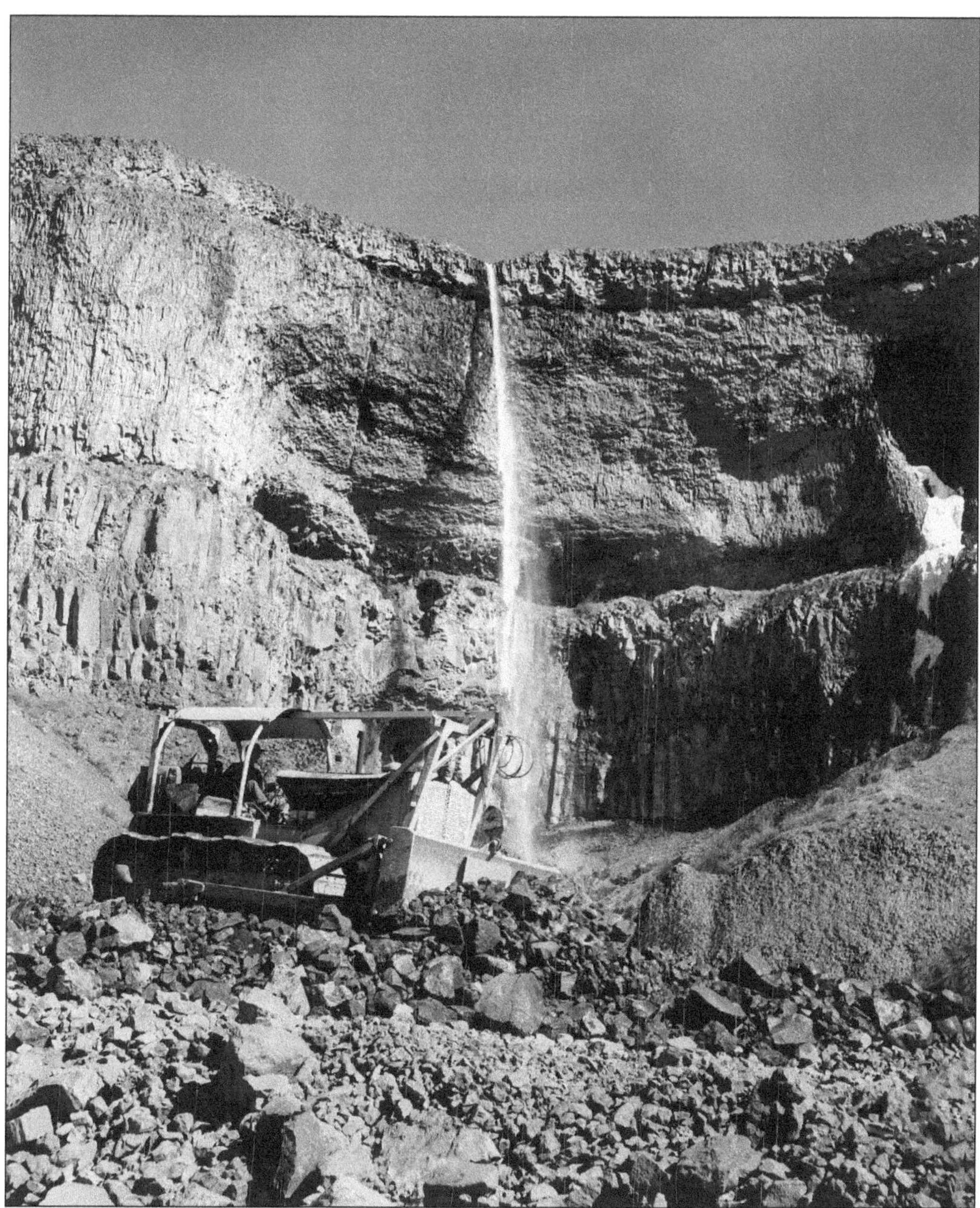

To replace the original Speedball Highway that would be flooded, the state started work at once on a replacement highway from Coulee City to Grand Coulee named Secondary State Highway 2F. The new highway would have to be elevated and placed closer to the east wall of the coulee to keep it out of the flood zone.

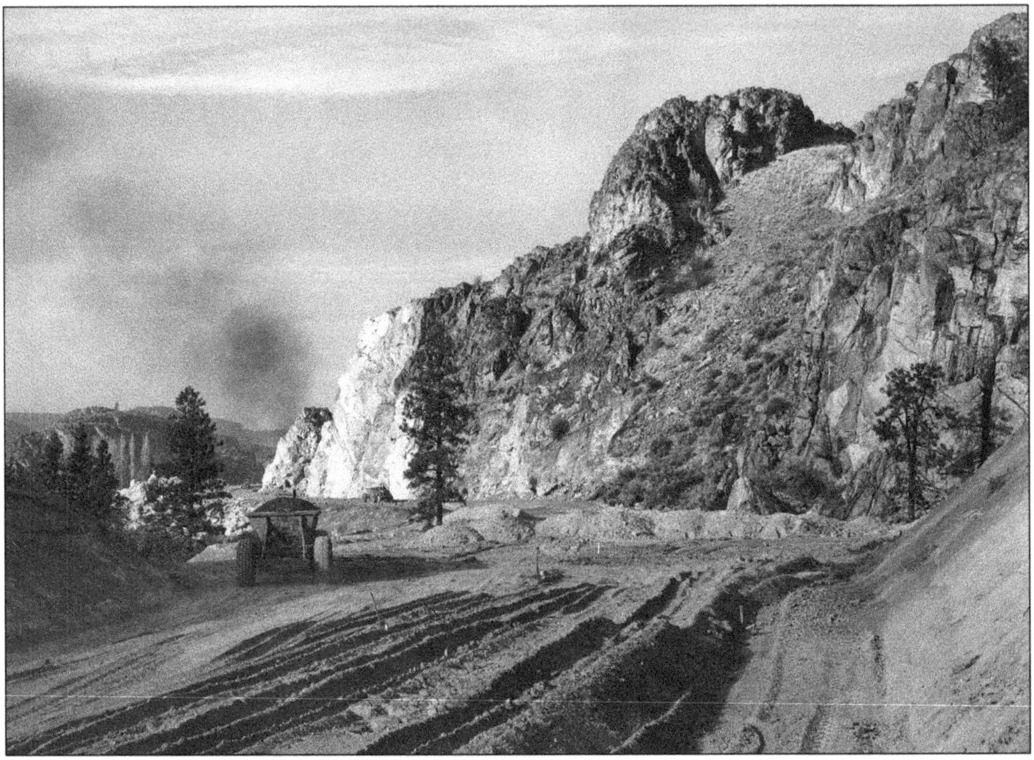

The construction of the new replacement highway in the late 1940s would blast through many rock outcroppings, add tons of fill to a dry shoreline, and travel through at least three old farmyards on its way from Coulee City to Steamboat Rock.

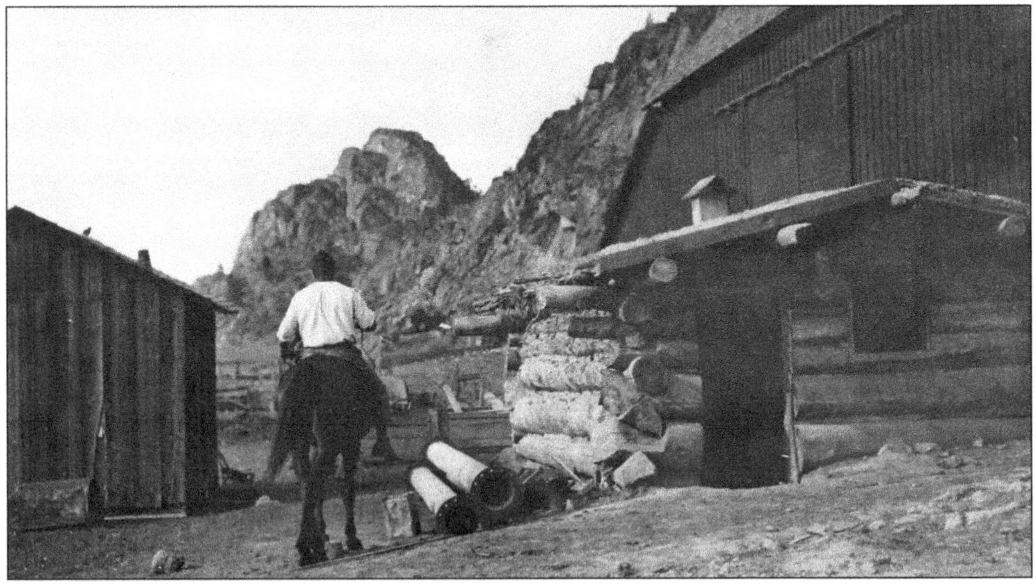

One of the farms the highway passed through was the old Fleet/Schrock Ranch that was later owned and lived in by George Baldwin and family at the foot of Castle Rock. All traces of the ranch were removed, root cellars filled in, and soon, the farmyard was crawling with bulldozers and earthmovers.

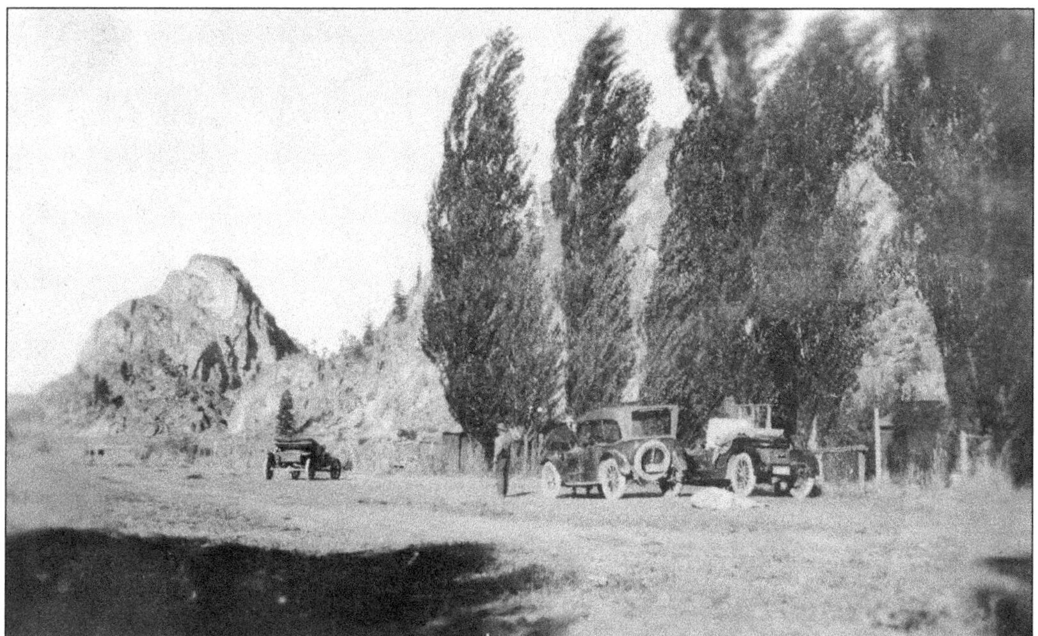

With the coming lake, the old Fleet/Schrock Ranch would soon be completely submerged under the water of the equalizing reservoir; only the raised land where the highway would run would be above the flood line.

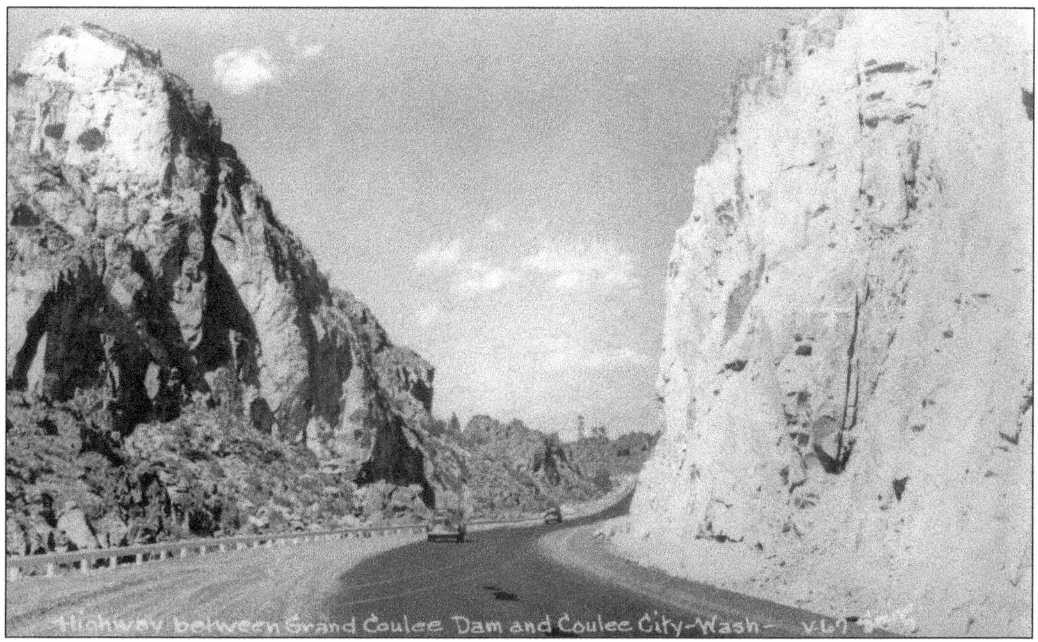

This picture shows the finished Secondary State Highway in the approximate spot where the Fleet/Schrock Ranch once stood. The sheared off-granite wall that was necessary for the construction of the new highway from Coulee City to Grand Coulee can be seen.

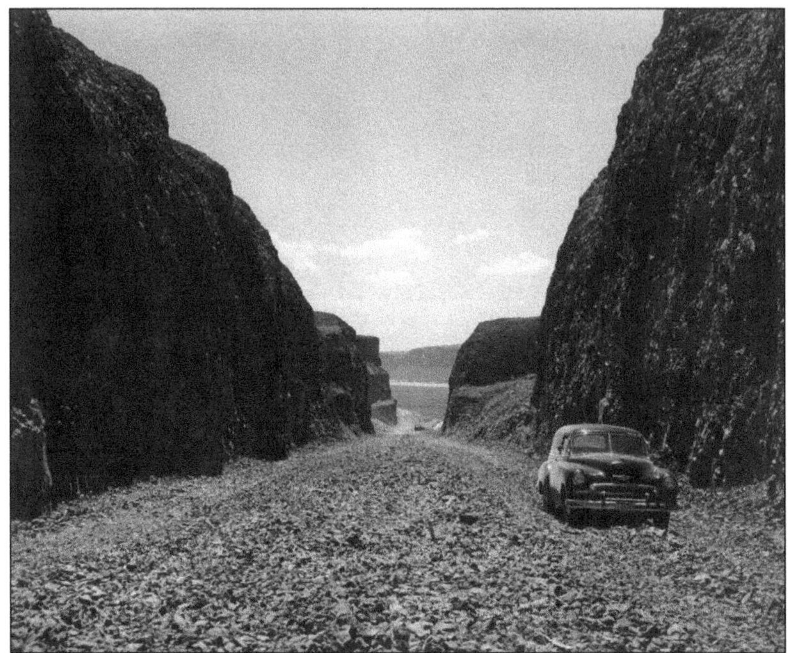

Due to unstable ground conditions at the south end of Salishan Mesa by the Alkali Sinks, the new highway would cut through the heavy basalt to the top of the cliff. The dynamited cuts and several hundred feet of fill would cost about a million dollars, earning it the name "Million Dollar Mile." The whole 27 miles of highway costs nearly $4 million (see page 71). (Courtesy of the *Star*.)

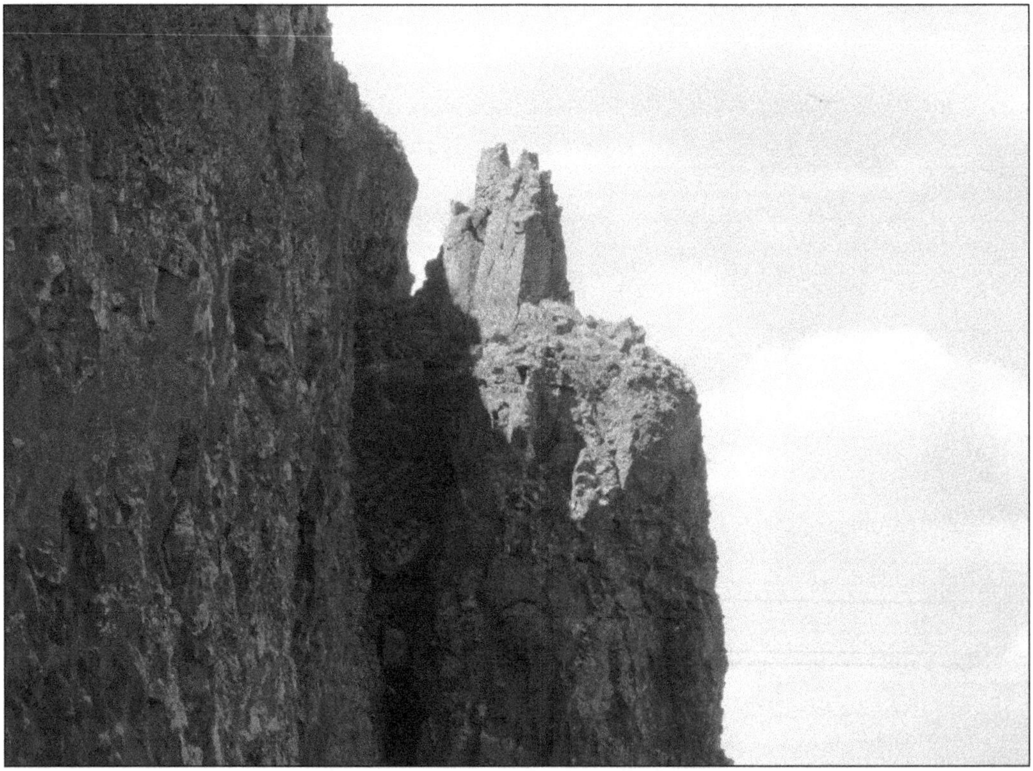

Some say it was the dynamite that caused Rabbit Rock's ears to crumble and fall apart, while others say it was done by people with guns, but the truth is probably a mixture of both. Rabbit Rock can still be seen today from the pull-off on the north end of Million Dollar Mile (see page 55). (Courtesy of J. Kemble)

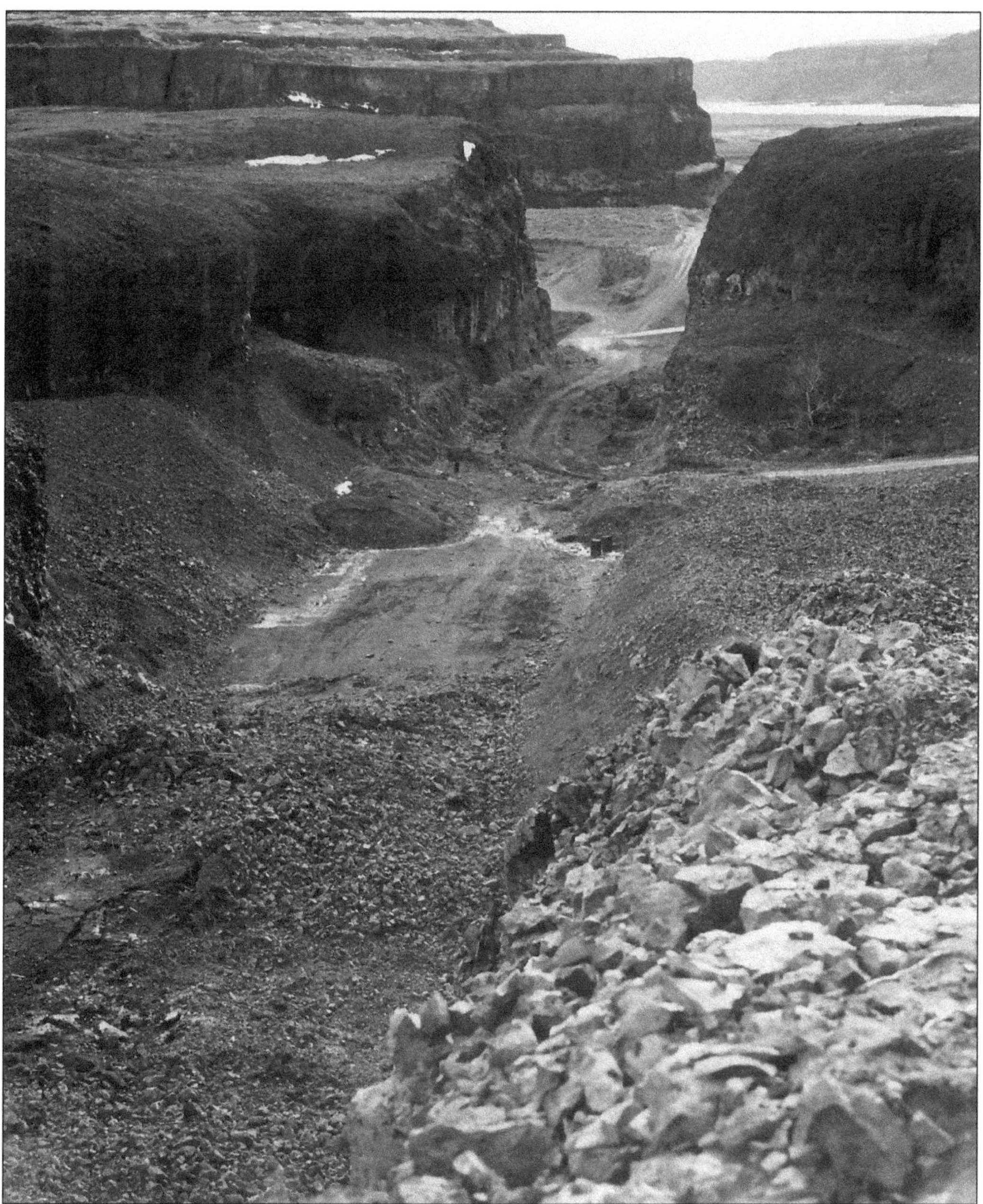

Construction of the Million Dollar Mile went all night, lit up by huge lights that cast eerie shadows everywhere. Early on, the build was inundated with a flood of rattlesnakes dug out of the basalt, slowing down the construction but not enough to put a stop to the work. (Courtesy of Gaylene [Pryor] Green.)

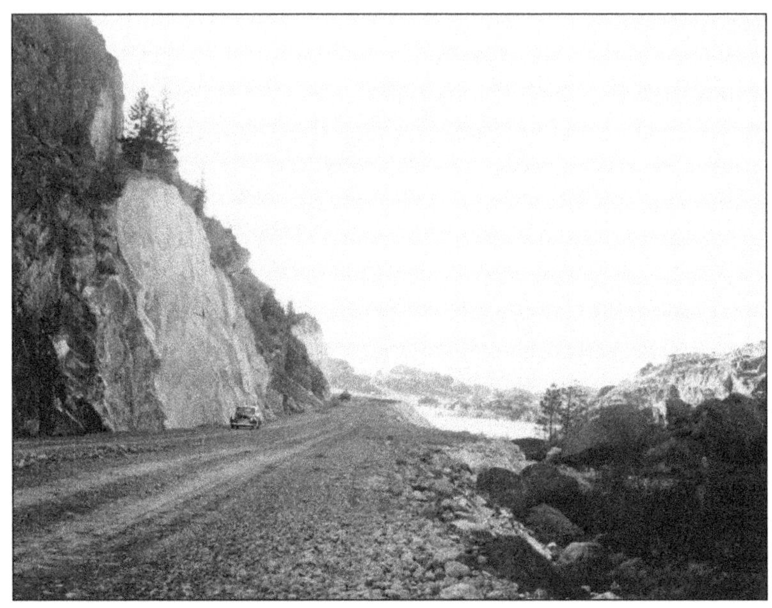

Secondary State Highway 2F was created to replace the Speedball Highway and run along the east coulee wall from Coulee City to the highway bridge in Grand Coulee, where it continued onto Omak with the name of Secondary State Highway 10F. The highway had to be elevated to keep it out of the waters of the coming equalizing reservoir. (Courtesy of Gaylene [Pryor] Green.)

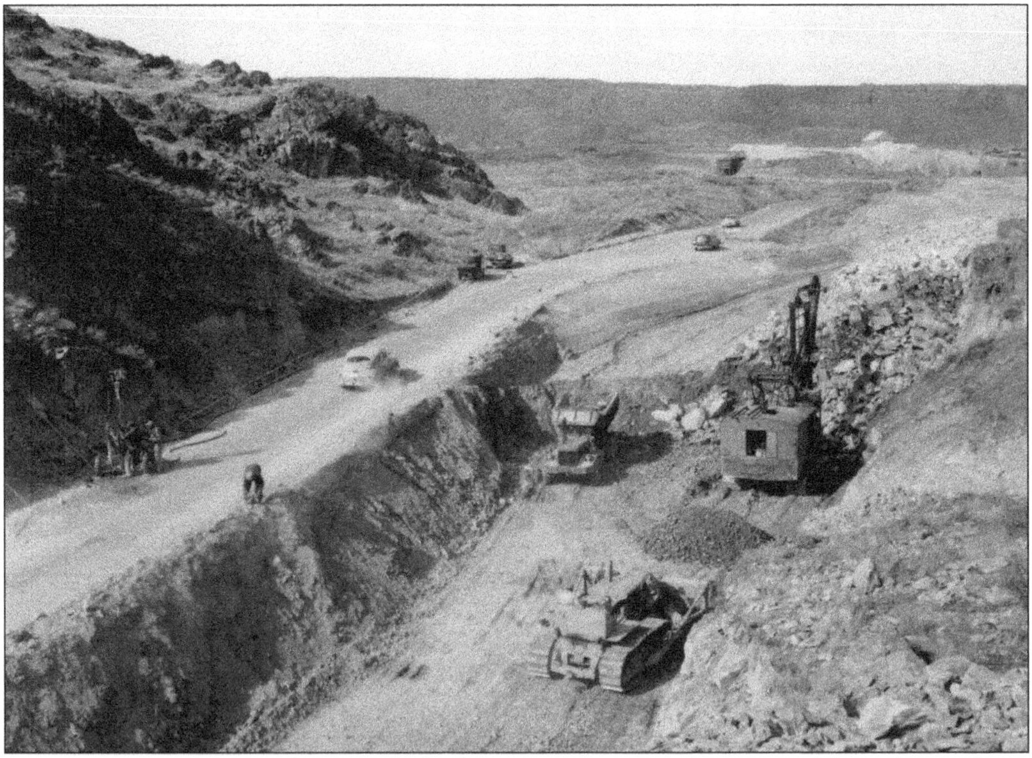

Once more to save time and money, the highway department used portions of the earlier roadway, the Speedball Highway. Some parts were preserved from necessity, like where the highway ran through a town like Electric City or Grand Coulee. Other times, parts became shorter renamed streets or roads to nowhere used by recreationalists. (Courtesy of Gaylene [Pryor] Green.)

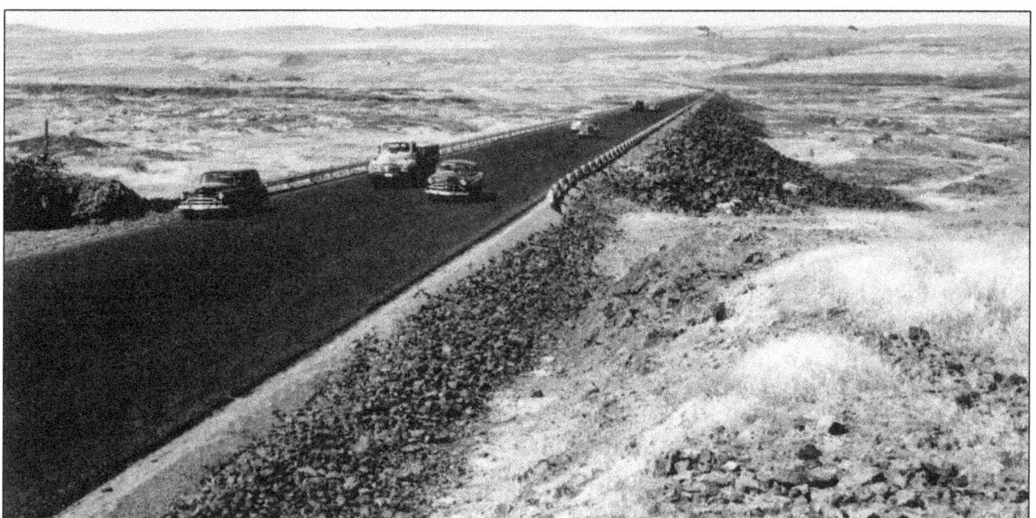

To create the equalizing reservoir, two earthen dams were constructed in the upper coulee, with one at the north end by Electric City or Delano Heights and the other at the south end by Coulee City. The highway would run across the dam at Coulee City, and it was named Dry Falls Dam and opened for traffic in 1950. (Courtesy of Gaylene [Pryor] Green.)

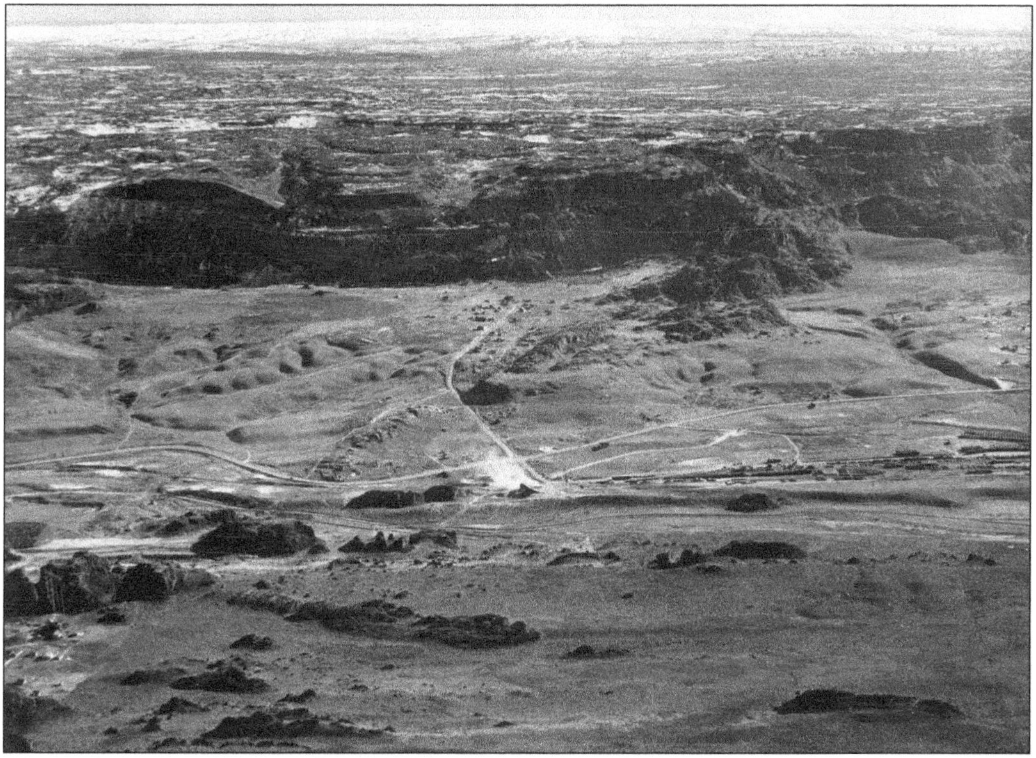

The earthen dam on the north end by old Grand Coulee was at the end of the main feeder canal, where water was pumped and released into the equalizing reservoir. It was much more modest in size and named North Dam. Now, it borders a park that is named North Dam Park. This aerial photograph shows where North Dam would eventually be. Delano Heights and Electric City can also be seen.

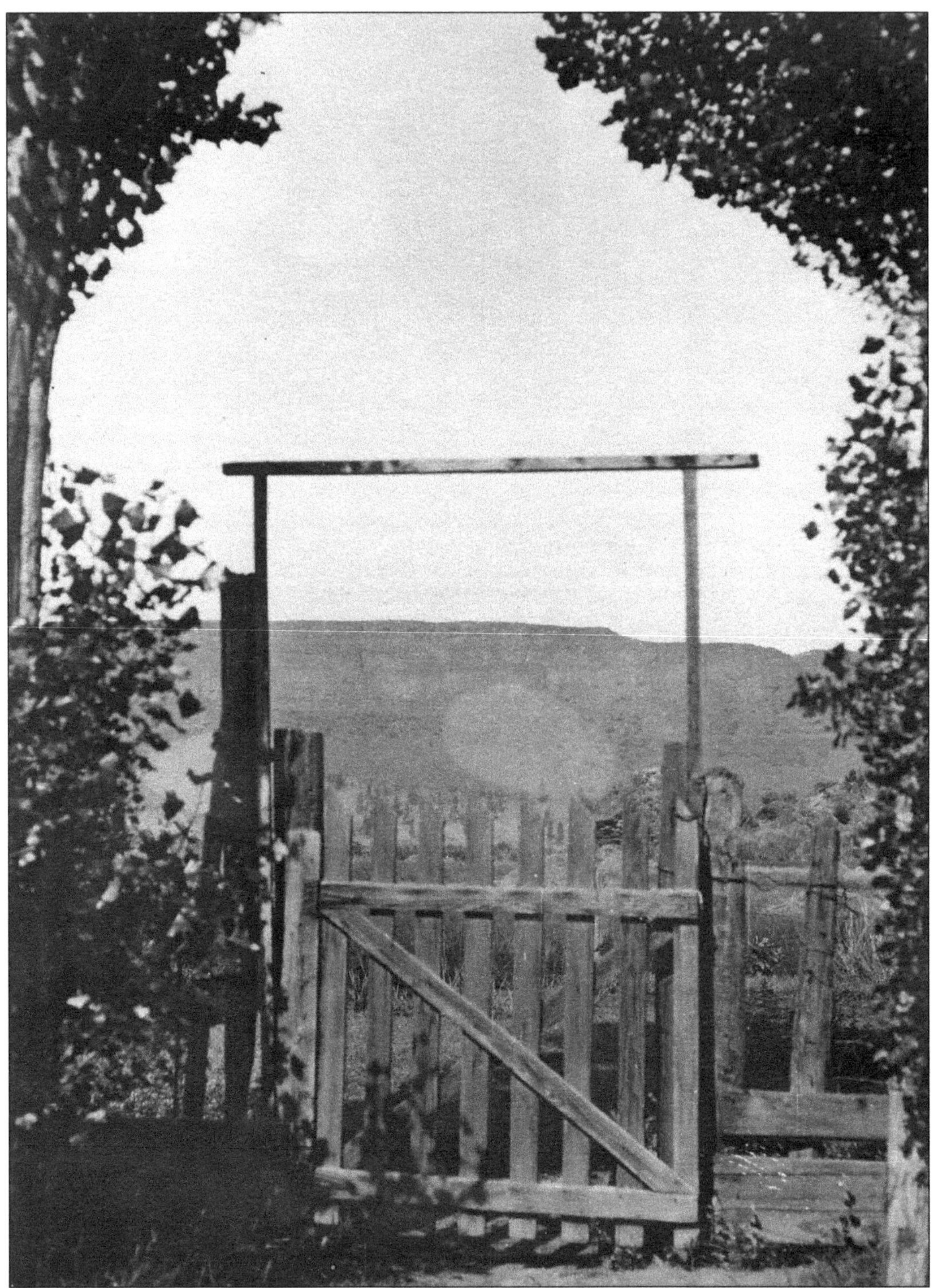

It was not just the highway and railroad that had to be moved—there were farms and people living in the coulee around Steamboat Rock, including the dwindling township of Rim Rock with its few residents. The people moved on, some to Coulee City and others to Electric City. The school was moved to Electric City, as was the great dance hall, which later became a roller-skating rink.

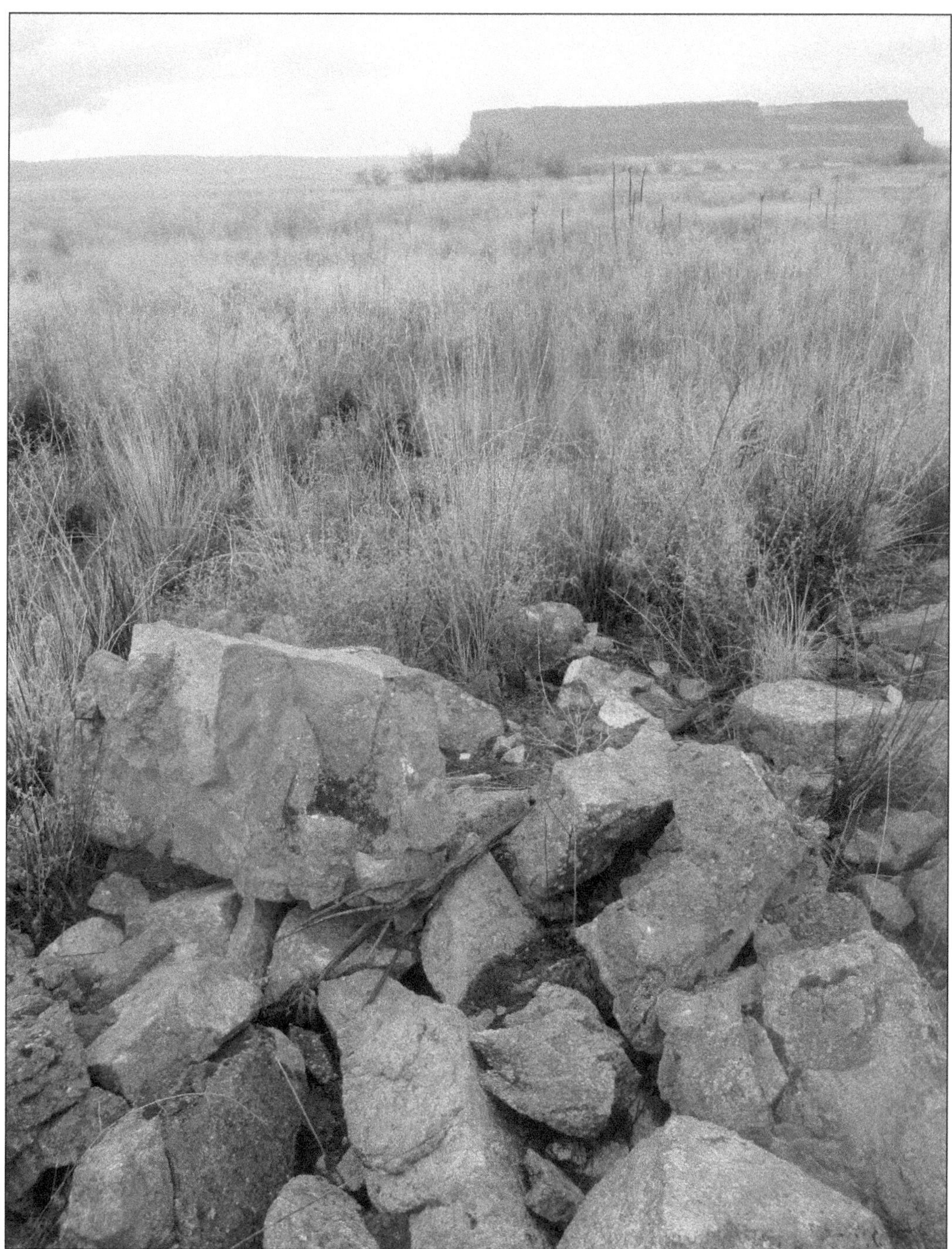

By 1950, all that was left was a stone building and a row of poplar trees to mark where Rim Rock once stood in the shadow of Steamboat Rock. Today, all that is left of the building is a pile of stones by the stumps of the poplar trees. (Courtesy of J. Kemble.)

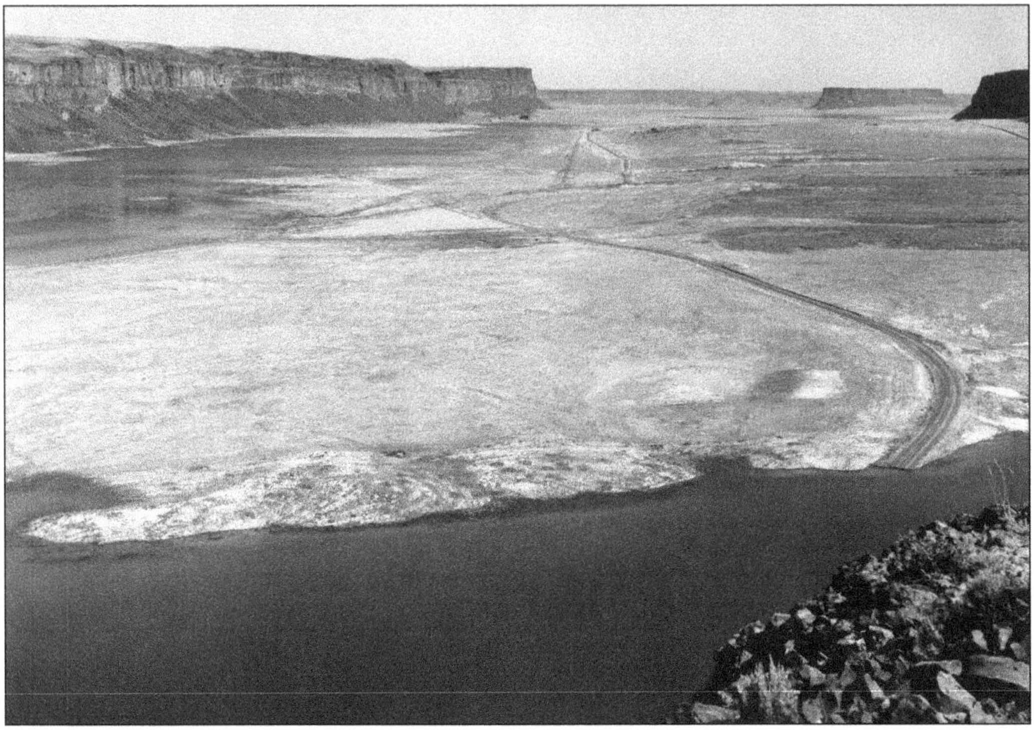

In the spring of 1951, work on the canals was finished, and the upper coulee was flooded with water diverted from the Columbia River. The equalizing reservoir was named after Grand Coulee Dam's chief construction engineer, Frank A. Banks. (Courtesy of Dan Bolyard.)

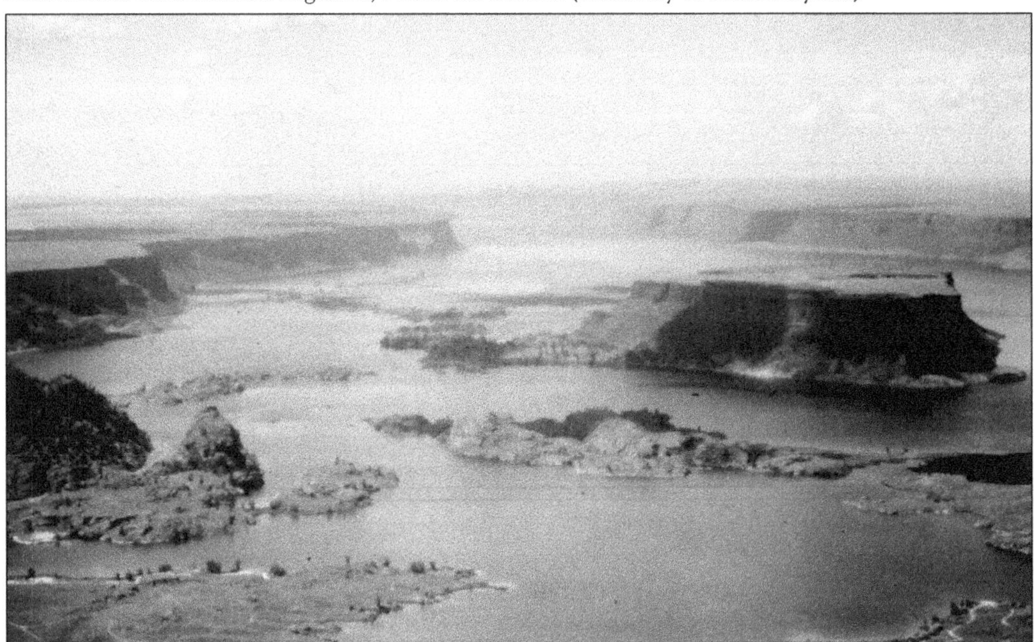

The reservoir created a huge lake that soon was filled with people taking advantage of Secondary State Highway 2F. The lake was stocked with fish by Washington State, and soon, people were traveling the new highway to enjoy a bounty of sun-filled recreation on the newly created Banks Lake.

Seven

Banks Lake

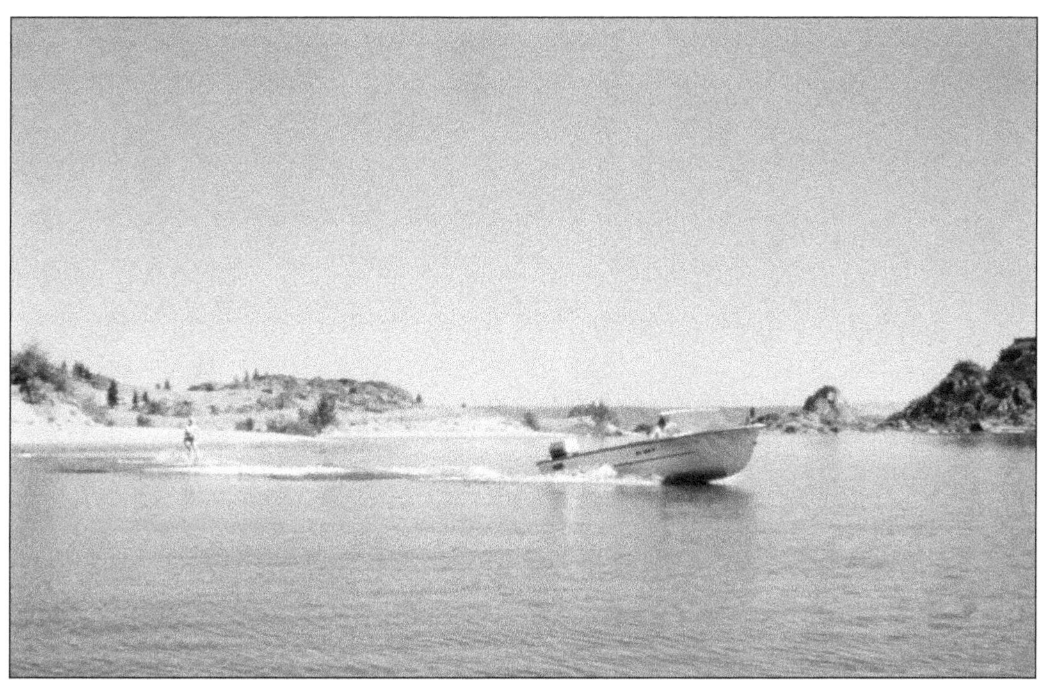

The equalizing reservoir named Banks Lake filled the upper coulee and set Steamboat Rock to sail once more. The lake is 27 miles in length and varies in width up to 5 miles. Banks Lake runs from the city of Grand Coulee, past Electric City, through Barker Canyon to the west of Steamboat Rock, and onto Coulee City.

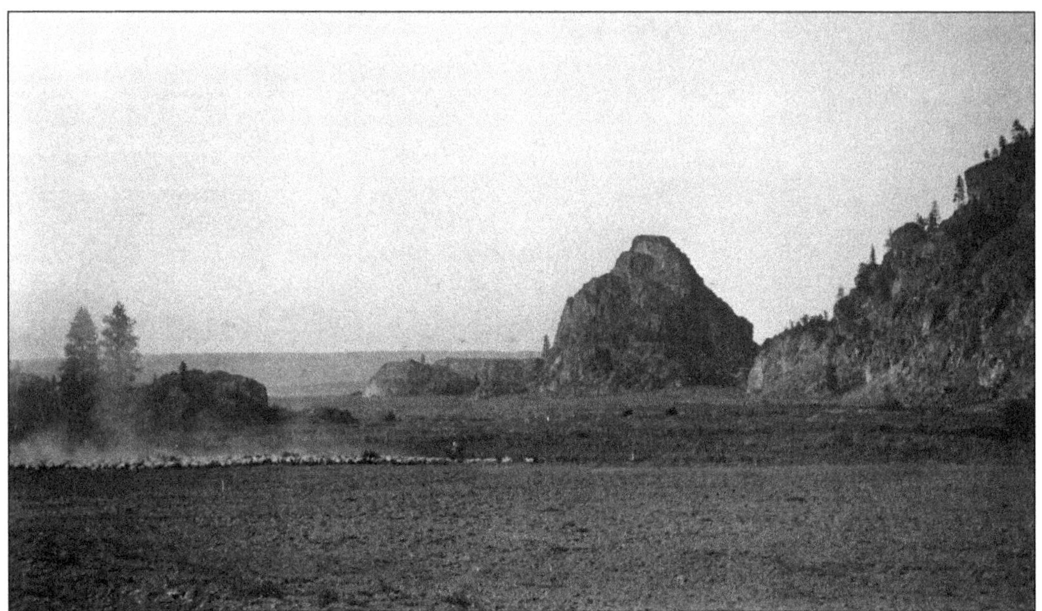

The waters from Lake Roosevelt behind the Grand Coulee Dam eventually filled most of the upper coulee, including much of the Lincoln Stock Company's pastures and fields. After the filling of Banks Lake, Steamboat Rock became situated at the end of a long peninsula, the easiest way to get to it became Secondary State Highway 2F, which ran down the east coulee wall.

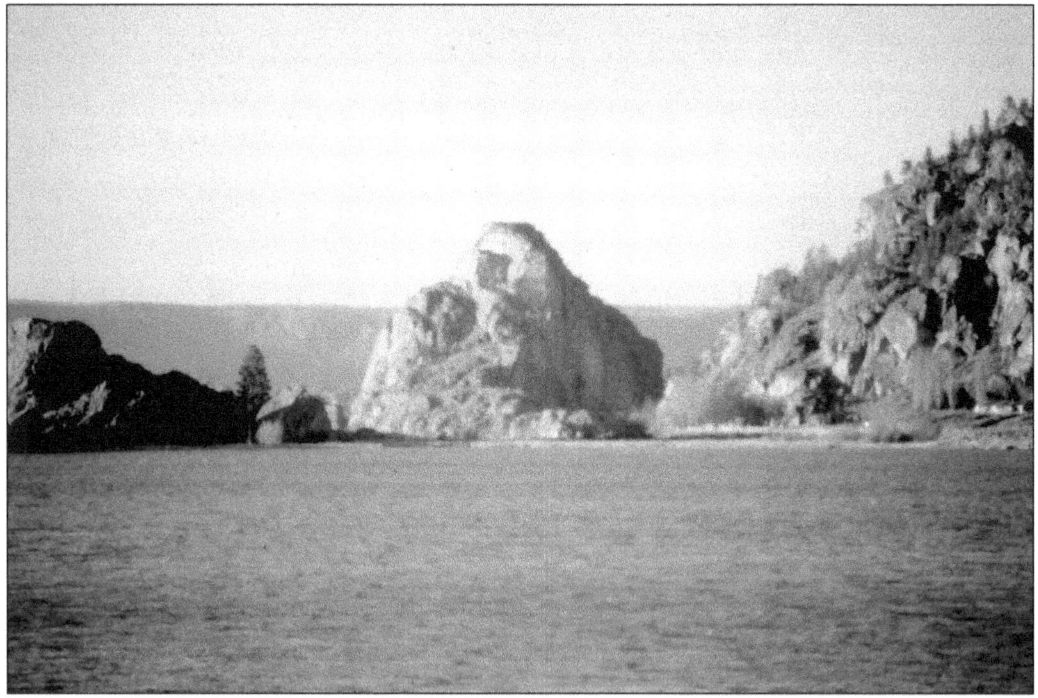

This picture, taken in the 1970s, shows the location of the Fleet/Schrock Ranch and the effects of the flooding of the upper coulee with the creation of Banks Lake.

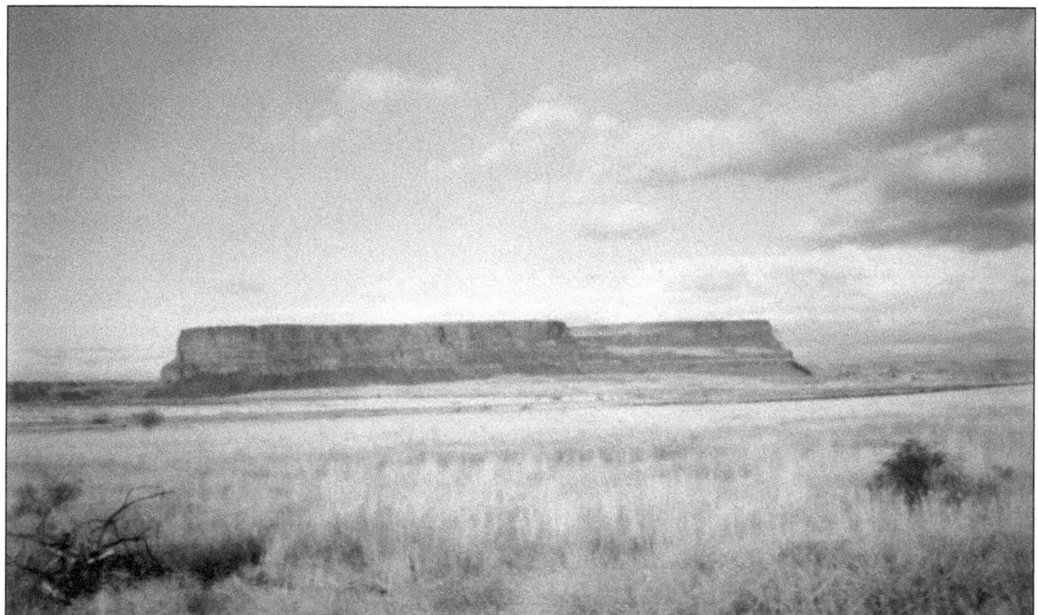

The land around Steamboat Rock, with its rich organic soil, luxuriant bunch grass, and seasonal lakes, would no longer struggle to find sources of water for irrigation; it would now hold water for irrigating hundreds of thousands of acres of crops.

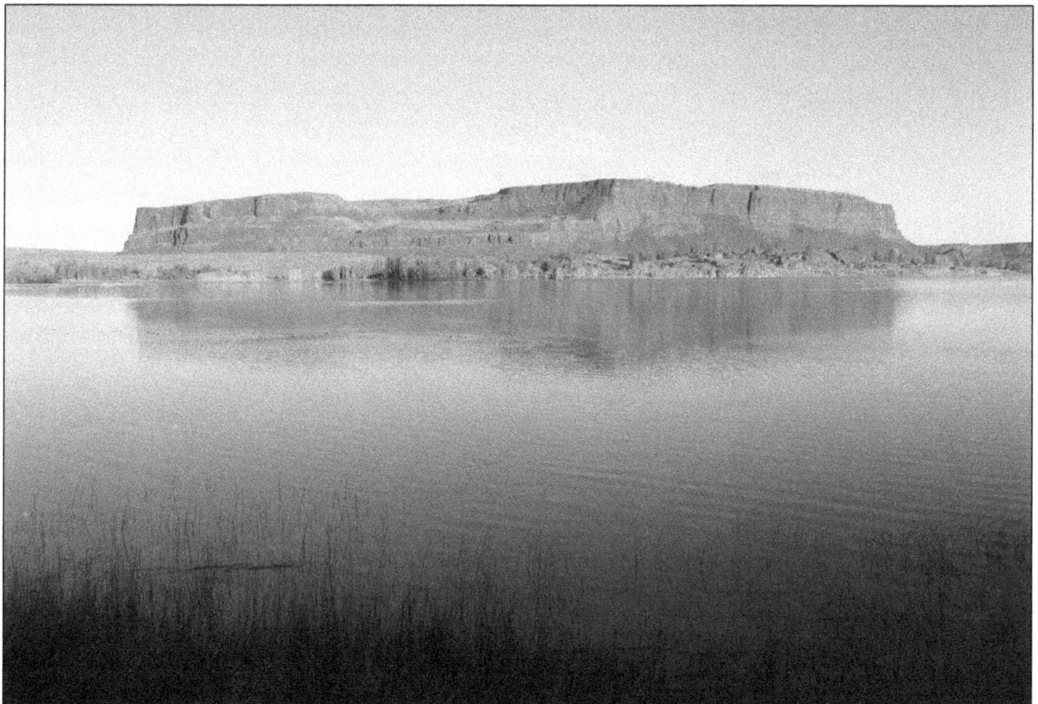

Landlocked for centuries, Steamboat Rock's community finally slipped below the waves as water, once more, filled the upper coulee for the first time in centuries. Compared to the water level during the Great Missoula floods, Banks Lake was just a puddle, not even touching the stately basalt walls of Steamboat Rock. (Courtesy of J. Kemble.)

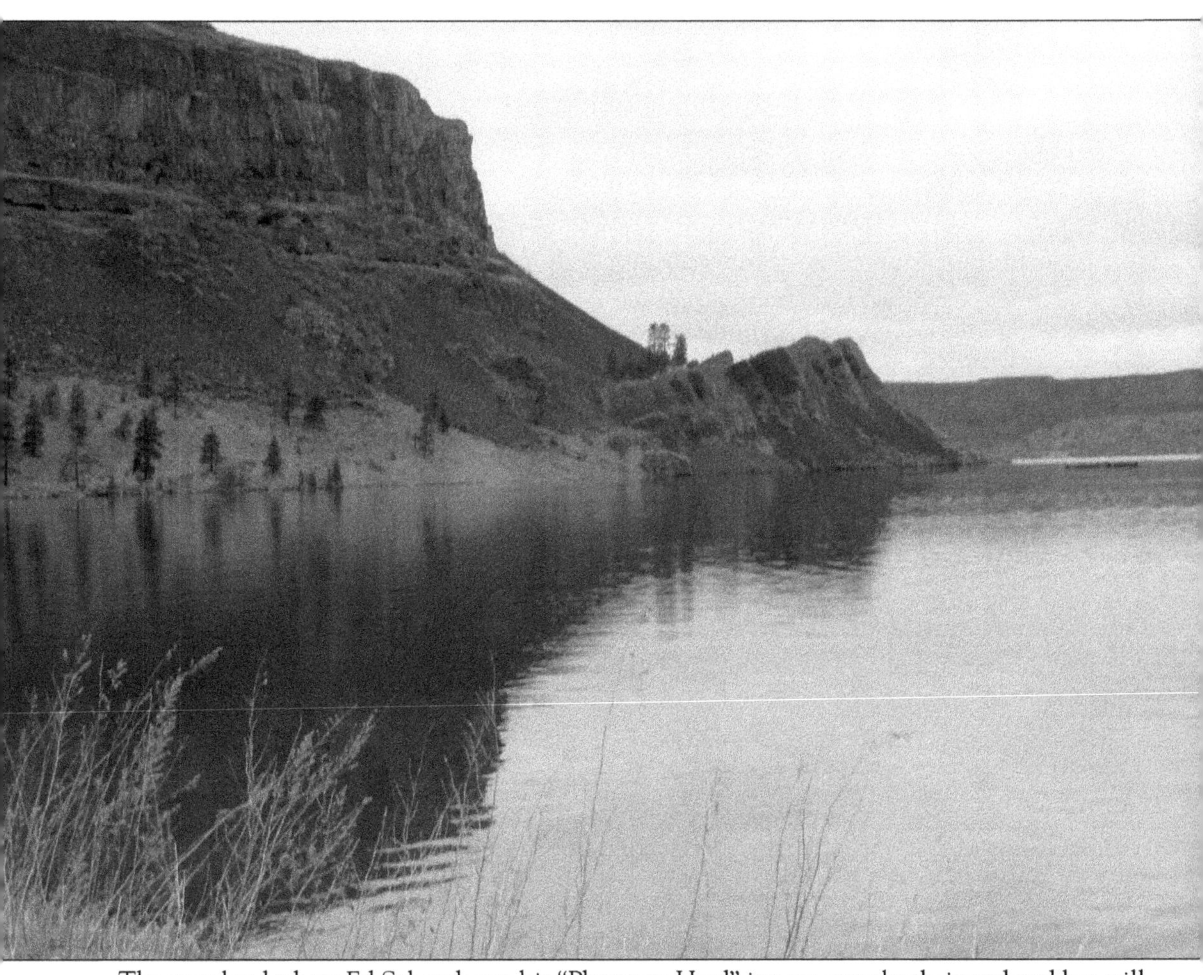

The very land where Ed Schrock ran his "Phantom Herd" is now completely inundated but still recognizable. Once, there were cattle here to feed the people of all over the country, but now a fish pen floats to stock the waters with a different type of protein (see page 26). (Courtesy of J. Kemble.)

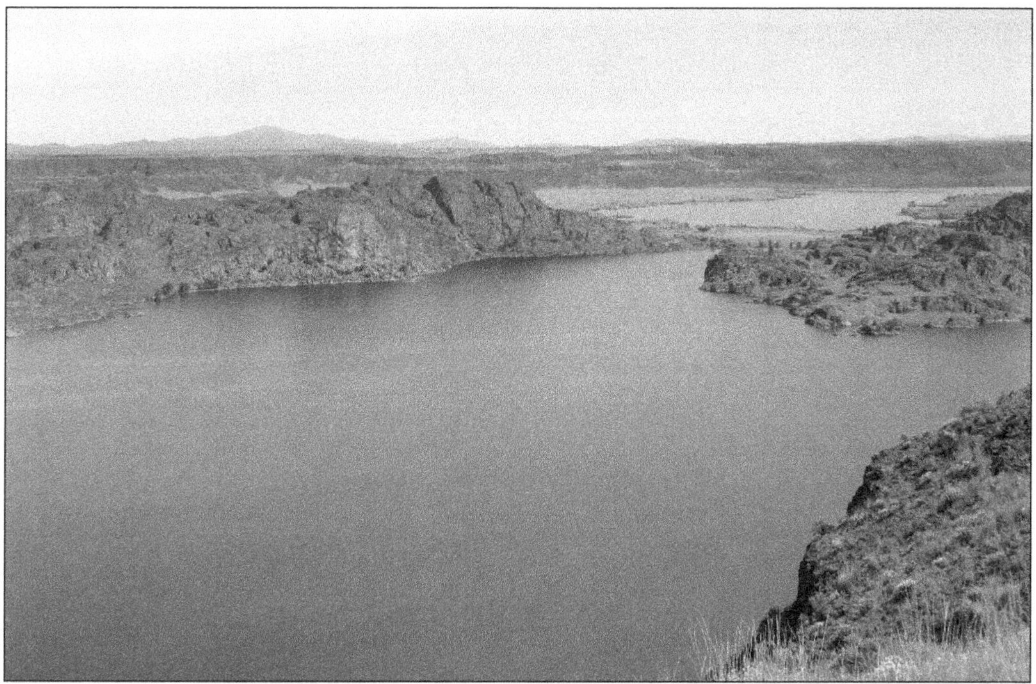

Devils Lake was also flooded but remains a popular fishing spot to this day, with its granite boulder shoreline vastly unchanged. Devils Lake itself has had a long noteworthy history. Before the first pioneers, it was a sacred place visited by indigenous people. Irrigation from Devils Lake helped define dry-land farming in the early 1900s, and by 1940 it was a favorite fishing spot for locals. (Courtesy of J. Kemble.)

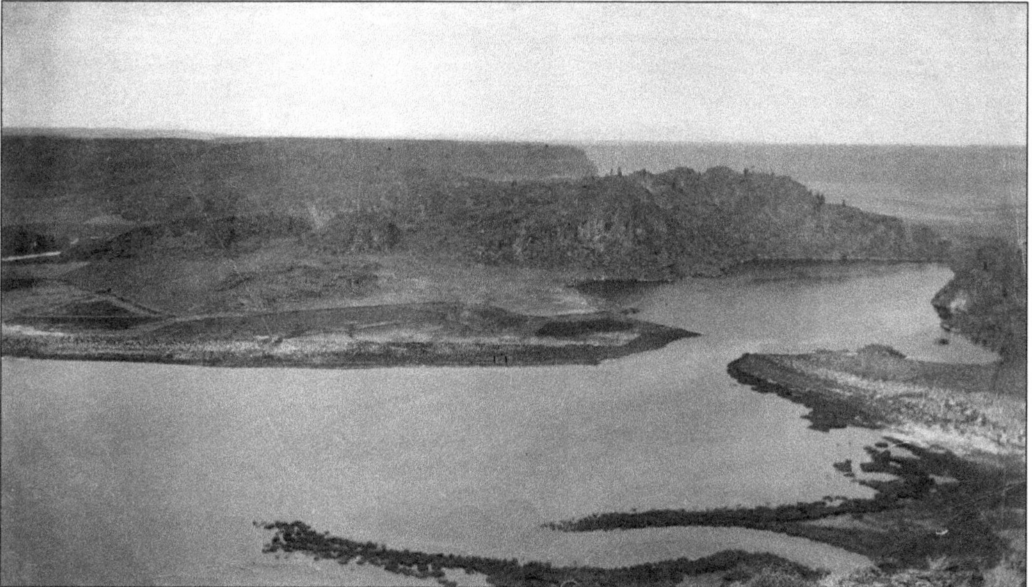

In the 1940s, rumors persisted that Devils Lake was bottomless, a rumor usually spread by children or to children by playful adults who also claimed the lake weed would draw one down to the bottom to never be found. This is a pre-flooded picture of Devils Lake taken from on top of Steamboat Rock that shows crops on the west shore.

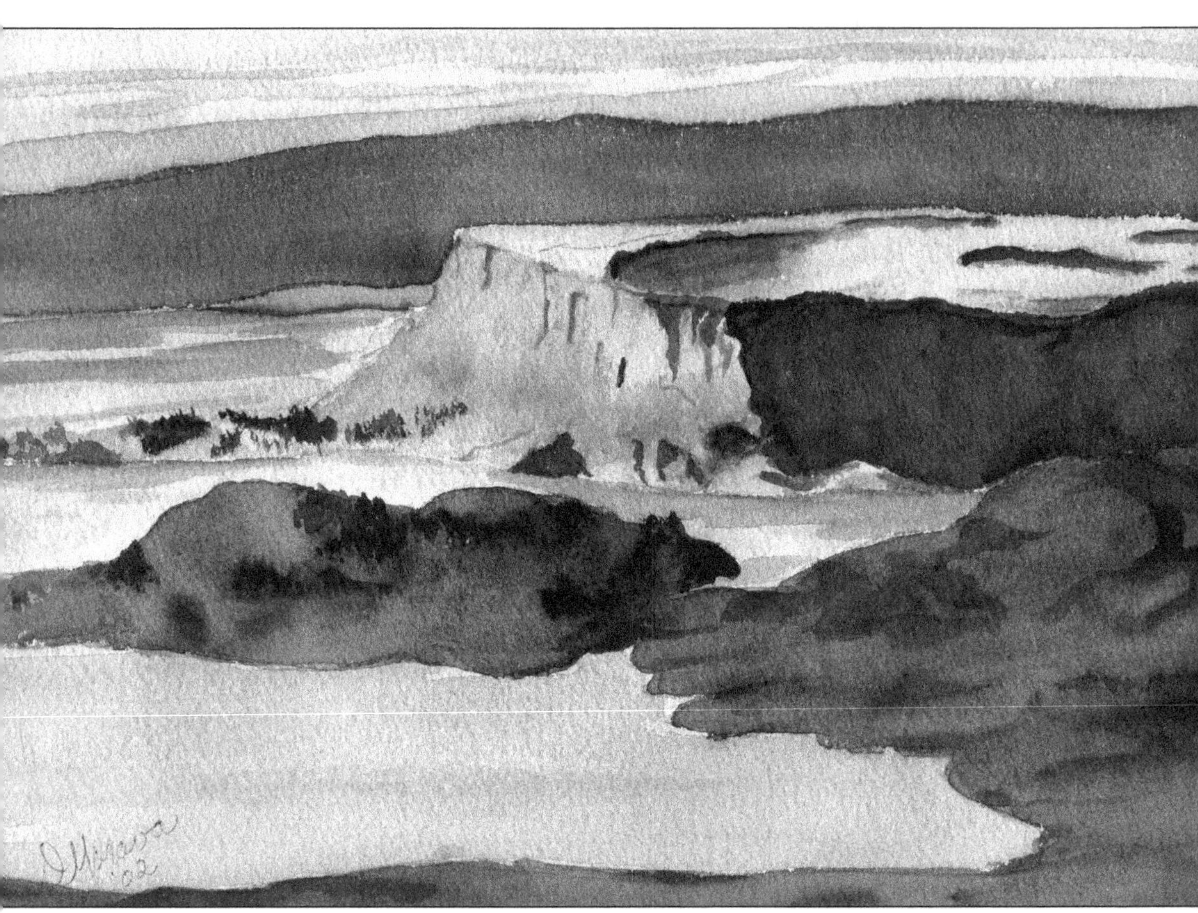

One of the great stories about the filling of Banks Lake is about the snakes invading Coulee City. As the waters of Banks Lake rose, the critters living in the coulee easily escaped the oncoming deluge—except the snakes. Unable to truly escape into the walls or holes, they moved down the coulee just ahead of the wave, building in number, and were not really noticed until they started to encroach on Coulee City. There was even a watch put up to keep an eye out for the varmints just outside of town, and children were told to stay inside the school during recess. (Courtesy of Darlene Morava.)

Eight

Parks and Recreation

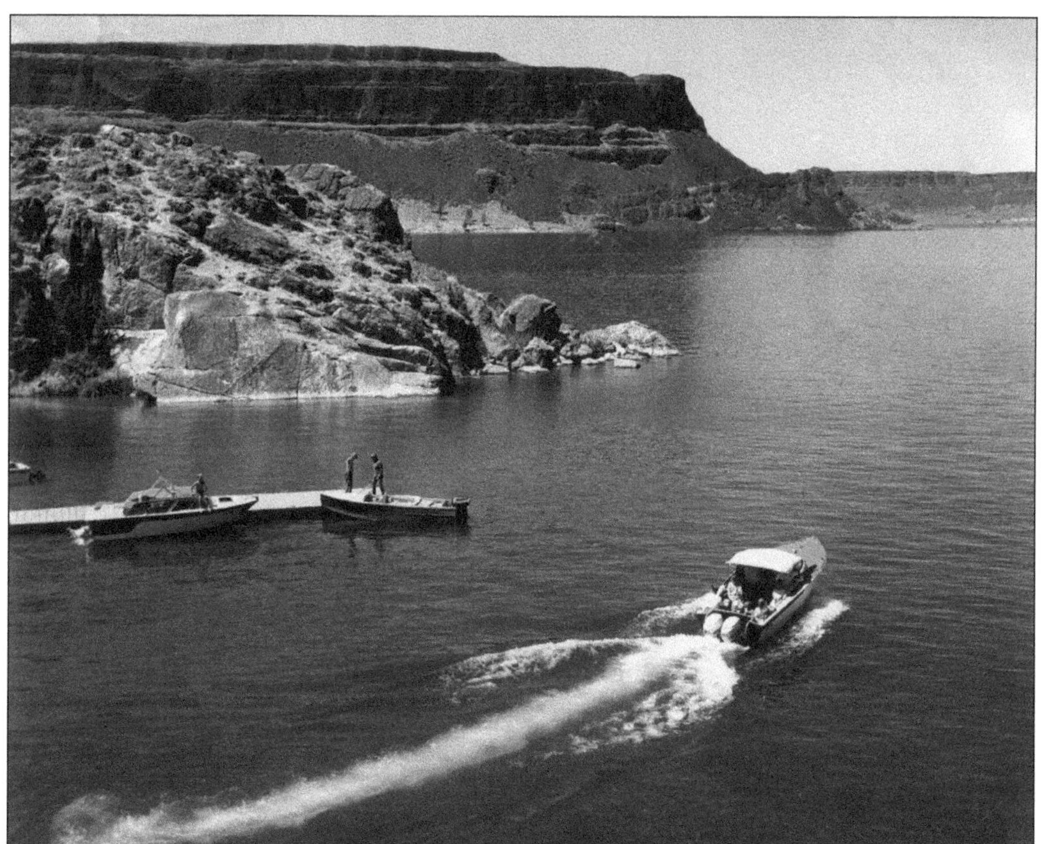

Since the creation of Sun Lakes in the late 1940s, the Grand Coulee had been a hot spot for recreation. Long, hot days and more than enough lakes and endless hiking possibilities made the area around Steamboat Rock a mecca for outdoor enthusiasts in the 1950s and 1960s. Almost immediately, people began boating, fishing, hiking, and exploring the new lake. (Courtesy of the *Star*.)

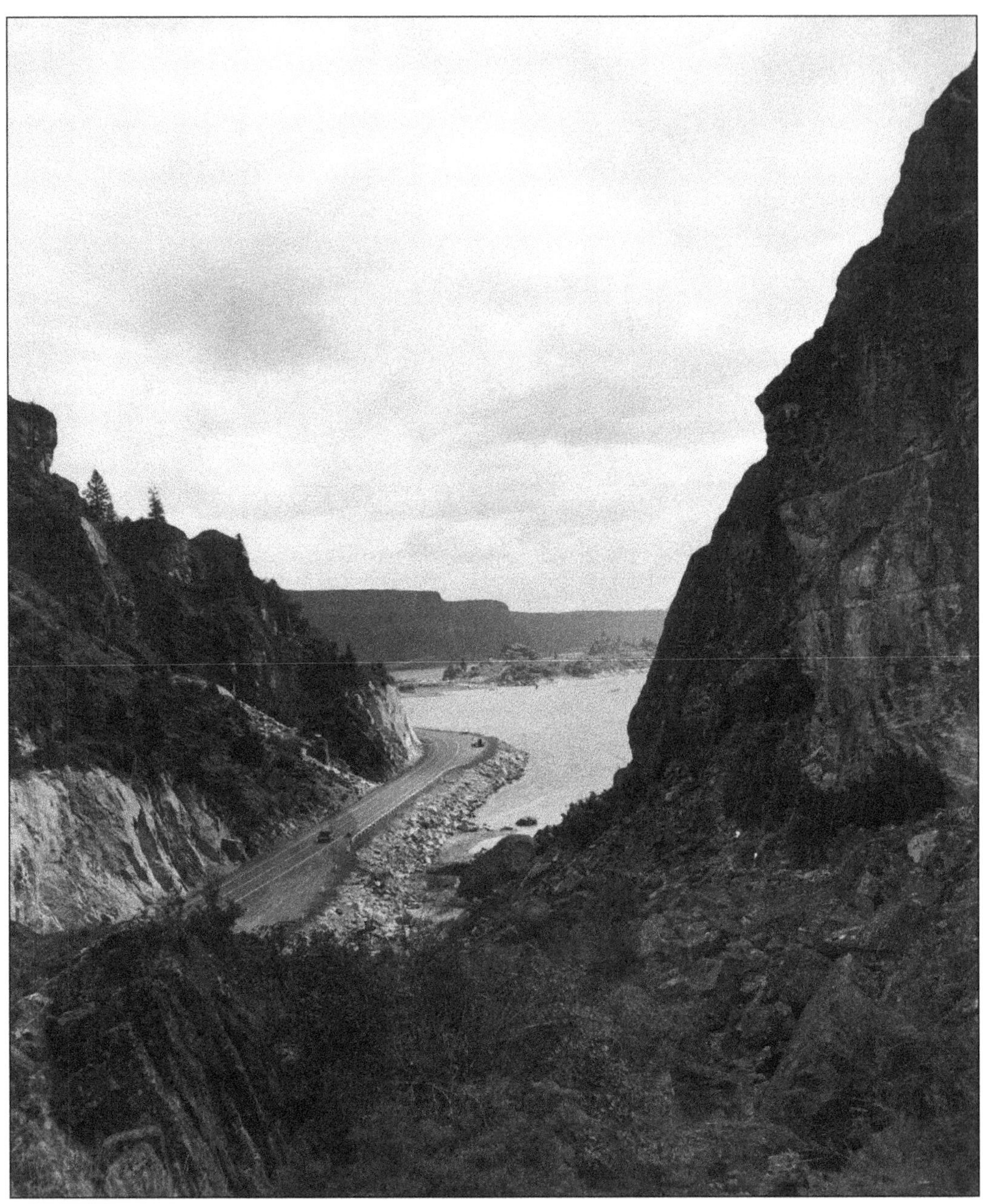

In 1964, Secondary State Highway 2F and 10F were combined to become State Route 155. The renumbering was due to the highway department revising its organization and deleting the primary and secondary road systems. (Courtesy of the *Star*.)

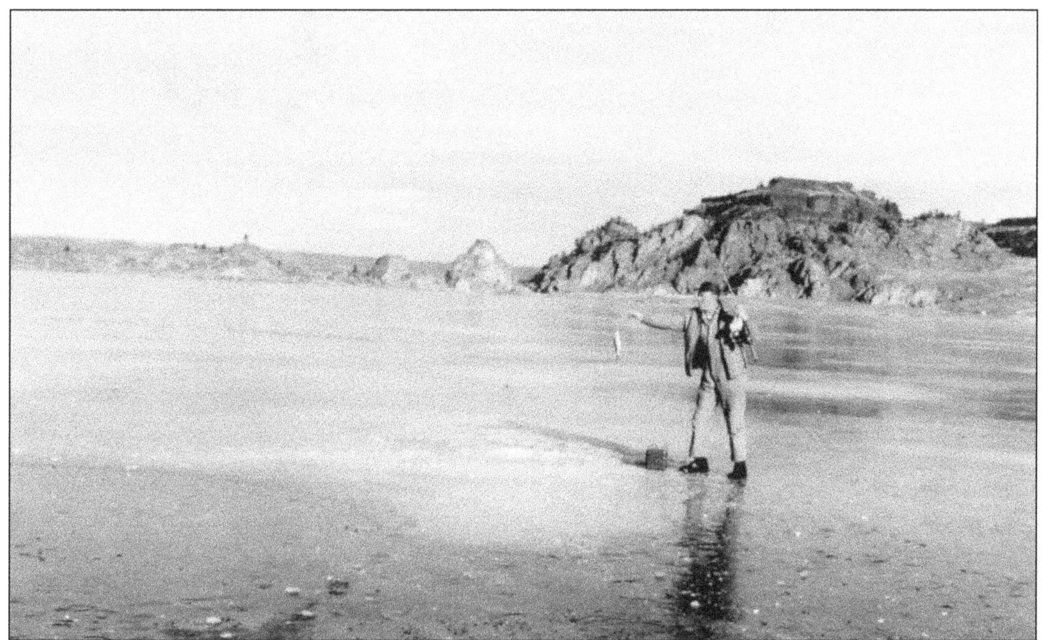

Fishing around Steamboat Rock was nothing new and, for decades, used to put food on the table. As time progressed and fewer and fewer people had to hunt or fish for their food, it became more of a recreational sport. Soon, fishermen could be seen all year round on Banks Lake. (Courtesy of Grant County PUD.)

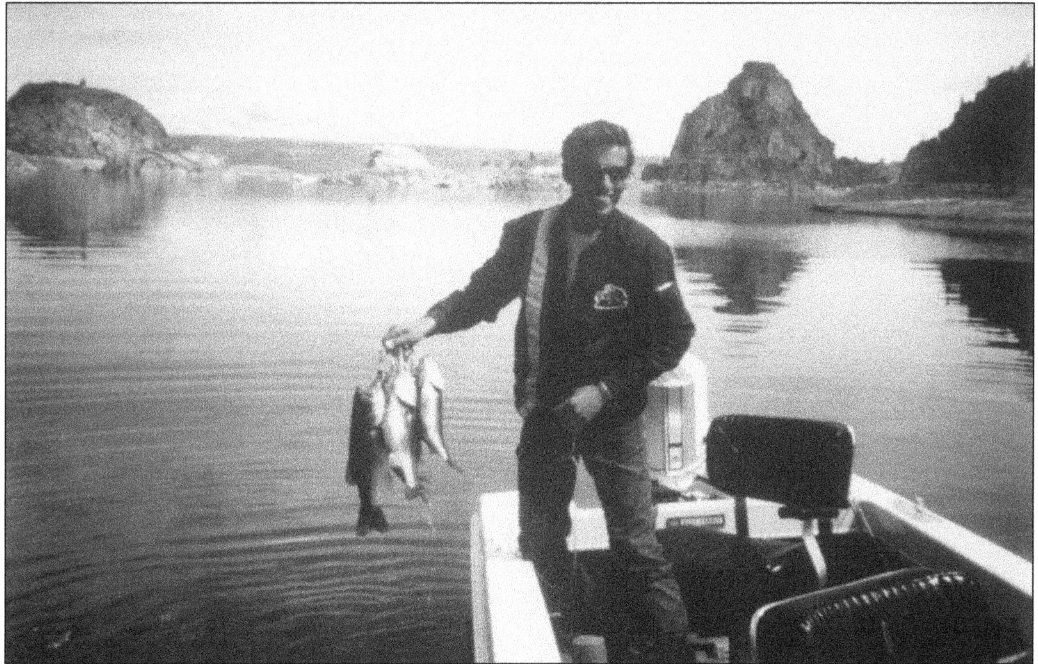

As people raced down the Speedball Highway in the 1930s and 1940s, they probably never thought that the road they were driving on would become a hot spot for catching fish. After the flooding, the slightly raised road attracted fish, making them an easy target for fishermen. (Courtesy of Steamboat Rock State Park.)

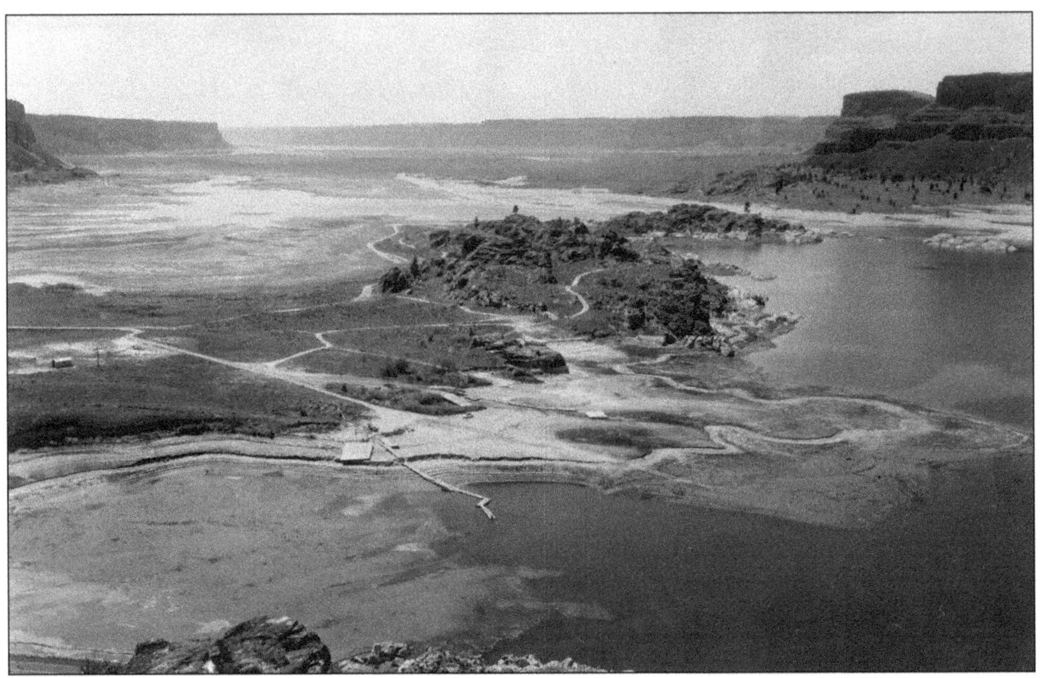

In 1953, the Steamboat Rock area was acquired from the Bureau of Reclamation, and by 1956, the area was officially designated as Steamboat Rock State Park. The first Steamboat Rock State Park was at the area now called Northrup Point and was little more than a rest area with a boat launch. Here, the original Steamboat Rock State Park is seen under construction during a drawdown. (Courtesy of Steamboat Rock State Park.)

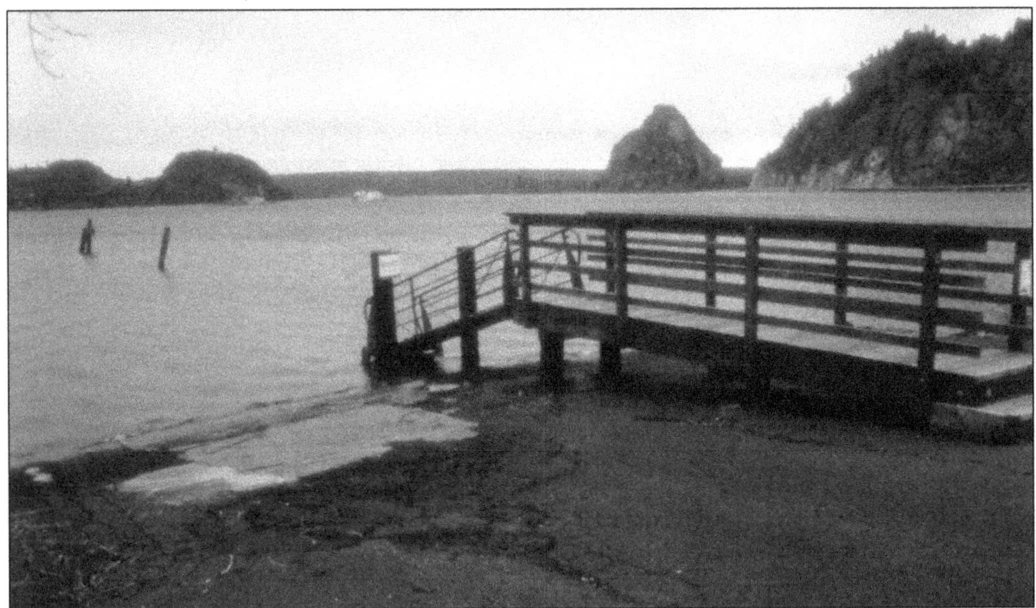

The original Steamboat Rock State Park's boat launch is located on old historic pastures of the Fleet/Schrock/Baldwin ranch at the base of Castle Rock. At first, it was just a basic boat launch, but as recreation in the area picked up, improvements were made. (Courtesy of Steamboat Rock State Park.)

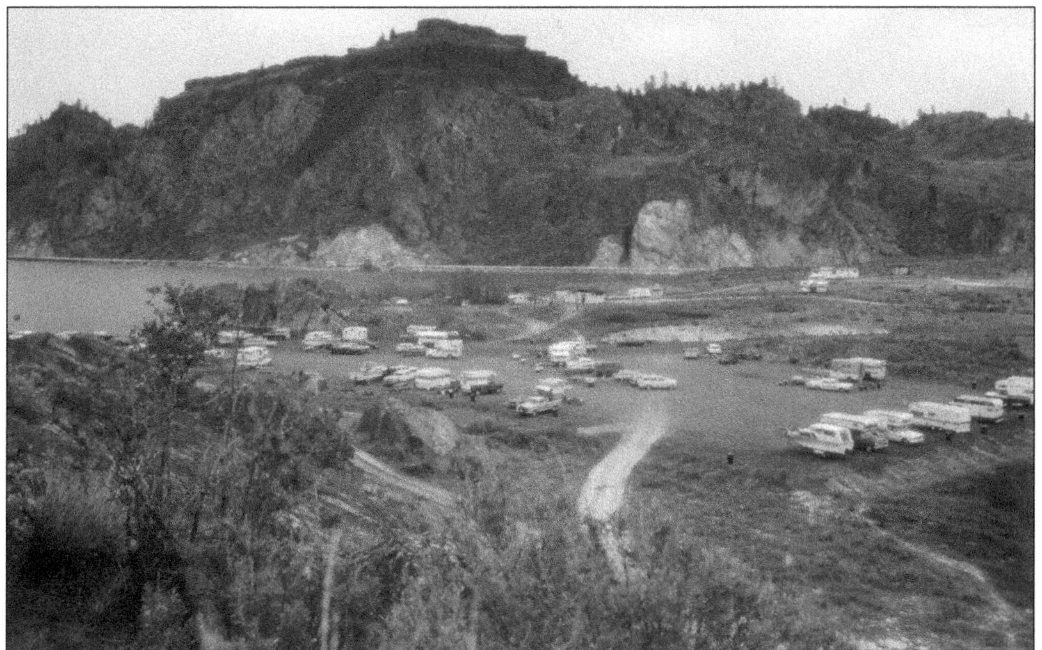

By 1968, Steamboat Rock State Park was little more than a boat launch and comfort station. It was often referred to as a pull-off or rest stop, but people would spend the night in campers, taking advantage of the facilities. By this time, everyone had a car, and traveling to distant locations for summer vacation had become the cultural norm. (Courtesy of Steamboat Rock State Park.)

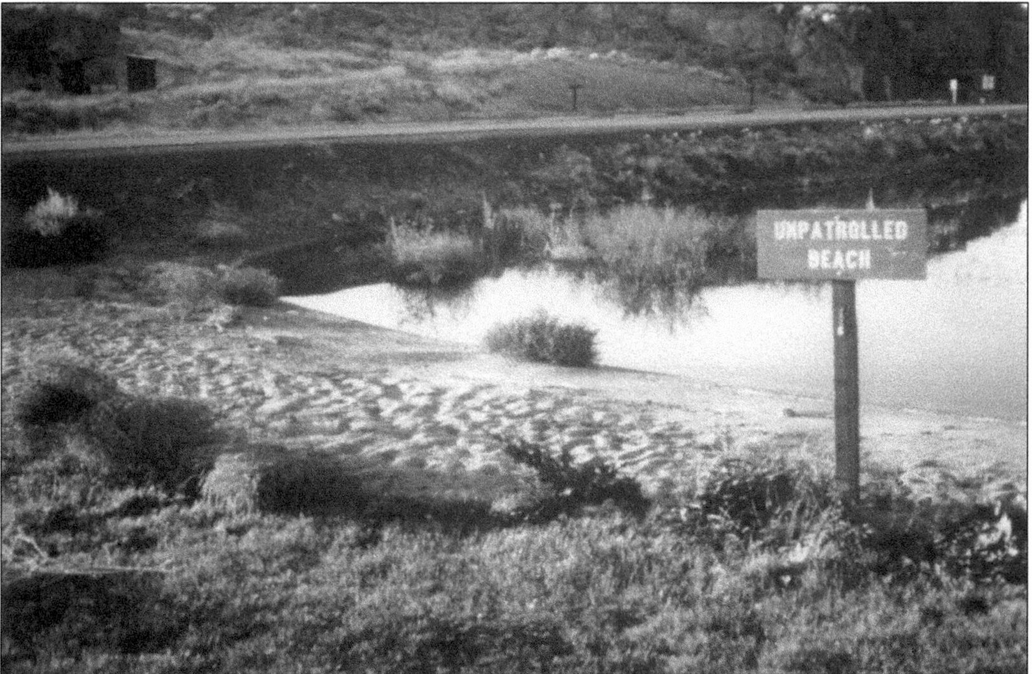

The original Steamboat Rock State Park had a small, unmanned beach for swimming and maintained yard for picnicking. The maintenance on the park at the time was relatively low, and the park itself is considered basic by today's standards. (Courtesy of Steamboat Rock State Park.)

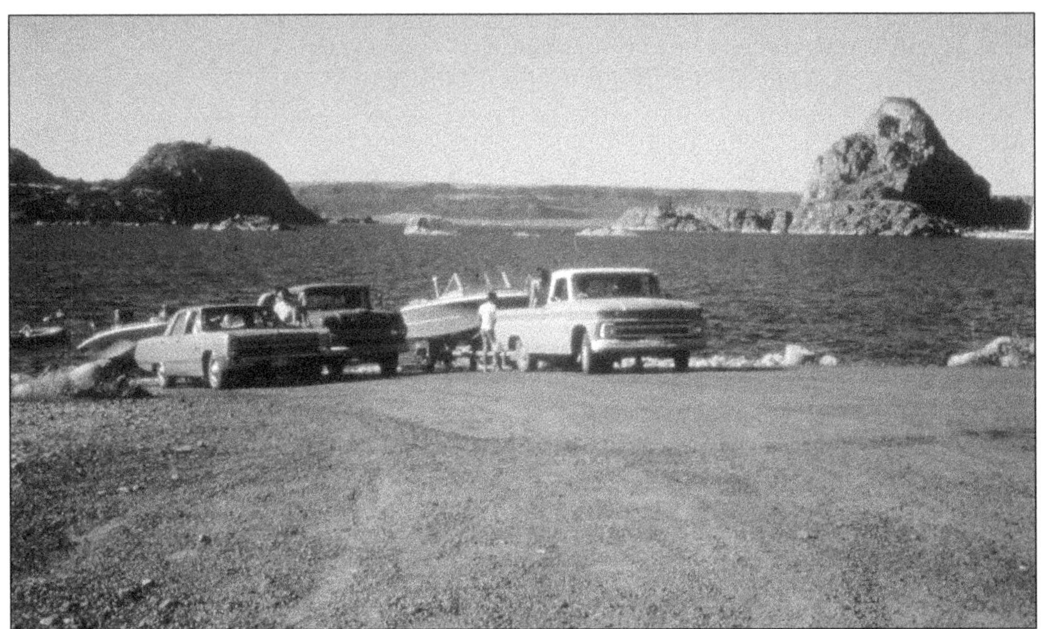

Recreation around Banks Lake was at an all-time high, with nearby Sun Lakes State Park overflowing and the little rest area around Steamboat Rock State Park seeing thousands of tourists. In 1967, the park was visited with over 137,000 people, and 1968 was even busier. (Courtesy of Steamboat Rock State Park.)

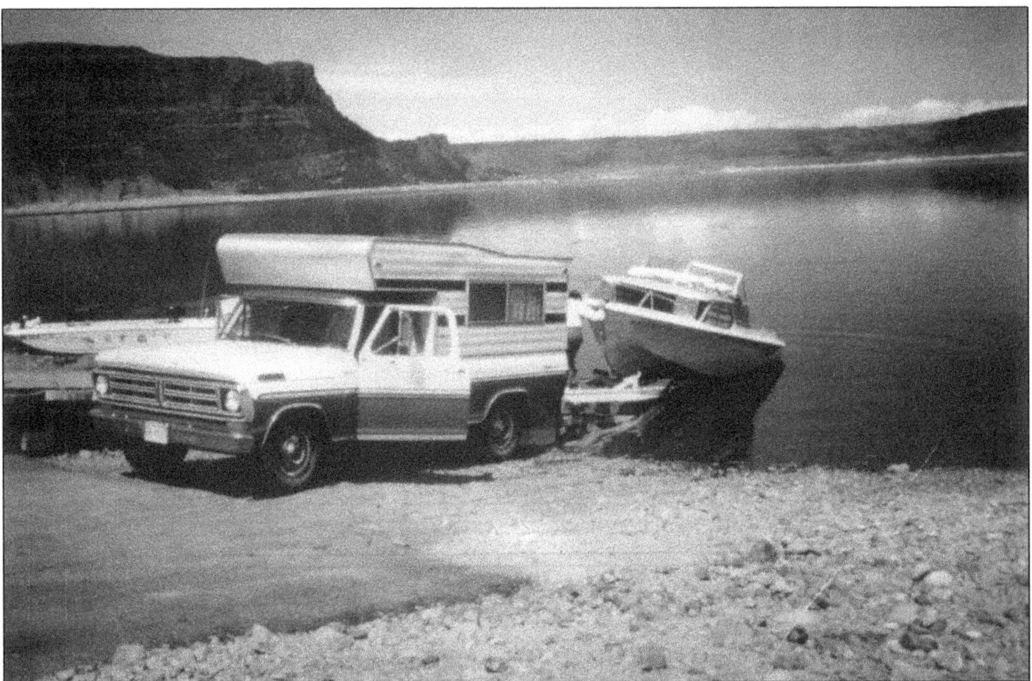

With nearby Spring Canyon National Park and Sun Lakes State Park operating at full capacity, people started sleeping in campers along the road, at rest stops and pull-offs all along State Route 155. Here, a man with a camper launches his boat in what was once the Ed Schrock Plus Bar Ranch at the base of Steamboat Rock. (Courtesy of Steamboat Rock State Park.)

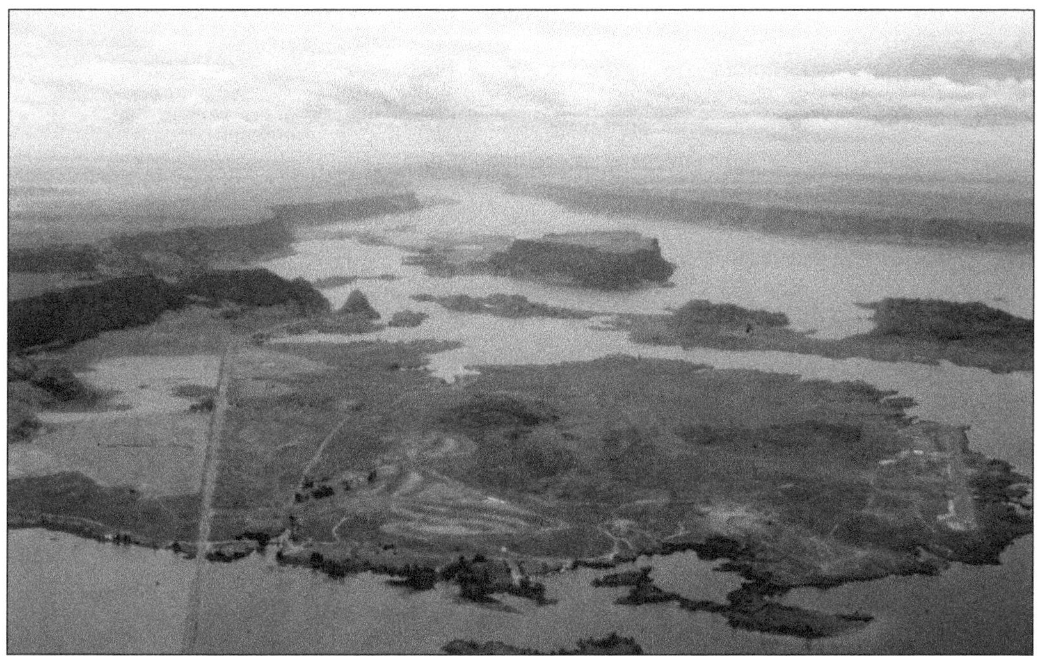

State parks commissioner Clair Greeley announced that the local area state parks attracted 2,727,709 visitors during the 1967–1968 fiscal year. Offering this as proof of a need for expansion on Steamboat Rock State Park, the push was on by both the local communities and the State Parks Department to expand Steamboat Rock State Park into something that would last generations to come. (Courtesy of Steamboat Rock State Park.)

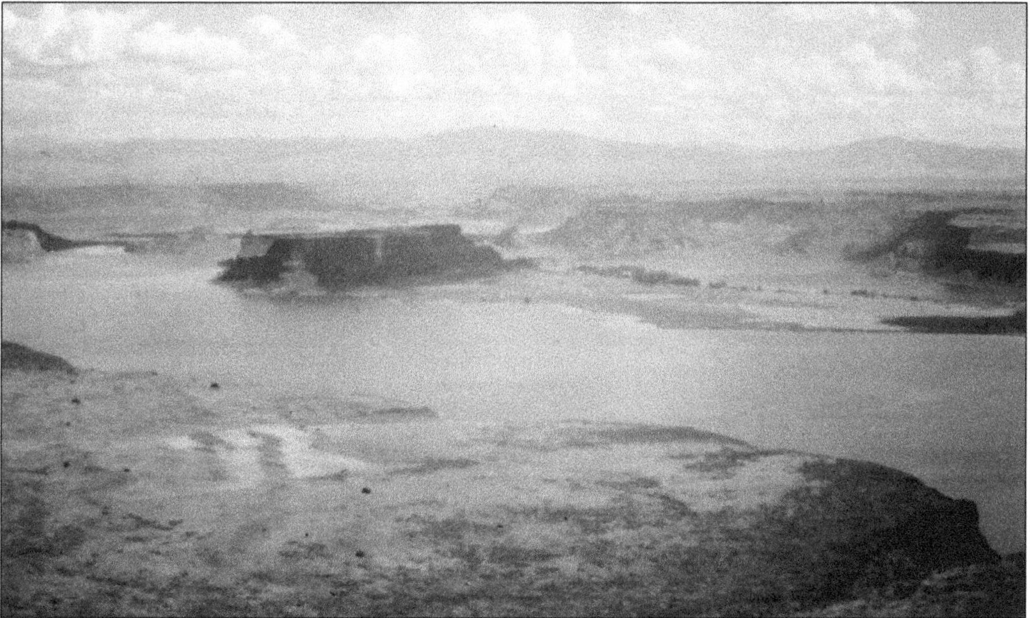

The main objective of the new plans to expand Steamboat Rock State Park would move the focus from Northrup Point and place it firmly at the base of Steamboat Rock. At first, some of those plans echoed sentiments heard in the past. One such plan was to create a landing strip for airplanes and helicopters with an adjacent campground. (Courtesy of Steamboat Rock State Park.)

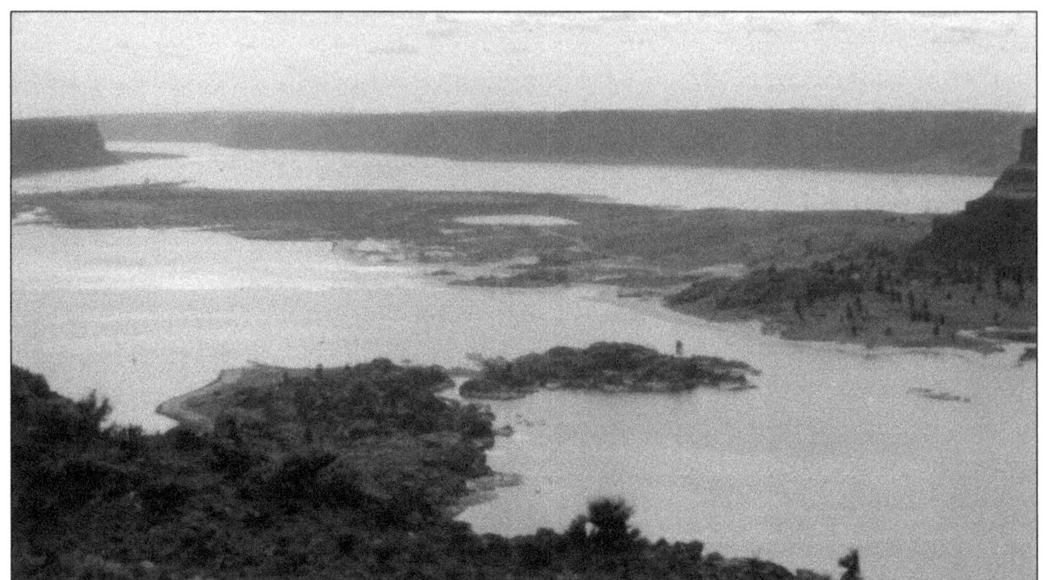

The same plans also called for a causeway-type bridge to be built from Northrup Point to Steamboat Rock, forming an inner lake. The area that was going to be the inner lake became known as the Devil's Punchbowl, creating confusion with Martin Falls, which was also called Devil's Punchbowl. Before flooding, Northrup Point was part of the cluster of rocks known as the Granite Hills. (Courtesy of Steamboat Rock State Park.)

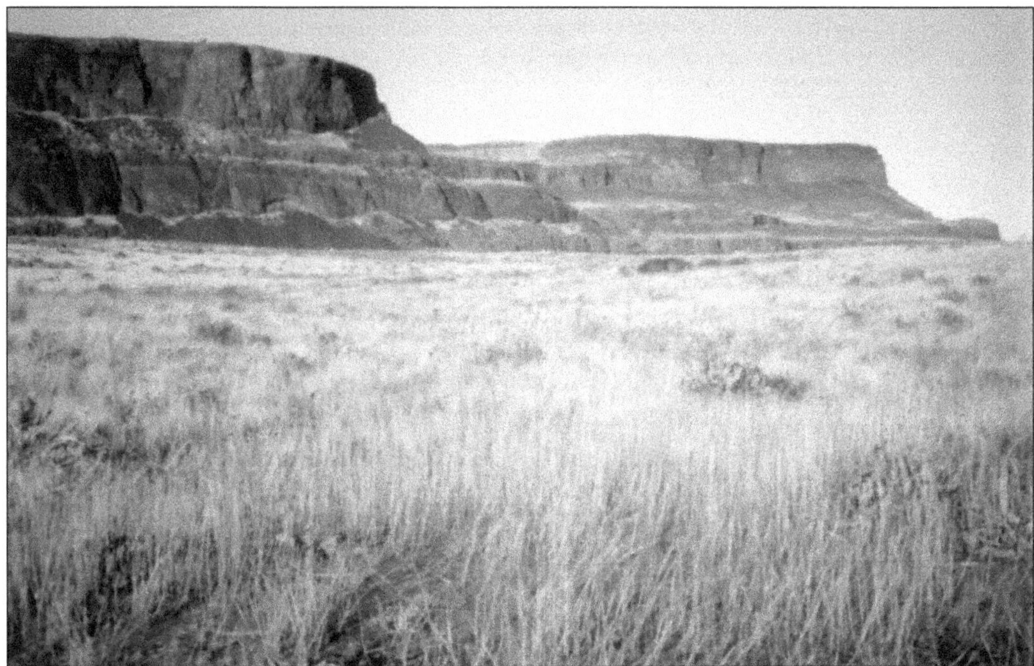

In 1969, the plans to expand Steamboat Rock State Park met a tangle in Olympia over funds; the Senate approved $400,000, but the House of Representatives turned it down, and the project fell into a stalemate, with improvements put on hold. By August, the legislature had approved $100,000 for the upkeep of the existing boat launch and comfort station at the original park. (Courtesy of Steamboat Rock State Park.)

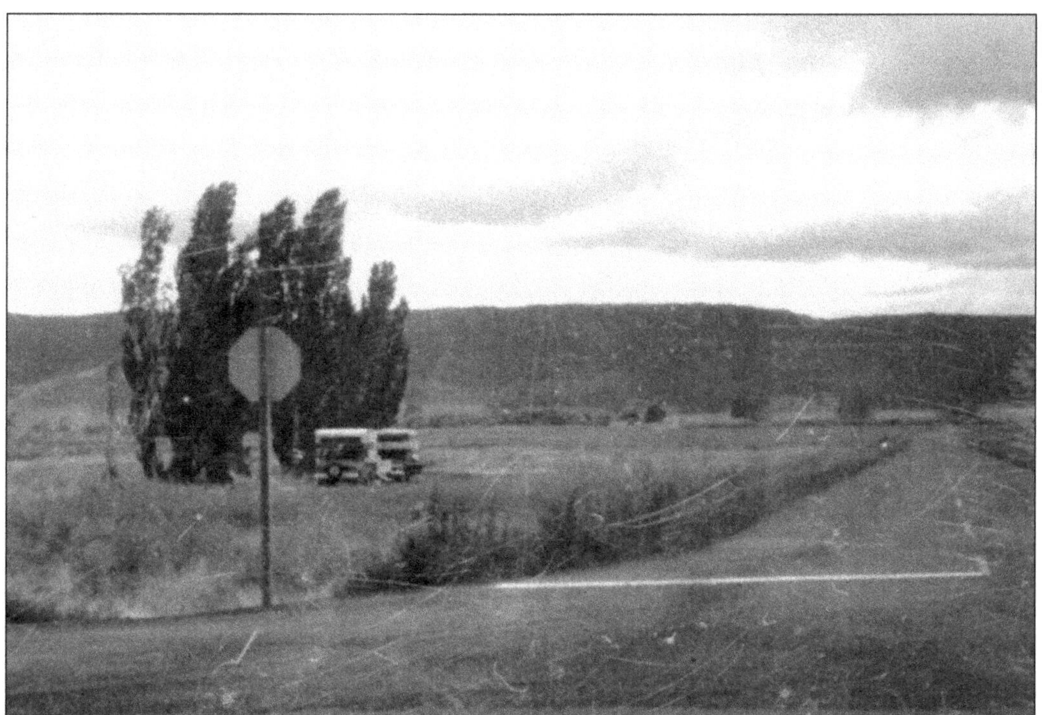

During this time, the fight for funds had spilled out into the local papers and had been taken up by members of the Grand Coulee Chamber of Commerce. Frustrated by the seeming lack of concern and slowness of which the state pursued the issue, the people took matters into their own hands and created a pull-off under a line of poplars on the peninsula to Steamboat Rock for campers and visitors. (Courtesy of Steamboat Rock State Park.)

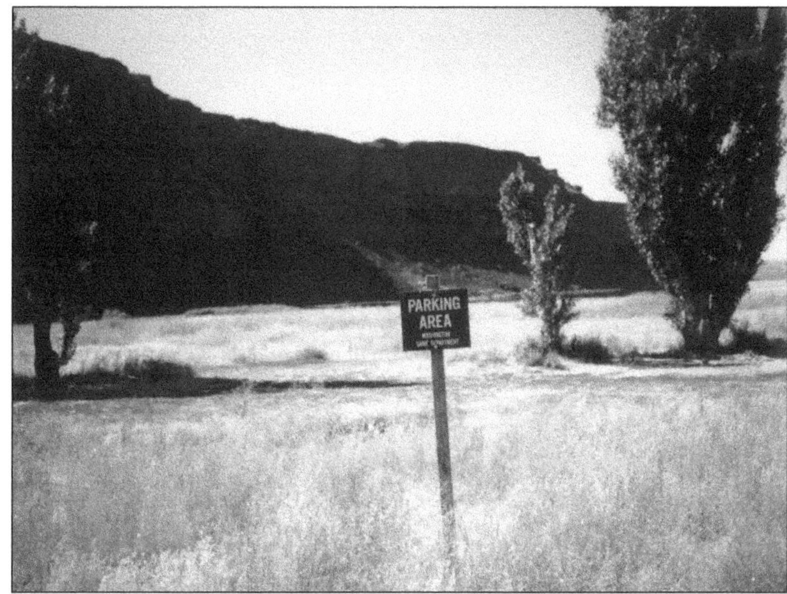

The poplars were originally planted as a windbreak, but in the 1970s they served as a meeting place for several generations. Now, the poplars are reduced to stumps due to old age, but the nearby body of water to the south of the stumps is called Poplar Bay in the memories of this historic spot. (Courtesy of Steamboat Rock State Park.)

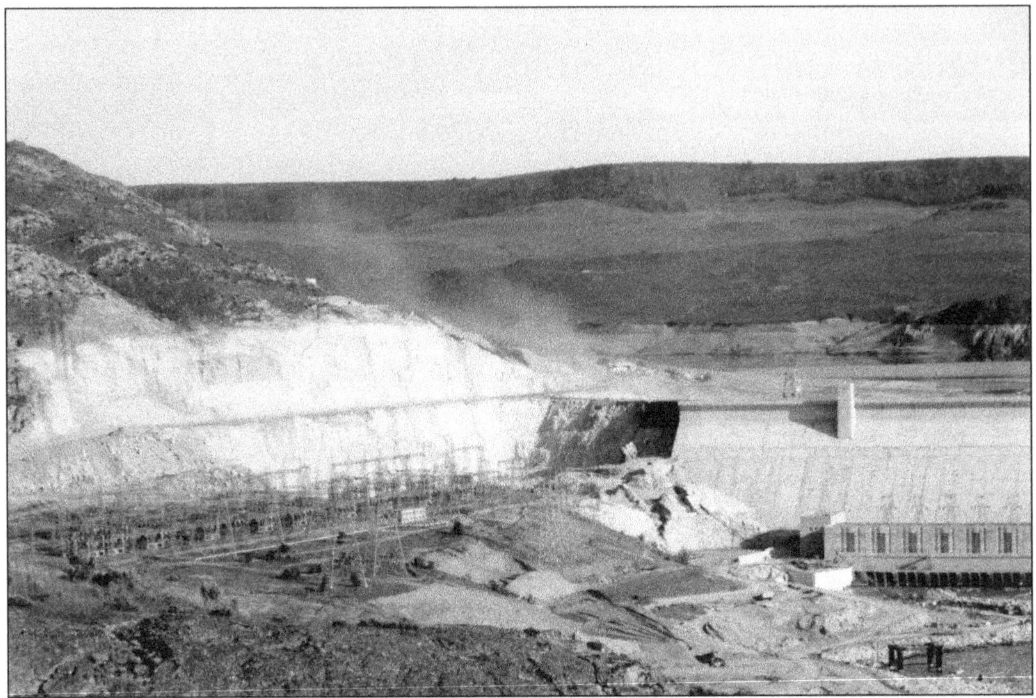

It was during this time that the construction of Grand Coulee Dam's third powerhouse got started, and the work had eliminated two local parks: one in Elmer City and one in Coulee Dam. The Grand Coulee Chamber of Commerce felt this also factored into the need to expand Steamboat Rock State Park. (Courtesy of Coulee Pioneer Museum.)

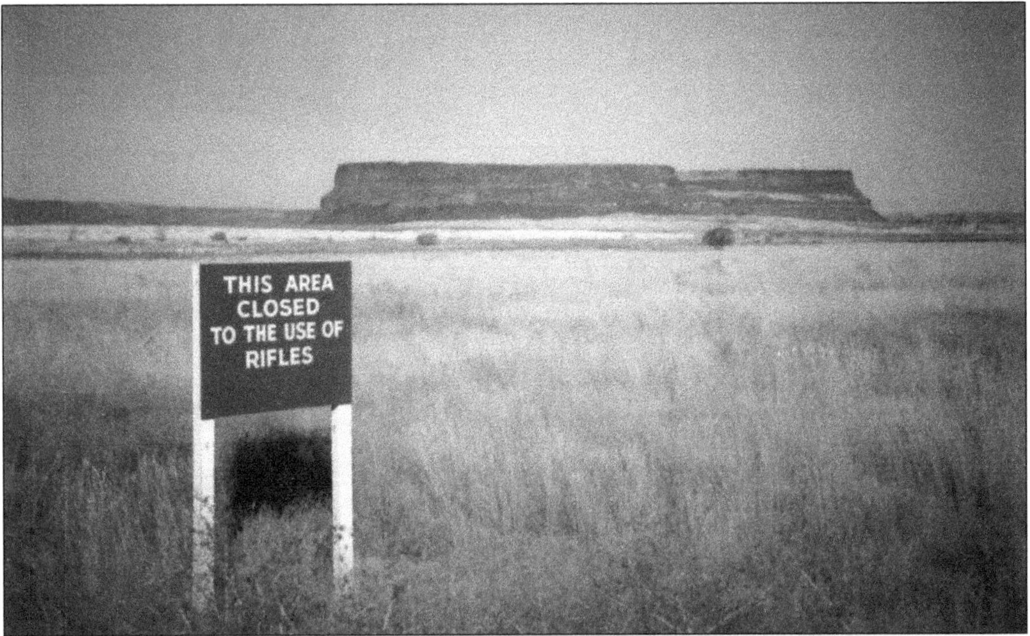

In early 1970, Deputy Director of Washington State Parks Richard Huebner announced that Steamboat Rock had been granted $730,000 to start expanding the state park to the base of Steamboat Rock for the 1971 vacation season. (Courtesy of Steamboat Rock State Park.)

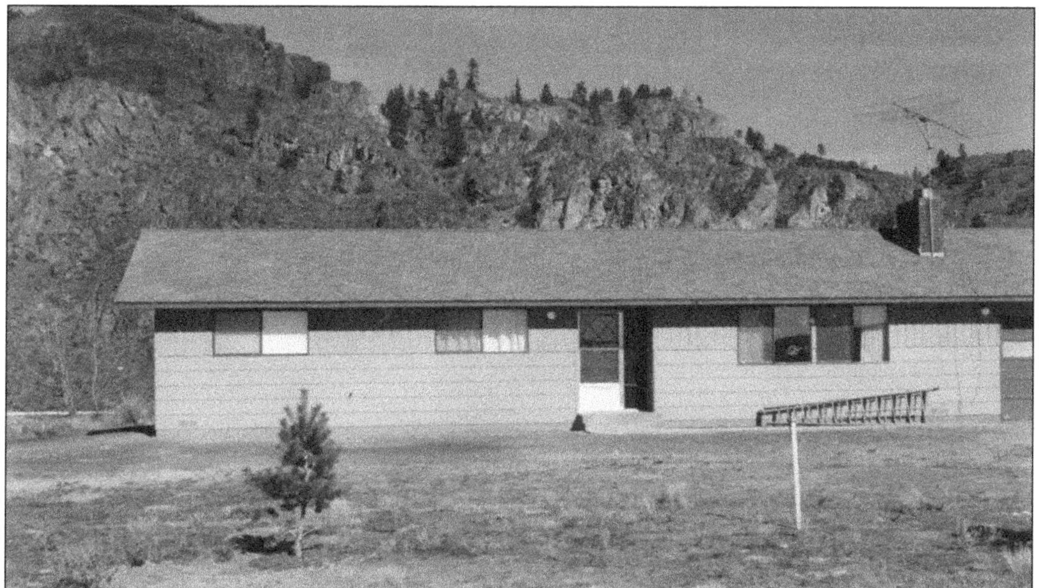

Robert Tucker became the first full-time Steamboat Rock State Park ranger in March 1970. Originally from Kansas, he was stationed at Fairchild Air Force Base. After leaving the Air Force, Tucker worked for the US Forrest Service and the Department of Natural Resources, before becoming a Washington State Park ranger. (Courtesy of Steamboat Rock State Park.)

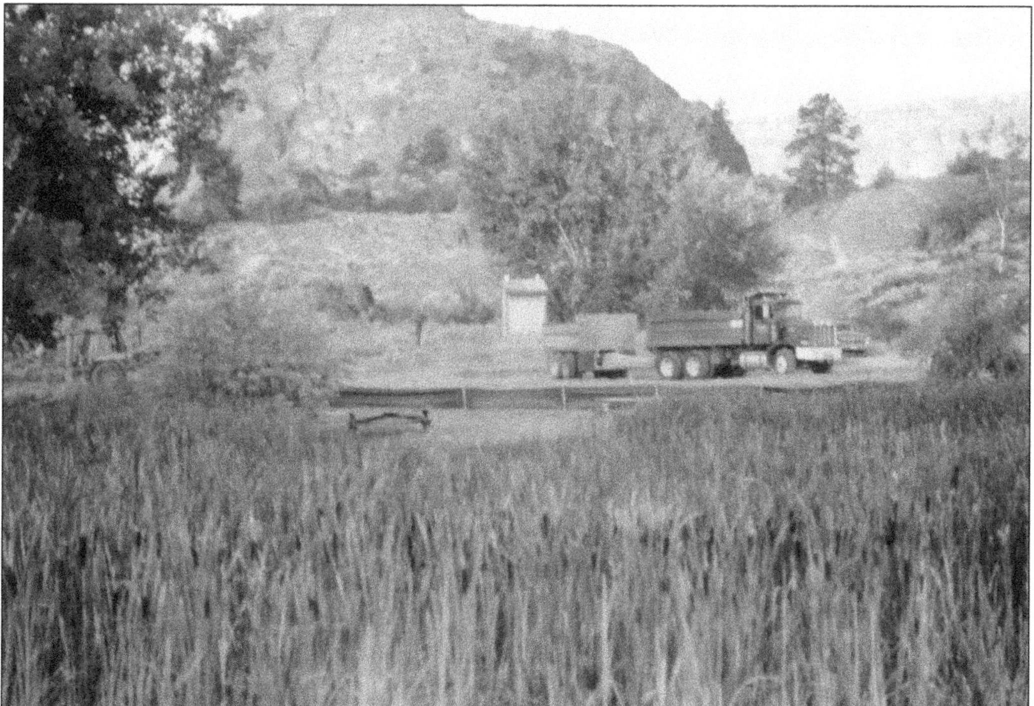

Robert Tucker, his wife, and two sons moved into a newly constructed ranger house and set up home. Of living at the state park, Robert said, "Here we have close-ups of the wonders of nature. We see them in their natural state and environment, no zoo could equal this." A true outdoorsman, Robert spent time improving trails and accommodations. (Courtesy of Steamboat Rock State Park.)

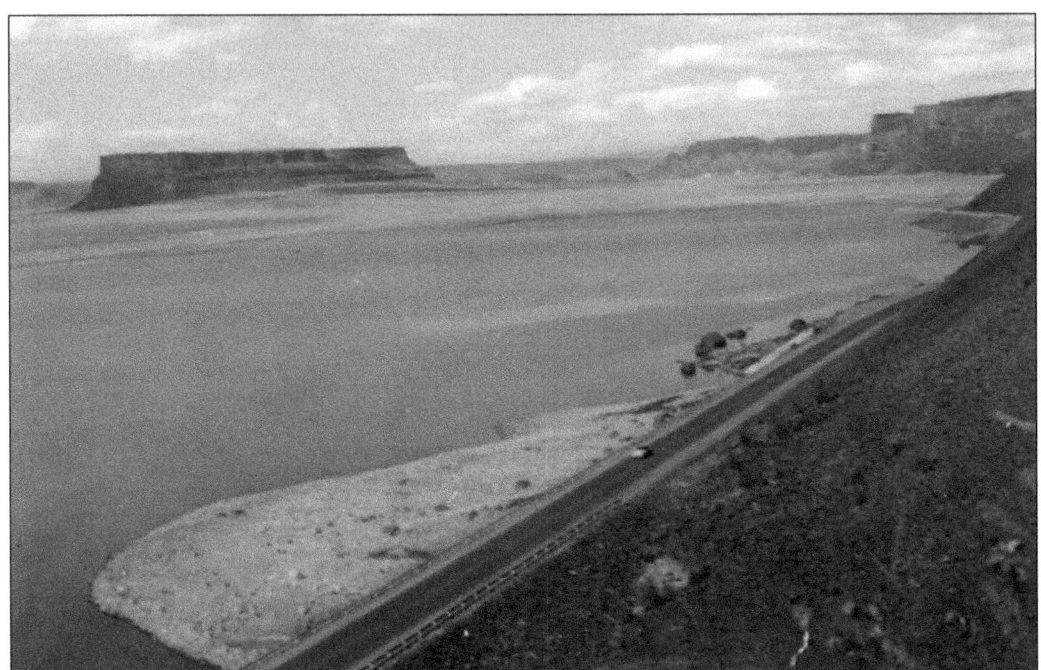

The new park plans were much more scaled-down than the landing strip and causeway from Northrup Point plans of the late 1960s. The new plans called for 50 camping units with utility hook-ups, 60 picnic spots, a swimming beach, a bathhouse, and a new road system out to Steamboat Rock from State Route 155.

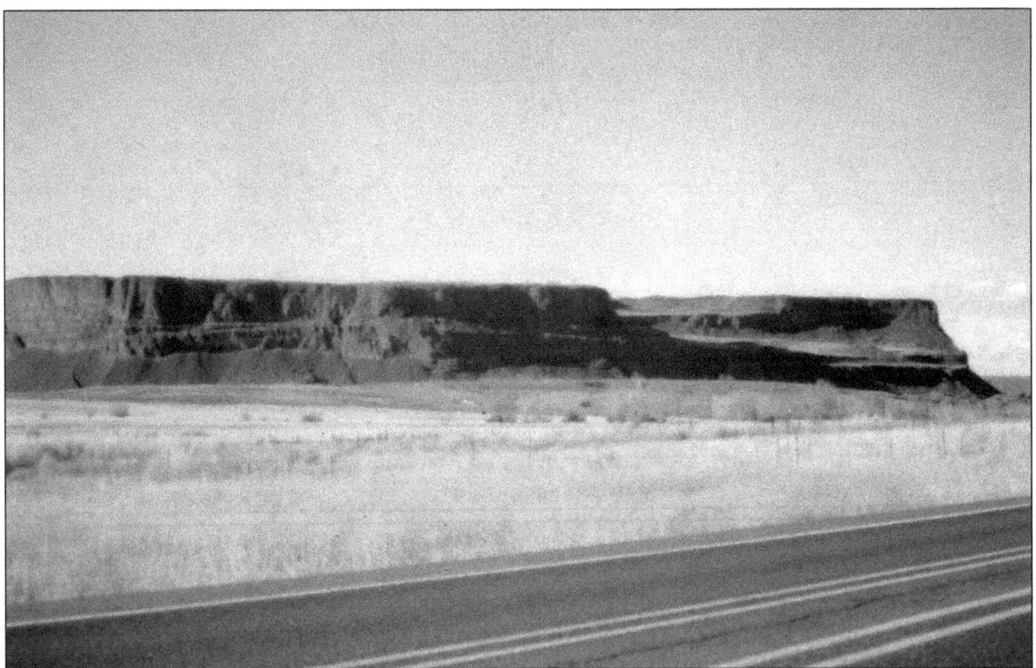

Despite a few funding issues at the beginning, work officially started on the Steamboat Rock State Park expansion in the spring of 1971 by N.A. Degerstrom Inc. of Spokane under contract by the State Parks Department. (Courtesy of Steamboat Rock State Park.)

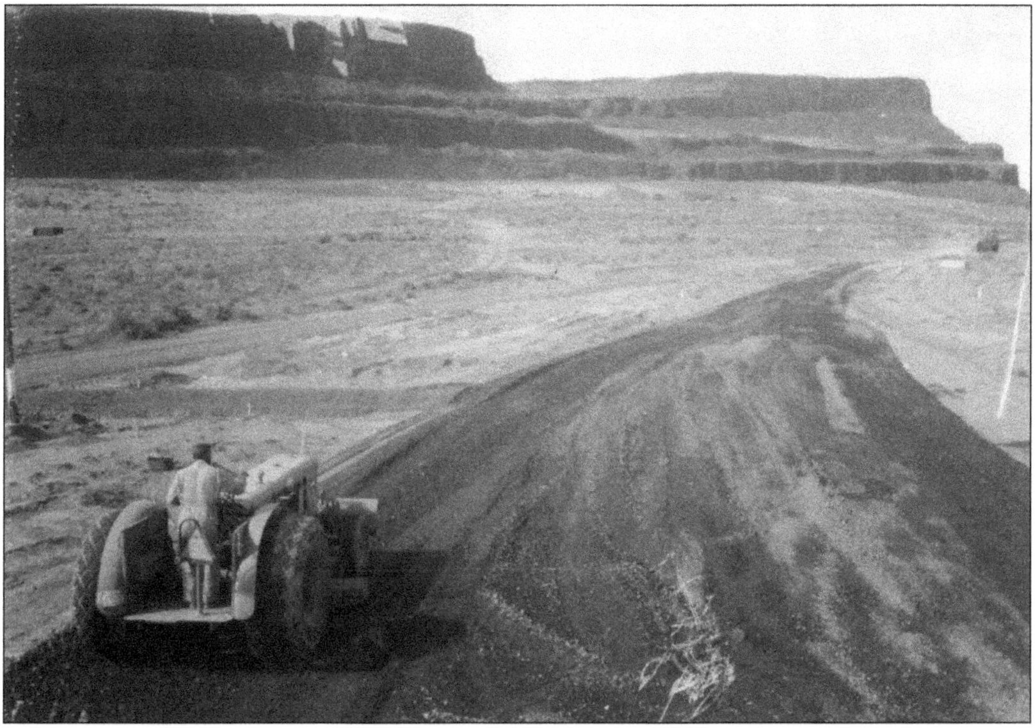

A new entrance road was provided by the State Highway Department. The new entrance road was paved with asphalt and turned off State Route 155 at the well-known Poplars. (Courtesy of Steamboat Rock State Park.)

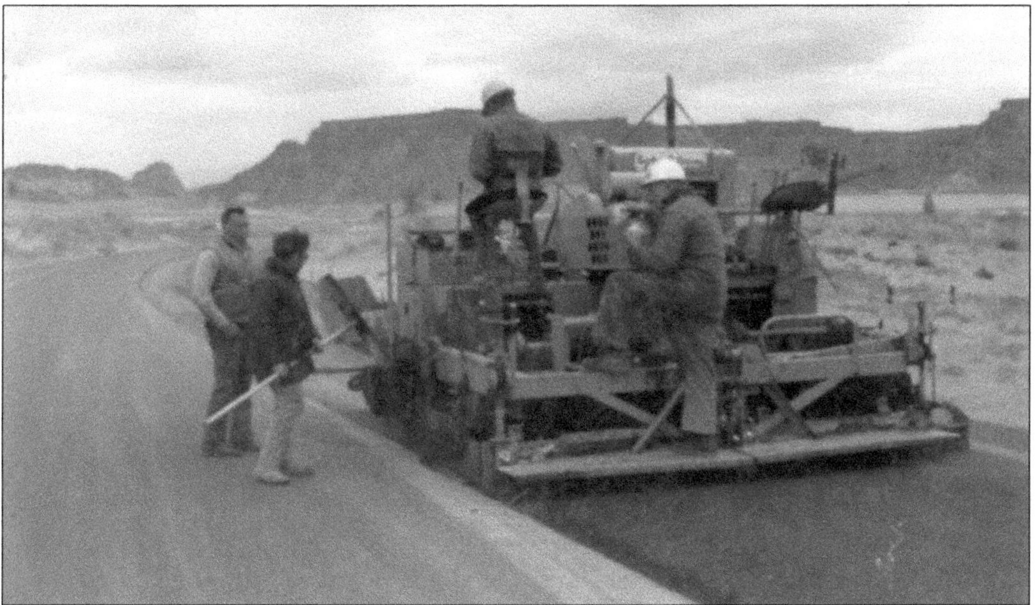

Two miles of double-lane black-topped road were finished by the State Highway Department the same year, using the top of the line and most modern equipment of the day. The new road to the unfinished park passed through fields of wheat as well as patches of sagebrush and sand dunes. (Courtesy of Steamboat Rock State Park.)

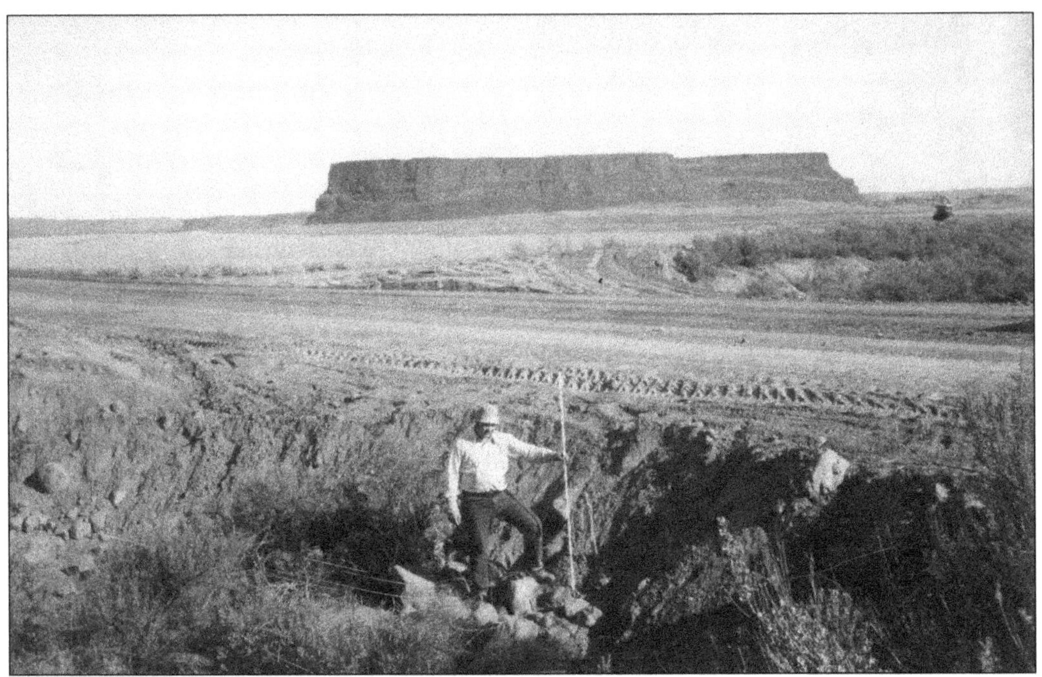

The new park entrance also cut through the old US Construction Railroad grade and Speedball Highway. The grade is marked by a deep rut running on either side of the new blacktop and is overgrown and forgotten. It is hard to recognize as an old railway since the tracks were removed back in the 1940s. (Courtesy of Steamboat Rock State Park.)

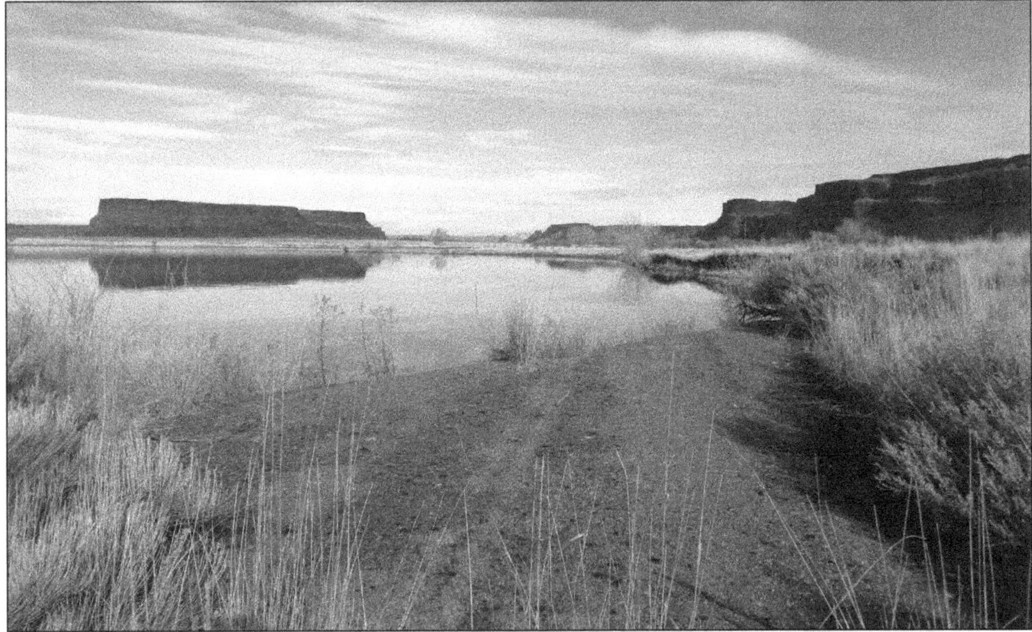

The Speedball Highway is easier to find and follow. The blacktop was built for durability and has stood up against the test of time well. It can be seen crossing the main entrance at the start and runs both directions into the lake. Bits and pieces of the road can easily be found running down the coulee and often into Banks Lake. (Courtesy of J. Kemble.)

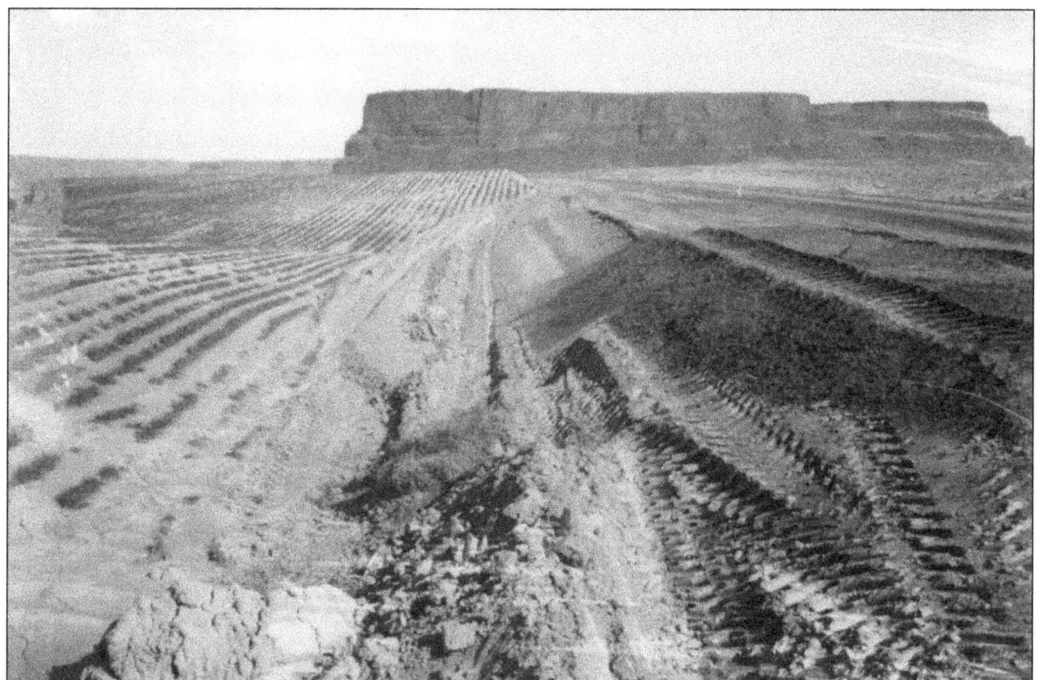

Farming was still happening in the coulee on the lands not flooded by Banks Lake, and this included right around the new entrance of Steamboat Rock State Park. The crops were mostly wheat, but sometimes other crops were grown. (Courtesy of Steamboat Rock State Park.)

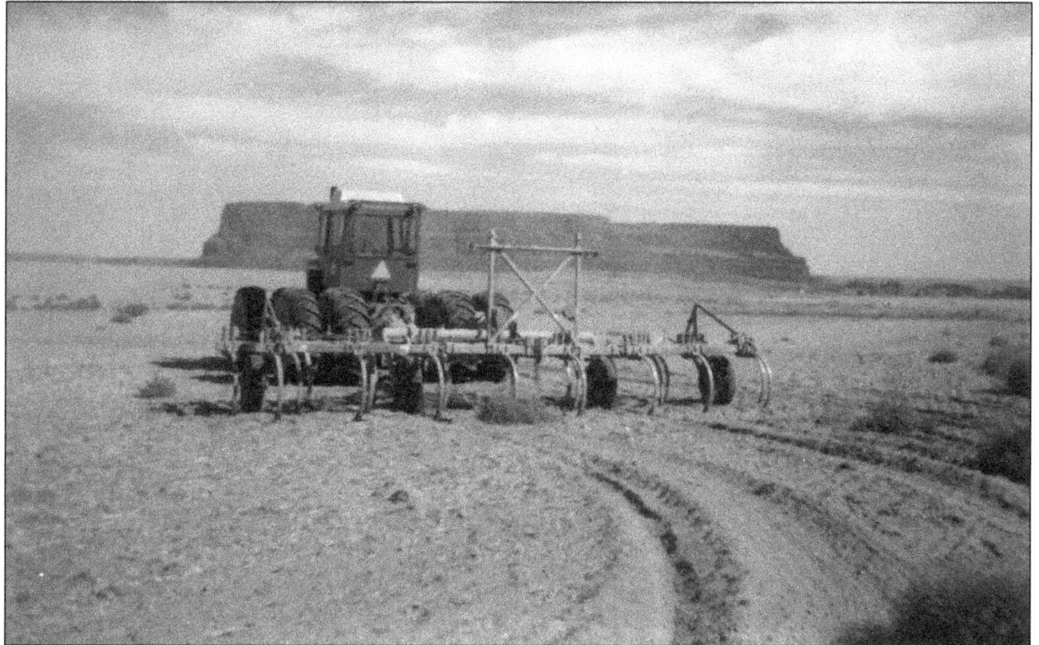

The farmers had leased the land from the USBR and farmed it for decades after the flooding of Banks Lake. At one time, driving down the long strip of road to the park would take one through fields of wheat where now they would pass through fields of sagebrush. (Courtesy of Steamboat Rock State Park.)

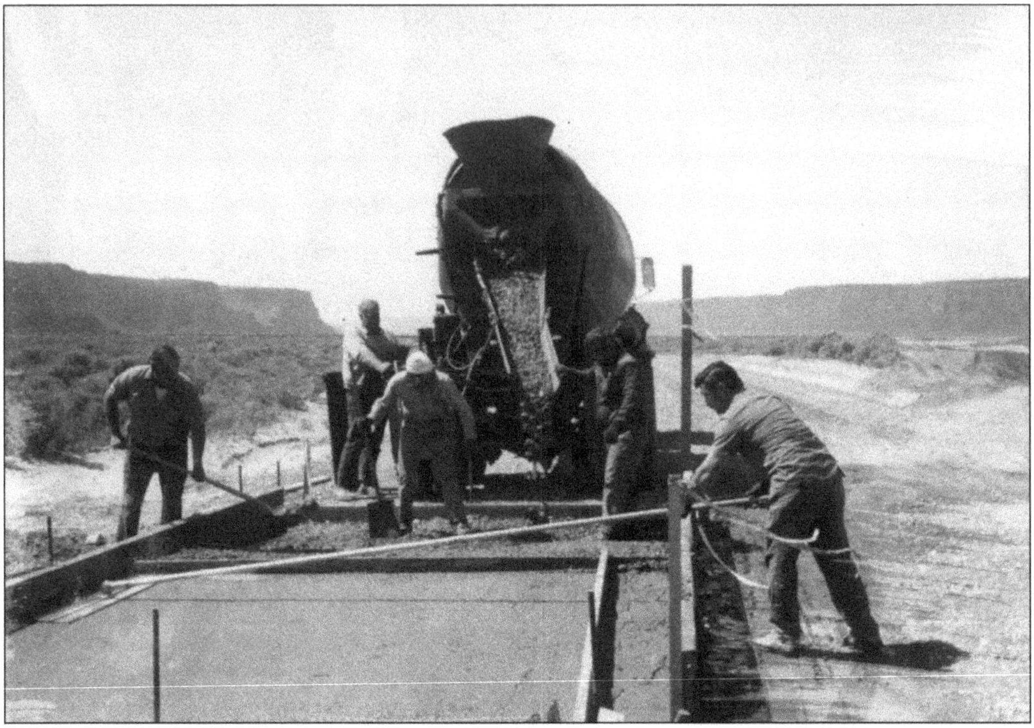

To protect the new asphalt roads from the heavy farm equipment that would need to work the land, the state installed concrete crossing zones. (Courtesy of Steamboat Rock State Park.)

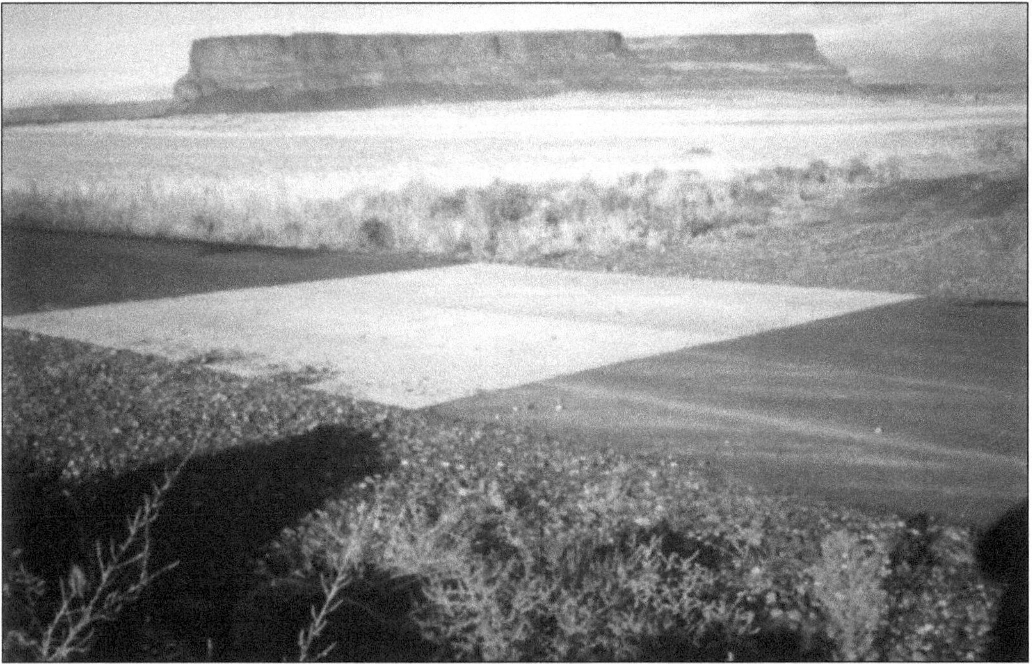

Even though the farms are now gone, these concrete crossings still dot the road in four different places as a reminder of earlier times when this land was used for agriculture—a time before recreation took over. (Courtesy of Steamboat Rock State Park.)

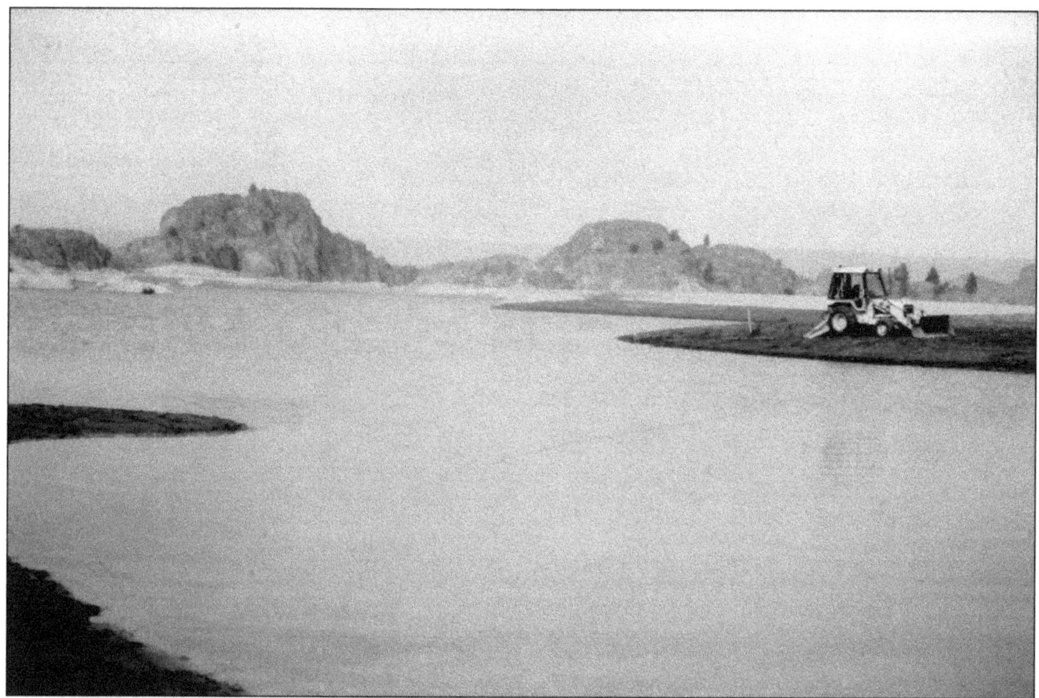

From 1971 through 1974, work continued on the expansion of the park to the base of Steamboat Rock. The park had become funded by both the Interagency Committee for Outdoor Recreation and the federal Bureau of Outdoor Recreation. (Courtesy of Steamboat Rock State Park.)

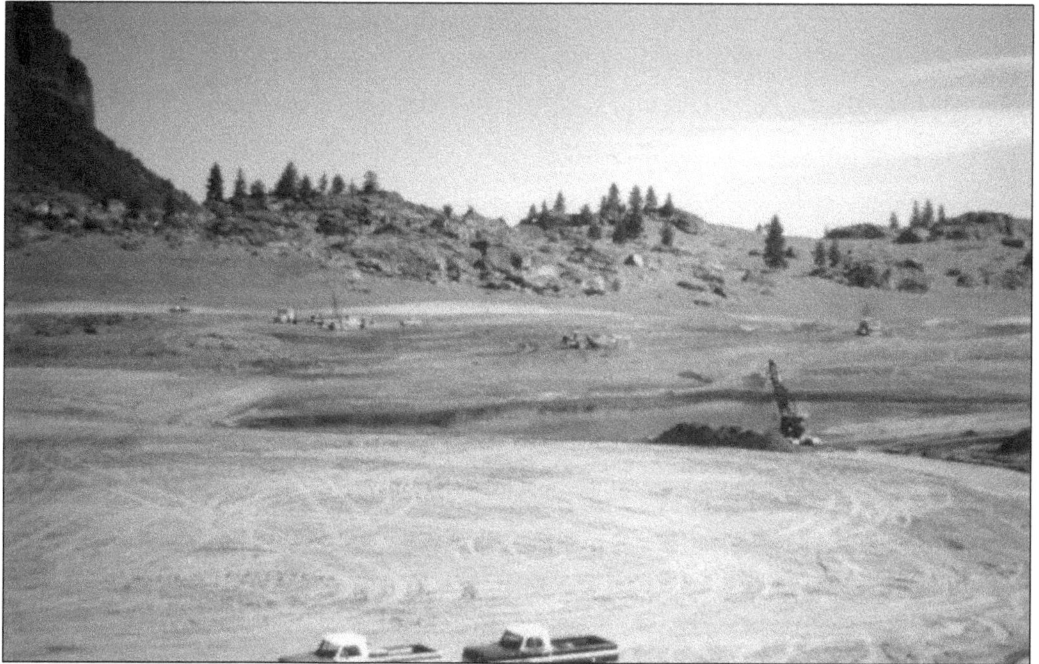

The building of the park took advantage of an early drawdown to create the Day Use area. This is an early picture of where the Day Use area ended up. Work on the boat launch parking lot and ramp area can be seen in the background. (Courtesy of Steamboat Rock State Park.)

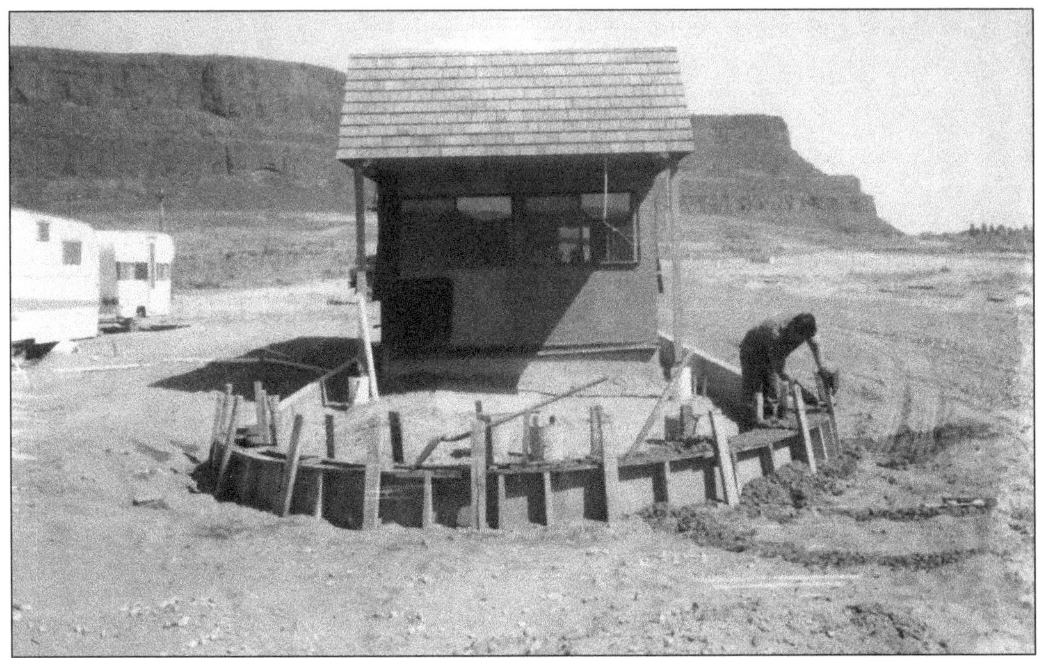

A lot of time had passed since the first pioneers heated their house with cast-iron wood stoves and rode horses over miles of open prairie. The new park would have electricity from cables running under the lake to the peninsula where Steamboat Rock State Park now sat on. Amenities would include a complete sewer system as well as running water and showers. (Courtesy of Steamboat Rock State Park.)

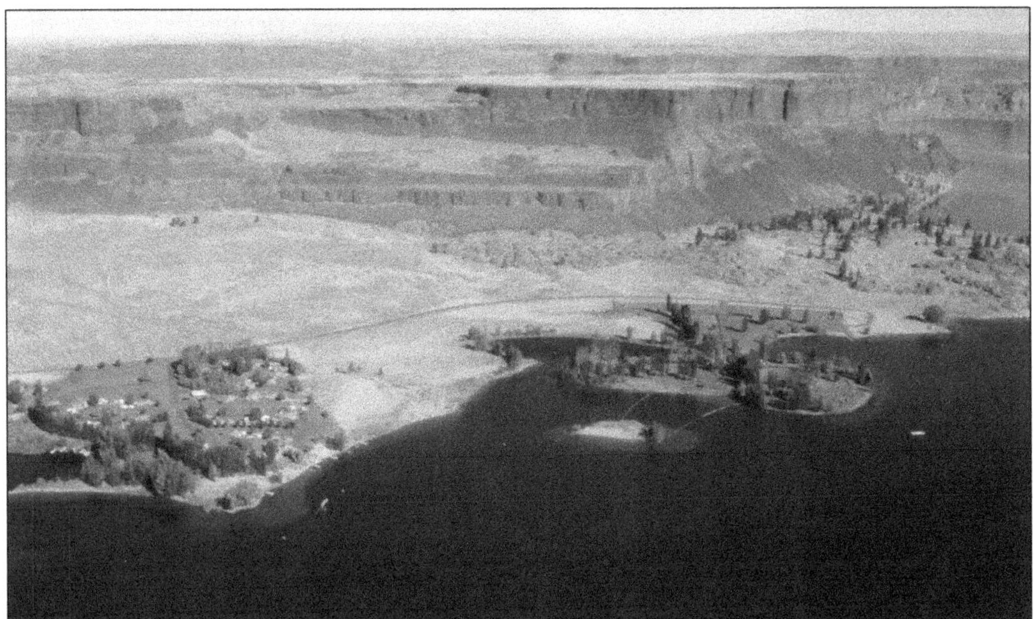

The new, expanded Steamboat Rock State Park would have a new boat launch, a concession stand, and a swimming beach as well as 100 camping spaces initially. The new park was built to the latest specifications of the time and was a fully modern facility, designed for both casual day use or overnight camping. (Courtesy of Steamboat Rock State Park.)

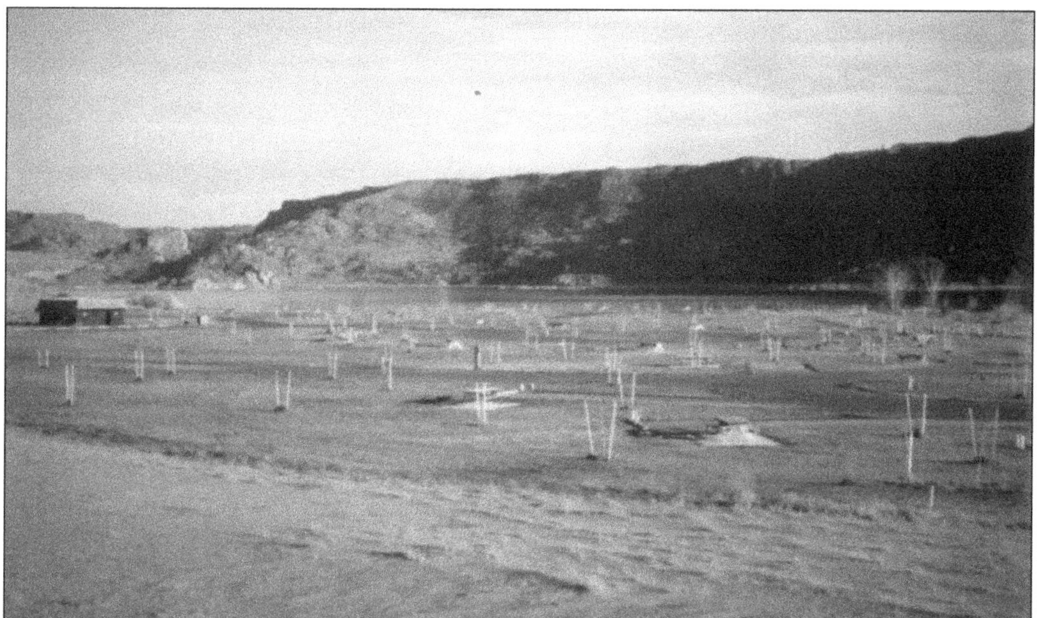

By 1974, work had been completed on the new Steamboat Rock State Park to include a new gate, multiple comfort stations, campgrounds, picnic areas, boat launch, and beaches; a Day Use area with a swimming beach was carved from sagebrush. Steamboat Rock State Park now had 100 campsites and was ready for the grand opening. (Courtesy of Steamboat Rock State Park.)

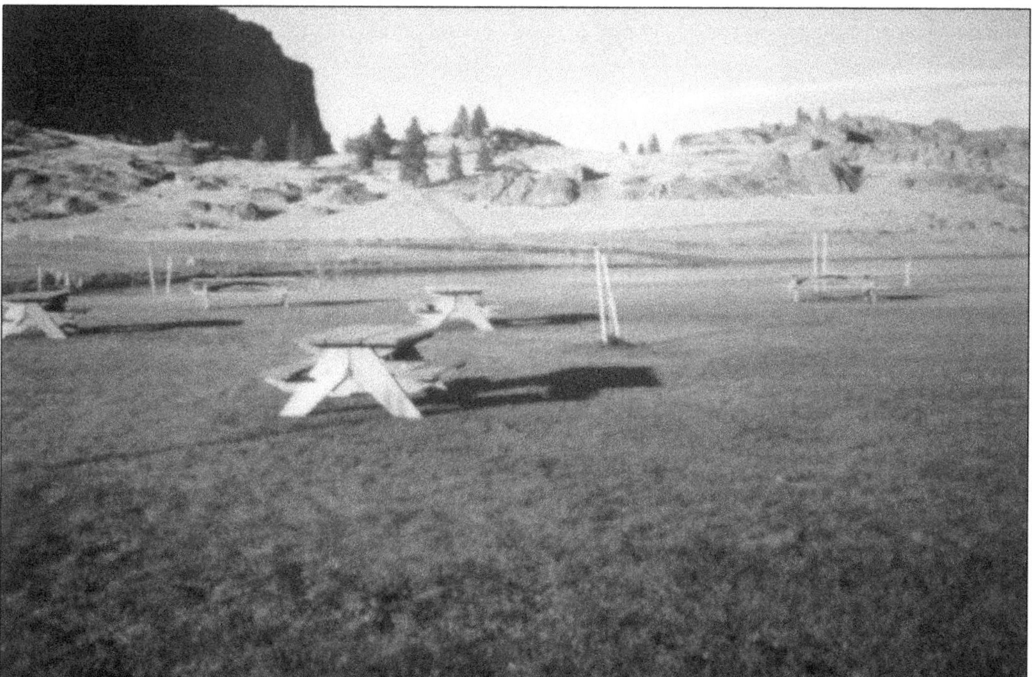

Jack Hilson of the *Star* newspaper and Grand Coulee Chamber of Commerce had long been an outspoken advocate for the expansion of Steamboat Rock State Park. Using his pull with the local newspaper, he urged people to attend the grand opening of the park and was invited to speak at the opening ceremony. (Courtesy of Steamboat Rock State Park.)

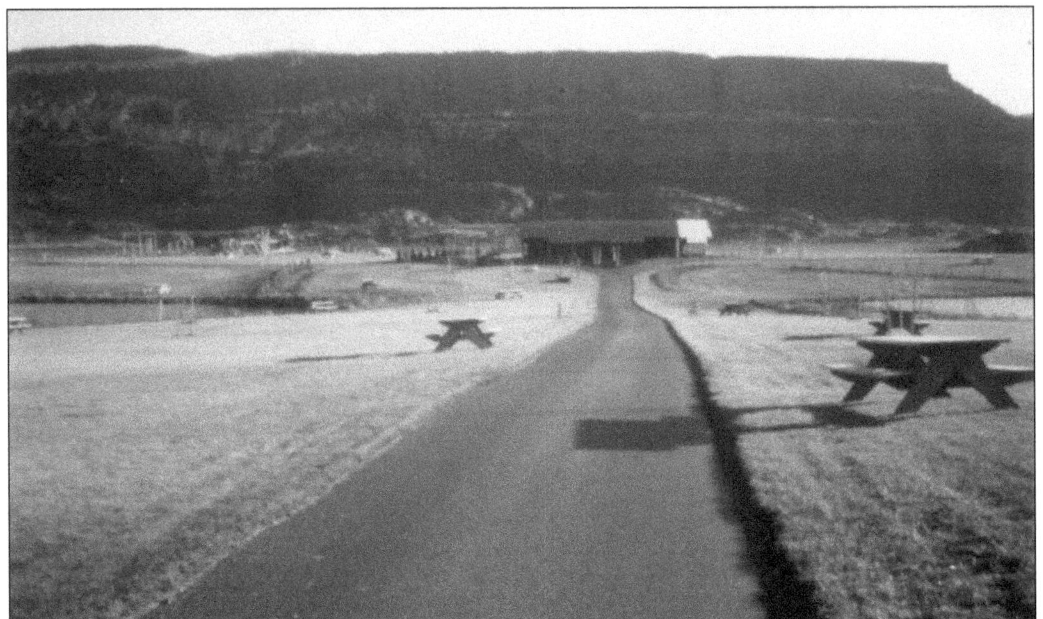

The Steamboat Rock State Park dedication was on September 15, 1974, in the new Day Use area. Charles H. Odegaard opened, and the ceremony included Congressman Thomas S. Foley and Sen. Clarence C. Dill, who spoke of the Grand Coulee Dam. Wilfred Woods, son of Rufus Woods, was also there to speak. A bronze plaque was presented by James G. McCurdy of the Washington State Parks and Recreation Commission. (Courtesy of Steamboat Rock State Park.)

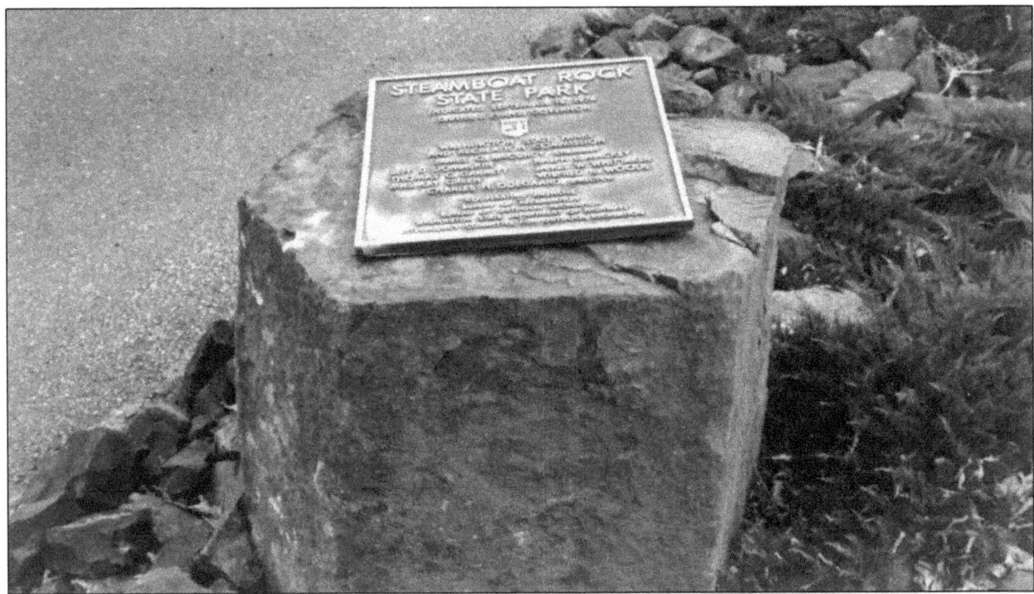

The bronze plaque was fastened to a piece of natural basalt pillar with the parks department crest; it listed the names of people behind the building of the park, including the agencies responsible: the Bureau of Reclamation, the Bureau of Outdoor Recreation, Washington State Department of Highways, and the Interagency Committee for Recreation. The plaque is still located in the Day Use area, close to the concession stand. (Courtesy of Steamboat Rock State Park.)

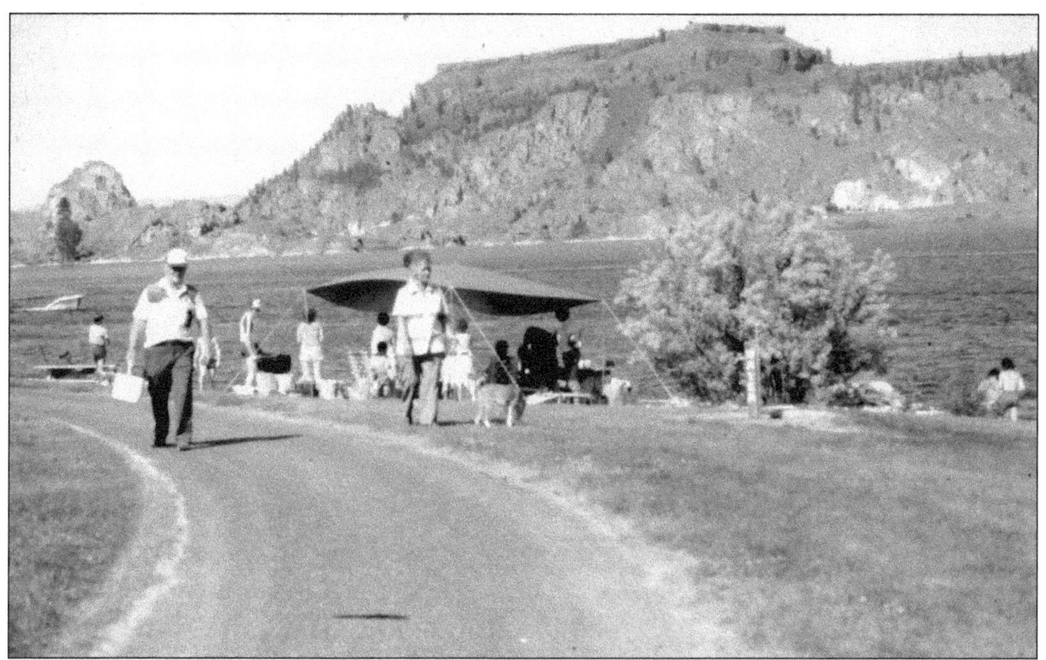

As of this writing, Steamboat Rock State Park covers 3,522 acres of land and 50,000 feet of shoreline and is open all year round. It has picnic grounds, public beaches for swimming, trails for hiking, boat launches, and fish-cleaning stations. (Courtesy of Steamboat Rock State Park.)

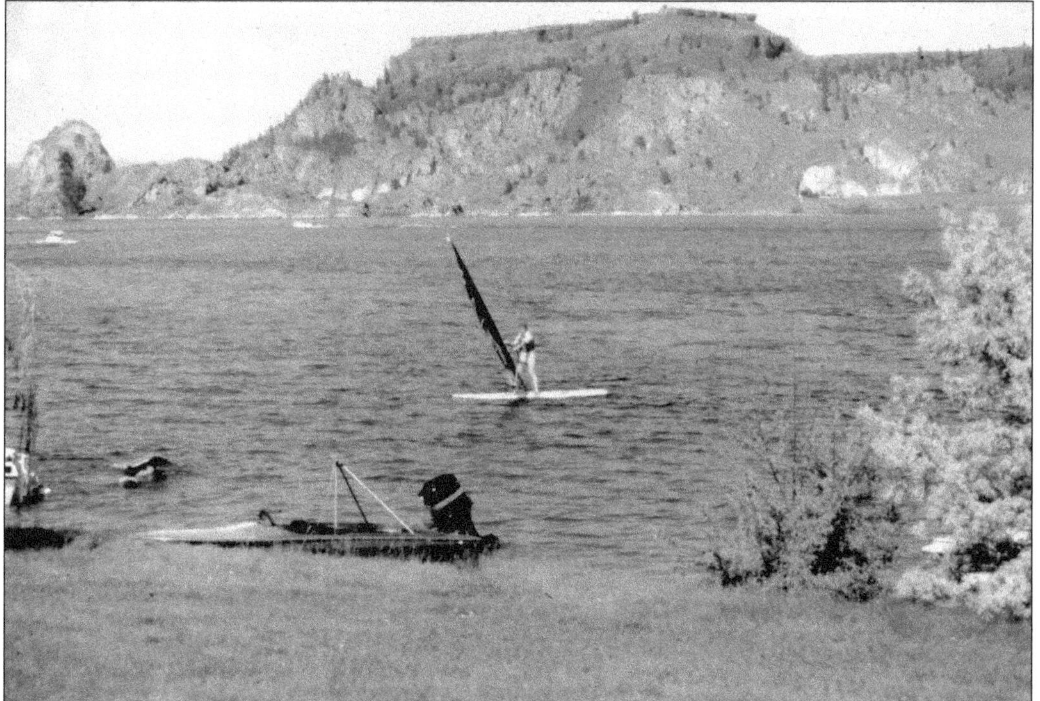

As time progresses, Steamboat Rock State Park continues to evolve and grow to match the world around it and remains one of the of Washington State's most popular tourist destinations. (Courtesy of Steamboat Rock State Park.)

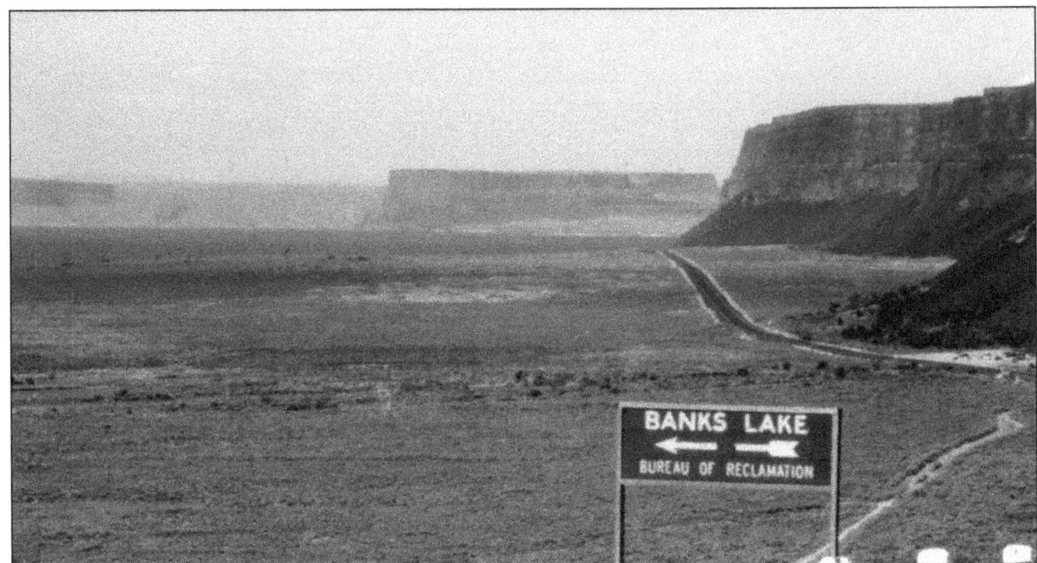

State Route 155 makes its way through Million Dollar Mile headed north toward Steamboat Rock. Taken in the mid-1970s, this picture shows the coulee after it was flooded with Banks Lake in 1951 and was taken from the pull-off by Rabbit Rock on the north face. Remnants of the Old Coulee Road can be seen intersecting with State Route 155, where the past meets the present on the road to Steamboat Rock. (Courtesy of Steamboat Rock State Park.)

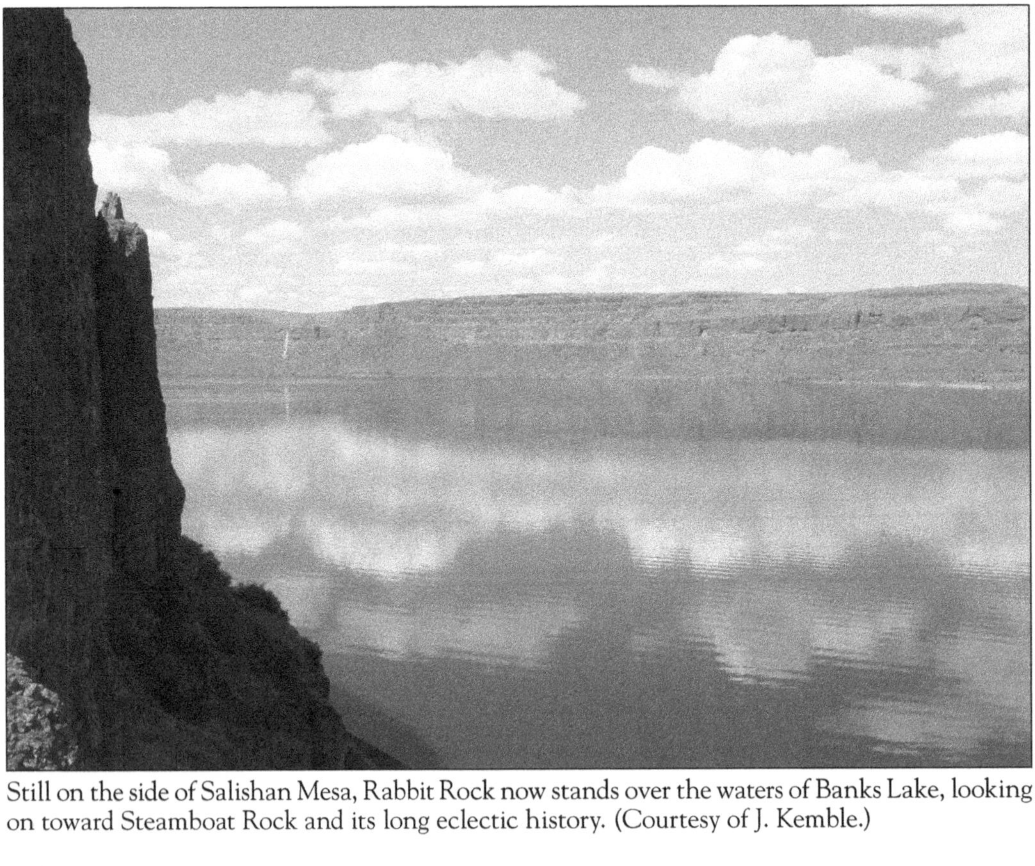

Still on the side of Salishan Mesa, Rabbit Rock now stands over the waters of Banks Lake, looking on toward Steamboat Rock and its long eclectic history. (Courtesy of J. Kemble.)

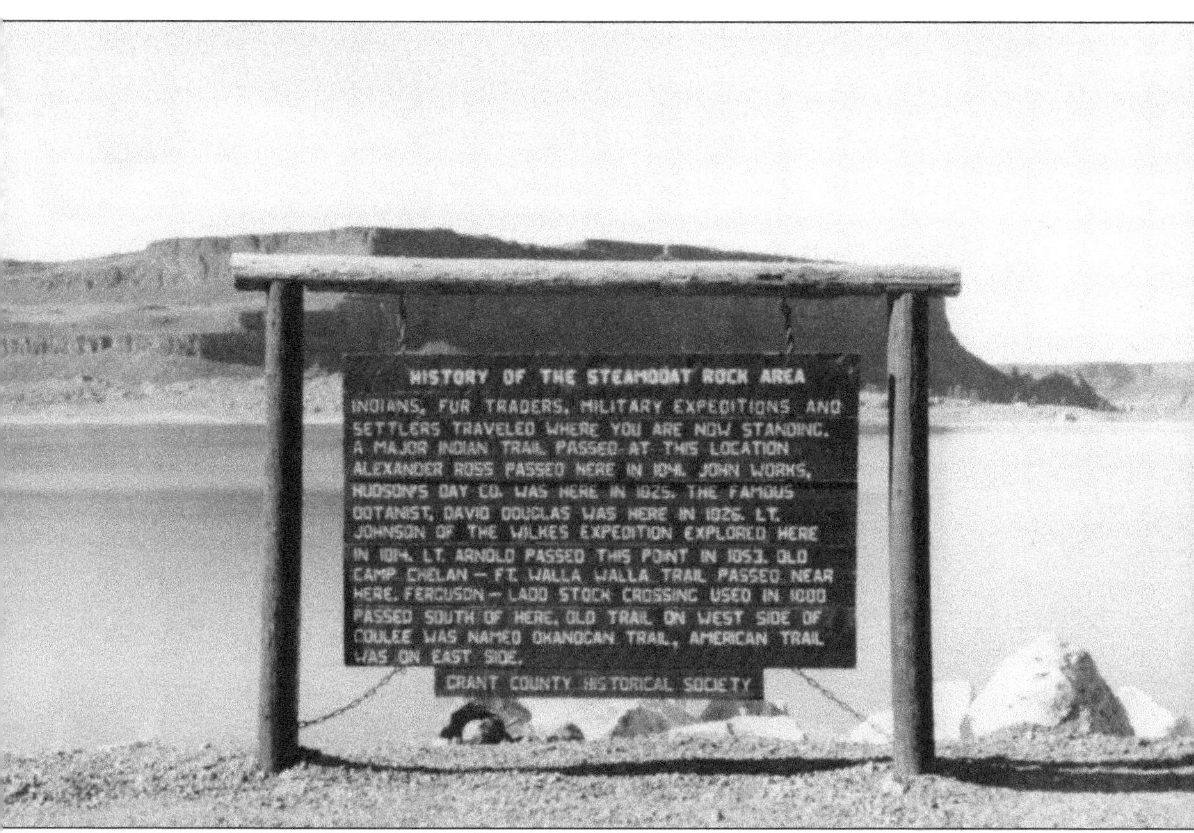

Located on a pull-off across from Steamboat Rock State Park is a historical marker that shares some of the earlier history of Steamboat Rock. The marker briefly covers an era before the contents in this book, when Steamboat Rock was a landmark and a curiosity for travelers, before the arrival of the first pioneers in the coulee (see page 14). (Courtesy of Steamboat Rock State Park.)

www.ingramcontent.com/pod-product-compliance
Lightning Source LLC
LaVergne TN
LVHW060626110826
845147LV00015B/950

9781467104715